Deterrence and the New Global Security Environment

Nuclear deterrence was the central organising mechanism for international security relations in the second half of the 20th Century. It effectively stabilised the security relations between the main protagonists of that period, the USA and the USSR and enabled them to be institutionalised through bilateral arms control agreements. This profound antagonism between the established nuclear-weapon states has subsided.

However in the 21st Century we are faced with new fears, prompted by a new global security environment characterised by the proliferation of all types of WMD and their delivery systems, as well as defensive systems. It appears to centre on regionally based sets of security problems, such as the Middle East and the threat from Iran and the threat posed by international terrorist organisations. In this environment the central role of deterrence, both nuclear and otherwise, appears to have diminished. This collection offers an important contribution and comprehensive analysis of the problems faced from a wide range of national perspectives and considers the place of deterrence in the international security relations of the 21st Century.

This book was previously published as a special issue of *Contemporary Security Policy*.

Ian R. Kenyon is a visiting Senior Research Fellow at the Mountbatten Centre for International Studies, University of Southampton, UK.

John Simpson is a Professor of International Relations at the University of Southampton, UK and Director of the Mountbatten Centre for International Studies.

Deterrence and the New Global Security Environment

Edited by Ian R. Kenyon and
John Simpson

Routledge
Taylor & Francis Group

First published 2006 by Frank Cass, an imprint of Taylor & Francis 2 Park Square, Milton Park, Abingdon, Oxon, OX14 4RN

Simultaneously published in the USA and Canada by Routledge
270 Madison Ave, New York, NY 10016

Routledge is an imprint of the Taylor & Francis Group

© 2006 Taylor & Francis Ltd

Typeset in Times by Techset Composition Limited
Printed and bound in Great Britain by Antony Rowe Ltd, Chippenham, Wiltshire

All rights reserved. No part of this book may be reprinted or reproduced or utilised in any form or by any electronic, mechanical, or other means, now known or hereafter invented, including photocopying and recording, or in any information storage or retrieval system, without permission in writing from the publishers.

The publisher makes no representation, express or implied, with regard to the accuracy of the information contained in this book and cannot accept any legal responibility or liability for any errors or omissions that may be made.

British Library Cataloguing in Publication Data
A catalogue record for this book is available from the British Library

Library of Congress Cataloging in Publication Data
A catalog record for this book has been requested

ISBN10: 0-714-65498-1 (hbk)
ISBN10: 0-714-68398-1 (pbk)

ISBN13: 978-0-7146-5498-0 (hbk)
ISBN13: 978-0-7146-8398-0 (pbk)

CONTENTS

Preface   vii

Foreword   ix

Notes on Contributors   xi

PART I: INTRODUCTION

Introduction   *Ian R. Kenyon and John Simpson*   xv

PART II: DETERRENCE THEORY

1. Deterrence and Deterrability   *Sir Michael Quinlan*   3

2. The Emergence of Stability: Deterrence-in-Motion and Deterrence Reconstructed   *Darryl Howlett*   10

3. Deterrence Asymmetry and Other Challenges to Small Nuclear Forces   *P.K. Ghosh*   29

4. Deterrence and Asymmetry: Non-State Actors and Mass Casualty Terrorism   *Wyn Q. Bowen*   46

5. The New Indeterminacy of Deterrence and Missile Defence   *Aaron Karp*   63

PART III: DETERRENCE PRACTICE – THE FIVE ESTABLISHED NUCLEAR WEAPON STATES

6. United States Nuclear Strategy in the Twenty-first Century   *James A. Russell and James J. Wirtz*   82

7. A Few Speculations on Russia's Deterrence Policy   *Alexander A. Pikayev*   100

8. Redefining Strategic Stability in a Changing World: A Chinese View   *Zhong Jing and Pan Zhenqiang*   114

9. France, the United Kingdom and Deterrence in the
   Twenty-first Century   *John Simpson*   127

PART IV: DETERRENCE PRACTICE – REGIONAL DYNAMICS

10. Positions on Deterrence in a Non-WMD
    Country: The Case of Germany   *Bernd W. Kubbig*   145

11. Regional Dynamics and Deterrence:
    South Asia (1)   *Waheguru Pal Singh Sidhu*   156

12. Regional Dynamics and Deterrence:
    South Asia (2)   *Naeem Ahmad Salik*   169

13. Regional Dynamics and Deterrence:
    The Middle East   *Alaa Issa*   192

PART V: CONCLUSIONS

Conclusions   *John Simpson and Ian R. Kenyon*   201

Index   215

Preface

The Mountbatten Centre for International Studies in the School of Social Science of the University of Southampton, England, was established in 1990 to explore significant trends in international security relations, including issues in global non-proliferation. In 1999, as part of its commitment to the study and support of the international regimes for the control of the proliferation of weapons of mass destruction (WMD), particularly the Nuclear Non-Proliferation Treaty, the Centre set up a project known as the Mountbatten Centre International Missile Forum to study, and to provide a forum for international expert discussion of the most common delivery system for WMD, missiles, including both the drivers for their acquisition and the means to control their proliferation. As part of the preparations for the 2002 Forum meeting it was decided to ask a group of scholars to consider, ten years after the end of the Cold War, whether the most prominent late-twentieth-century concepts of deterrence, such as Mutually Assured Destruction, still had validity and what were the new problems facing current strategic thinkers. The resulting papers, written by a group of scholars and practitioners from around the world, offer insights into how strategic thinking has evolved over the past decade and the many different strategic challenges confronting states in different regions of the world. Following an unforeseen delay in publication, the authors updated their papers, where appropriate, for this publication.

Foreword

TIMOTHY GARDEN

After 1945, the world learned to live in the shadow of nuclear catastrophe. Deterrence theory was developed in think tanks; the nuclear powers responded with ever more diverse methods of nuclear weapon delivery. Deterrence preserved an uneasy peace between the West and the Soviet Union. Many hoped that the end of the 20th Century would see a decline in the importance of nuclear forces.

Arms control and other measures have had real successes in slowing the spread of nuclear weapons. Yet there remained a hard core of countries that still sought to join the nuclear club: Israel, India and Pakistan succeeded. Others, notably North Korea and perhaps Iran continue such development work. And for those that find the nuclear path too difficult, biological weapons offer an easier route to strategic capability. Already, we have been close to nuclear conflict between India and Pakistan. Yet deterrence seems to have continued to shape their actions.

In the United States, the debate over missile defences showed the growing concern over reliance on deterrence for national safety. The terrorist attacks on Washington and New York of 11 September 2001 have brought a heightened sense of insecurity. While deterrence can work against hostile powers, how can it influence the actions of terrorists prepared to die for their cause? The greatest nightmare is that such fanatical terrorists might themselves gain access to weapons of mass destruction. The 2002 USA National Security Strategy looks to a more proactive doctrine with pre-emptive elimination of the threat replacing a dependence on deterrence.

This volume is published at a key moment. The reader can access the role of deterrence in so many areas of potential conflict. While new strategies of defence and pre-emption may have a part to play, the underlying requirement for deterrence in a nuclear world remains.

Lord Timothy Garden is visiting professor at the Centre for Defence Studies at King's College London, where his current research is on transatlantic security issues and on international terrorism. He was a pilot in the Royal Air Force, was assistant chief of the UK defence staff and then the air marshal commandant of the Royal College of Deference Studies in London. After retirement from the military, he went on to be Director of the Royal Institute of International Affairs at Chatham House. He writes and broadcasts on security policy issues.

Notes on Contributors

Wyn Q. Bowen is Director of Research, Defence Studies Department, King's College London, at the UK Joint Services Command and Staff College (JSCSC), and Deputy Director (Research Coordination) of the International Policy Institute at King's. Prior to joining King's in July 1997, he spent two years as a Senior Research Associate of the Center for Nonproliferation Studies, Monterey Institute of International Studies, California. He has served as Specialist Advisor to the House of Commons Foreign Affairs Committee for inquiries into 'The Decision to Go to War in Iraq' (2003) and 'Weapons of Mass Destruction' (2000). In 1997–98, he served as a weapons inspector on several missile teams in Iraq with the UN Special Commission. He has written widely on security-related issues most recently including, with Joanna Kidd, 'The Iranian Nuclear Challenge', *International Affairs*, March 2004.

P.K. Ghosh is a Commander in the Indian Navy and a Defence Analyst. He is a Communication and Information Technology specialist and commanded the warship *INS Ghorpad*. He has been a senior member of the faculty in the School of Maritime Warfare and Tactics (a naval think tank) for three years. Currently a Research Fellow at the Institute of Defence Studies and Analyses (IDSA) he has been awarded the Professor DS Kothari Chair at the USI for conducting research on BMD issues. He specializes in nuclear strategy and ballistic missile defence and has written, lectured and presented papers extensively on these subjects. Some of his recent publications include: 'Economic Dimension of the Strategic Nuclear Triad', *Strategic Analysis* (April–June 2002); 'Response to Missile Defence Shield: Chinese Options and Strategies', *Issues and Studies*, Vol.39, No.4, December 2003; and 'Layered Defence Concept: Some Architectural Options for an Expanding Ballistic Missile Shield', *Contemporary Security Policy*, Vol.24, No.3 (December 2003).

Darryl Howlett is a Senior Lecturer in International Relations at the University of Southampton in the United Kingdom where he teaches courses on Arms-Control, Disarmament and International Security. He has also taught at the universities of East Anglia and Sussex, and from 1987 to 1995 he was the Information Officer for the Programme For Promoting Nuclear Non-Proliferation (PPNN). He has published widely in the area of arms control, disarmament and international security and has been a speaker or *rapporteur* at conferences in Australia, Germany, France, Spain, Sri Lanka, Nepal, Zimbabwe, Venezuela, United States and Kazakhstan.

Alaa Issa is Counsellor at the Permanent Mission of Egypt to the United Nations, New York. From 1999 until 2002 he served as Director for Disarmament Affairs at the Ministry of Foreign Affairs, Cairo. From 1997 until 2002 he served in the cabinet of the Foreign Minister, Cairo. His publications include: 'The Drivers behind Missile Proliferation', Monterey Institute of International Studies, CNS Occasional Paper No.7, July 2001.

Ian R. Kenyon is a Visiting Senior Research Fellow at the Mountbatten Centre for International Studies, University of Southampton and Co-Director of the Centre's Missile Forum Project. He was for 20 years a member of the United Kingdom Diplomatic Service, specializing in arms control and disarmament and from 1993 to 1997 was Executive Secretary of the Preparatory Commission for the Organisation for the Prohibition of Chemical Weapons in The Hague.

Aaron Karp is Senior Faculty Associate with the Graduate Program in International Studies at Old Dominion University and Assistant Professor at the US Joint Forces Staff College, both in Norfolk, Virginia. He also is Consulting Editor for the *Small Arms Survey* in Geneva.

Bernd W. Kubbig is Director of the Internet Project 'Ballistic Missile Defense Research International' of the Peace Research Institute Frankfurt (PRIF) and Coordinator of US-related research at PRIF. In 1993, he had an Academic Year of the German Marshall Fund of the United States. He has just edited the Special Volume 'Toward a New American Century? The US Hegemon in Motion', *Amerikastudien*, Vol.46, No.4 (2002). Among his recent publications is 'Positioning Europe as a Credible Actor in the Ballistic Missile Defense Game: Concepts and Recommendations', PRIF Report No. 56, Frankfurt am Main 2000.

Alexander A. Pikayev is the Director of the Department for Arms Control and Conflict Resolution, Institute of World Economy and International Relations, and Deputy Chairman, Committee of Scientists for Global Security. From 1994 to 1997 he worked in the Duma Defense Committee as a senior staff member. From 1997 to 2003 he was Co-Chair of the Non-Proliferation project at the Carnegie Moscow Center and edited the *Nuclear Proliferation Journal* there. He has published widely in both Russian and English on the subjects of nuclear and chemical arms control. He is frequently consulted by the media on strategic issues affecting Russia.

Sir Michael Quinlan in his main career was a British civil servant, primarily in the defence field, and much involved with United Kingdom and NATO nuclear-weapons policy, doctrine and arms control. He retired in 1992 as Permanent Under-Secretary of State for Defence, and from later in 1992 until 1999 was Director of the Ditchley Foundation. His writings include *Thinking About Nuclear Weapons* (Royal United Services Institute for Defence Studies, 1997) and *European Defense Cooperation* (Woodrow Wilson Center Press, 2001). He is a Visiting Professor in the Department of War Studies at King's College London.

James A. Russell is the US Office of the Secretary of Defense Fellow in the National Security Affairs Department at the Naval Postgraduate School, Monterey, CA. While in the Defense Department, he served as the country director for Saudi Arabia, Kuwait and the United Arab Emirates in the office of the Assistant Secretary of Defense (ISA-NESA). His most recent publication is 'Nuclear Strategy and the Modern Middle East', *Middle East Policy*, Vol.XI, No.3 (Fall 2004).

Naeem Ahmad Salik is a Brigadier in the Pakistan Army, currently serving as Director, Arms Control and Disarmament Affairs Directorate at the Strategic Plans Division, Joint Staff Headquarters. He holds an M.Sc. in Strategic Studies from University of Wales, Aberystwyth, UK, and an M.A. in History from the University of Punjab, Pakistan. In addition to his varied military experience, he served as Associate Professor at the Department of Defence and Strategic Studies, Quaid-i-Azam University, Islamabad, 1994–96 and continues to teach there as a visiting Professor. He lectures regularly at The National Defence College, Pakistan Naval War College, National Institute of Public Administration and other military training institutions. He has published extensively on the nuclear policies of India and Pakistan, the nuclear and ballistic missile programmes of Pakistan, technology and warfare, the non-proliferation regimes, confidence building measures and nuclear deterrence and stability. He was a visiting fellow at Henry L. Stimson Center, Washington, DC, 1995 and Center for International Security & Cooperation (CISAC), Stanford University, 2004.

Waheguru Pal Singh Sidhu is Faculty Member, Geneva Centre for Security Policy. He directs the 'Iraq Crisis and World Order' and 'Kashmir: New Voices, New Approaches' projects at IPA. He has written extensively on South Asian security issues in general and on confidence-building measures in particular, including, with Jing Dong Yuan, 'A Languid but Lethal Arms Race', *Disarmament Forum*, No.2, 2004; *China and India: Cooperation or Conflict?* (Lynne Rienner, 2003); and *India's*

Nuclear Use Doctrine, Planning the Unthinkable: New Proliferators and the Use of Weapons of Mass Destruction, Peter R. Lavoy, Scott Sagan and James J. Wirtz (eds) (Cornell University Press, 2000).

John Simpson is Director of the Mountbatten Centre for International Studies and Professor of International Relations at the University of Southampton. His research and writing has focused upon the UK military use of nuclear energy and global nuclear non-proliferation issues. He has participated directly in disarmament and non-proliferation diplomacy through his membership of the UN Secretary-General's Advisory Board for Disarmament Matters from 1992–98 and as Programme Director of the International Programme for Promoting Nuclear Non-Proliferation (PPNN) from 1987–2002.

James J. Wirtz is Chairman of the Department of National Security Affairs, Naval Postgraduate School, Monterey, California. He is Section Chair of the Intelligence Studies Section of the International Studies Association and President of the International Security and Arms Control Section of the American Political Science Association. His most recent publication is *Balance of Power: Theory and Practice in the 21st Century* (Stanford University Press, 2004).

Zhong Jing is currently a lecturer at the Teaching Division for Military Technology and Arms Studies, National Defense University (NDU), PLA, which is the top institution of military learning in China. She received her MA degree at the NDU in 1999, and from then has shifted interests to subjects on arms control and non-proliferation from a technology perspective. She has published six books and dozens of articles in such periodicals as *Military Arms Science Studies, Military Science and Technology, Balance of Military Power, The Challenges of the Revolution in Military Affairs, Turn the Newly Equipped Arms and Equipment into Combat Effectiveness.*

PART I: INTRODUCTION

INTRODUCTION

IAN R. KENYON AND JOHN SIMPSON

For they have sown the wind and they shall reap the whirlwind
Hosea 8 vii

The advent of nuclear weapons in 1945 was almost universally regarded as having changed the nature of global warfare and of the mechanisms for preventing war. After their use in Hiroshima and Nagasaki, and the advent in the early 1950s of thermonuclear weapons of theoretically infinite explosive power, nuclear weapons increasingly were regarded as purely instruments of deterrence – means to prevent war rather than tools for fighting a war – although their credibility in the former role was seen to require, paradoxically, detailed preparations for the latter. This credibility in turn depended on the availability of an effective delivery system, which from the 1960s onwards increasingly meant a ballistic missile.

Sitting ready to deliver Armageddon was thus virtually the only role played by ballistic missiles capable of carrying a payload of 500 kg for a distance of more than 300 km (the definition of a missile used by the Missile Technology Control Regime (MTCR)).[1] Any attempt to acquire a ballistic missile capability, particularly one more advanced than the basic SCUD, was assumed to indicate an intention to acquire weapons of mass destruction, most probably nuclear weapons. For these reasons any attempt to understand the regional and global dynamics of both nuclear proliferation and missile proliferation needs to embrace an understanding of current concepts of nuclear deterrence, as well as the motivations that drive states to commit the substantial resources and to accept the political risks involved in their acquisition.

The dynamics of the Cold War were simple but very effective. As long as the two superpowers each had the ability to visit massive destruction on each other, which translated into possession of an assured 'second strike' capability,[2] any use of nuclear weapons carried the likelihood of escalation to all-out nuclear war and, therefore, involved unacceptable risks. The slogan coined by President Reagan in the 1980s that 'a nuclear war cannot be won and must never be fought', became part of the stock in trade of speechwriters in the United Nations and elsewhere and seemed to reflect a universally accepted view. The only question seemed to be how to manage the superpower relationship in a way that maintained a stable balance, controlled the danger of accidental triggering of a holocaust and limited the numbers of nuclear systems of each side. The main tools developed for this purpose were a series of bilateral arms control agreements characterized by steadily increasing complexity and intrusiveness in their verification provisions.

At the same time, the system of military blocs in Europe had the effect of reducing the motivation for additional states to acquire nuclear weapons. Both bloc leaders provided politically and technically credible guarantees that if these non-nuclear weapon states were attacked, they would respond in kind against the aggressor. This in turn generated a relationship of what was known as extended deterrence, which was seen to negate the need for them to own such nuclear weapons.

Despite these efforts at moderating the superpower arms race, the economic burden of trying to match the United States in military power was undoubtedly one of the factors that caused the collapse, first of the East/West confrontation and then, on 25 December 1991, of the Soviet Union itself.[3] However, the changes in strategic thinking stimulated by the new political configurations in Europe and elsewhere were slow to take place. Although symbolic gestures were made to de-target strategic missile systems, the basic force structures of the main players did not immediately undergo any fundamental change. A priority task, achieved surprisingly quickly and easily, was to ensure that only Russia emerged from the break-up of the Soviet Union as a nuclear weapon state. Belarus, Kazakhstan and Ukraine duly transferred the nuclear warheads deployed on their territories to Russia, and joined the NPT as non-nuclear weapon states. In addition, efforts were made to strengthen physical security over the nuclear weapons and the stocks of weapon useable materials produced by the former USSR, to ensure that they did not fall into the wrong hands.

During the Cold War period, the international language of nuclear debate differentiated clearly between 'vertical' proliferation and its 'horizontal' twin. Vertical proliferation was the increase in numbers and sophistication of the weapons developed and deployed by the established technology holders, and horizontal proliferation the dissemination of this technology to others. Despite relations between the United States and the Soviet Union going through some very difficult phases after 1949, it was striking that, whatever the temperature of the overall relationship might be, the two states continued to cooperate closely over the problem of nuclear proliferation and the health of the Treaty on the Non-Proliferation of Nuclear-Weapons (NPT).[4] Whilst they considered such weapons essential both for their own security, and as the means of ensuring that the Third World War never happened, neither wished to see any new players enter the nuclear arena. They were assisted in this by a large group of medium and small sized states, who had concluded that their individual security would be enhanced if they collectively renounced the nuclear option.

INTRODUCTION

The NPT turned this idea of limiting the number of nuclear-weapon states into international law. The Treaty was opened for signature in 1968, by which time only five states had joined the nuclear club. The line was formally held at this level for 30 years. The negative political consequences of a test by India in 1974 of what the Indian government declared to be a 'peaceful' nuclear device resulted in almost a quarter of a century passing before such an action was repeated by India or any other non-nuclear weapon state. In the 1960s it had been confidently predicted that there would be at least 20 nuclear weapon states by the year 2000. In fact, by then only India and Pakistan had tested and gone on to declare that they were deploying nuclear weapons. Israel had refrained from testing[5] but was generally regarded as also having a nuclear weapon arsenal. Apart from these three, the NPT achieved universal adherence in 2002.

The end of the Cold War generated a major shift in perceptions of where the main nuclear dangers were to be found. While the threat from a bilateral nuclear holocaust and its consequences receded, and thus the need for deterrence to prevent it, concerns over nuclear weapon proliferation moved to the forefront of the global strategic agenda. Near-universal adherence to the NPT had not proved to be an effective guarantee of non-proliferation. For any treaty is only as strong as the relationship of trust between its parties, reinforced by their belief in the effectiveness of its verification mechanisms, as the cases of Iraq and the DPRK have demonstrated. How, therefore, was deterrence to operate in this new context?

Once the world ceased to be divided into two armed camps, a whole new set of questions became apparent (some of which had been there all along but had been obscured by Cold War issues). These included:

- How much nuclear weaponry was enough for the United States and Russia, if nuclear deterrence was in the process of being supplanted by a new, cooperative relationship between them?
- Was there still a role in the new environment for twentieth-century style bilateral and multilateral arms control diplomacy and formal treaties?
- Did the move away from a potentially apocalyptic set of East–West deterrent relationships mean that certain types of nuclear weapon were now usable against a state (a 'proliferator') attempting to acquire weapons of mass destruction (WMD),[6] or a 'small' nuclear-weapon state?
- How did the states with small nuclear capabilities and those previously provided with extended deterrence guarantees fit into this new picture?
- What salience should be attached to deterrence through nuclear weapons possession as compared to through possession of other WMD or the threat of use of advanced conventional technologies?
- Could a state with a small nuclear capability deter the use by a major nuclear power of its advanced conventional capabilities?

- Did the same rules apply to the India/Pakistan confrontation as had governed US/USSR relations?
- What role did deterrence play in the Middle East?

And last but not least,

- Did theories of deterrence have any role in helping the world community face up to the new dangers highlighted by the events of 11 September 2001?

These were some of the questions that our authors, sitting in different parts of the world, have been asked to address in order to provide a systematic coverage of the many issues that are emerging over the future of deterrence. This coverage starts by asking what does the concept of deterrence imply both theoretically and in practice. It then moves on to examine how deterrence, and the ideas of the stability it could generate through concepts such as Mutual Assured Destruction (MAD), evolved during the Cold War period.

There then follow three analyses of specific problems arising in the post-Cold War international strategic environment. First, how do the small, non-aligned nuclear weapon states cope with the problems of the asymmetry of nuclear and conventional military force, and the vulnerability of their modest arsenals. Second, to what extent is the concept of deterrence applicable to threats of mass casualty attack from non-state actors. And third, why is missile defence, once condemned as destabilizing to deterrence, now considered a useful element of strategic stability. Does the explanation lie in a movement to a situation where deterrence can no longer be regarded as a single, holistic set of activities, but has to be differentiated into a number of different forms, each of which has a distinct nature? Moreover, might actions to bolster deterrence in one of these areas actually degrade its operation elsewhere?

An attempt is then made to assess the problems facing the governments of the established nuclear weapon states and their allies in the new century and how they are facing up to them. These problems include:

- The United States, in its new relationship with Russia, equipped with a vast arsenal designed for the bipolar Cold War but faced with the problems of proliferation of WMD to the states it categorizes as 'the axis of evil' and the need to combat a new level of mass terrorism;
- Russia, left as custodian of the Soviet arsenal but without the economic resources to maintain it, seeking a new relationship not only with the United States but with NATO, China, and its southern neighbours and confronting its own terrorist problem in Chechnya;

- China, with its small strategic nuclear forces vulnerable to the anti-missile systems under development by the United States and also concerned over potential terrorism problems; and
- France and the United Kingdom, in a much improved threat environment in the short term, proving reluctant to move away from nuclear weapon status while the medium term future remains uncertain.

There are contributions on how deterrence can be viewed in different regions – from Western Europe on the new problems faced by Germany, with US nuclear weapons still based on its territory, politically uncertain of their future military role in its security. And, finally, from two areas that are at the heart of regional concerns over nuclear war: South Asia and the Middle East. It is perhaps in these last papers that the degree to which we are now living through an increasingly complex transitional age can best be appreciated. For if there are now at least three differing forms of deterrence relationship, two of which may be operative in these two regions, as well as the liberating consequences of the third in allowing for low-risk (and low casualty) nuclear weapons use, how are the two Cold War aims of preventing nuclear war and proliferation to be achieved in the twenty-first century?

NOTES

1. The exceptions were the use of conventional explosive warheads on V2s aimed at London and Antwerp in 1944 and the SCUD type missiles used against each other's cities by Iran and Iraq in the First Gulf War and by Iraq against Israel and Saudi Arabia in the Second Gulf War.
2. A 'second strike' capability is a set of weapon systems that could be guaranteed to survive a first strike by the opponent, such as submarine based systems.
3. For a full account see: Jack F. Matlock, Jr, *Autopsy of an Empire: The American Ambassador's Account of the Collapse of the Soviet Union* (New York: Random House, 1995).
4. The NPT was opened for signature simultaneously in London, Moscow and Washington on 1 July 1968 in order to ensure that all states of the world, regardless of their allegiance at that time, could have an opportunity to sign. (A particular problem was the recognition or otherwise of China and Taiwan.) Thereafter the US, UK and USSR, as the depository states were required to convene the five-yearly NPT Review Conferences.
5. There are those who believe that the double flash observed in the South Atlantic by a US satellite in 1979 was a test conducted jointly by South Africa and Israel. See David Albright and Corey Gay, 'A Flash from the Past; South Africa – Nuclear Proliferation', *Bulletin of the Atomic Scientists*, Vol.53, No.6 (Nov.–Dec. 1997), p.15 quoted by Roy E. Horton, *Out of South Africa: Pretoria's Nuclear Weapon Experience*, ACDIS Occasional Paper (University of Illinois at Urbana-Champaign, Aug. 2000).
6. Weapons of Mass Destruction were defined by a Resolution of the United Nations Commission for Conventional Armaments, dated 12 August 1948 as: 'atomic explosive weapons, radioactive material weapons, lethal chemical and biological weapons, and any weapons developed in the future which have characteristics comparable in destructive effect to those of the atomic bomb or other weapons mentioned above'.

PART II: DETERRENCE THEORY

Deterrence and Deterrability

SIR MICHAEL QUINLAN

Si vis pacem, para bellum. The concept of deterrence goes back a long way – it was not new even when the Romans formulated that Latin axiom: 'If you want peace, make ready for war'. Deterrence arises from basic and permanent facts about human behaviour: that in our decision-making we customarily seek, whether explicitly or not, to take into account the probable consequences of our actions; that we refrain from actions whose adverse consequences seem to us likely to outweigh the beneficial ones; and that we exploit these universal realities as one means of helping to influence others against taking action that would be damaging to ourselves.

It is, however, only since the colossal shock of the nuclear revolution burst upon us that deterrence has become so special and salient a concept as it is now in discourse about international security. The possibility of some such revolution had been hazily glimpsed before: Henry Adams wrote gloomily in 1862 – 'some day science shall have the existence of mankind in its power, and the human race commit suicide by blowing up the planet'. Another remarkable American, Wilkie Collins – not, perhaps, a normal source in strategic studies – took the thinking a little further, and more operationally, in 1870 in the context of the Franco-Prussian War – 'I begin to believe in only one civilising influence – the discovery, one of these days, of a destructive agent so terrible that War shall mean *annihilation*, and men's fears shall force them to keep the peace'. The reality he thus foreshadowed came to pass in 1945. It was thereafter fairly quickly and generally recognized that old-style defence, in the form of physically warding off attack, could no longer play as large a part as it customarily had in security. In face of the vast new destructive power, only virtually impermeable defence would be good enough; and such a standard was simply not attainable. So deterrence had to step forward. From then onwards deterrence theory, centred upon nuclear weapons, accumulated libraries-full of writing. But however elaborate the analysis and the intellectual architecture become, they have to rest ultimately on the simple paradigm of human behaviour summarized earlier. Some of the writing has occasionally failed to maintain its grasp of that, and has as a result understood the operation of deterrence inaccurately or too narrowly. To help prepare the ground for later consideration of whether and how deterrence can continue to work in today's and tomorrow's world, we might note five propositions which are virtually self-evident if thought about lucidly, but which seem, nevertheless, from time to time to be overlooked.

Proposition one is that deterrence works by displaying the prospect of costs in terms of values prized by the 'deterree'. For almost every society known to history, physical existence and physical assets are not the only such values; and instruments for executing physical destruction – that is, primarily, military instruments – are therefore not the only possible instruments of deterrence. Political, economic, social, judicial and even religious or similar ones can also sometimes make a contribution.

Proposition two is that for effective deterrence the costs displayed do not have to be in the same currency, or even of the same magnitude, as the actions we seek to prevent. Opponents may be of widely different sizes and value-systems, yet deterrence can still work between them. In the course of debate during the Cold War on the morality of possessing nuclear armouries, anti-nuclear ethicists occasionally argued that because the Soviet Union must be supposed to have a counter-population nuclear-strike policy, and because counter-population strike would always be immoral, no Western nuclear planning adequate to underpin deterrence could be morally legitimate. But there was a basic fallacy in that argument. Deterrence seeks to influence a comparison made, before the event, in the mind of the adversary; and the comparison relevant to his decision-making is not between harm inflicted and harm suffered, but between the net balance of advantage to him if he undertakes the objectionable action and the net balance of advantage to him if he does not. For example, deterrence '*du faible au fort*', as French analysts used to put it, is an entirely valid notion. Neither Britain nor France could have obliterated the Soviet Union as it could them; but to pose merely fearful damage as the cost of their obliteration was in concept a perfectly valid approach. (It might be added for completeness, since this too is a point sometimes missed, that the comparison to be influenced is not between 'before' and 'after', but between the future 'if I do' and the future 'if I don't'.)

Proposition three is that effective deterrence has two main components, not just one. It undoubtedly requires that the adversary perceive the existence of capability and general will to use it to exact in one form or another costs unacceptable to him. But it also requires that he understand clearly and credibly what is the action from which he must refrain. That was one of the key reasons why the East/West deterrent stand-off in Europe proved so secure, at least once the Berlin issue had been stabilized; the Iron Curtain was deeply unpleasant, but its line and its importance were unmistakable. The breakdowns of deterrence most evident to Western countries since the Second World War include the crises in Korea, Cuba, the Falkland Islands and the Gulf. In at least three if not all four of those instances the existence of adequate power was unmistakable, and the breakdown resulted not from misperception of that but from failure – whether blameworthy or not – to get across to the adversary in advance a clear sense of what we would refuse to acquiesce in.

Proposition four is an important partner of proposition three. Deterrence does not require that we specify precisely what form our non-acquiescence will take. It requires only that we make plain that the objectionable action will not be allowed to stand, that we have the power to prevent its doing so, and that we have the resolve to implement from among the means available to us whatever we find necessary for the purpose. Over-exact specification may actually weaken deterrence, for instance by helping our adversary in one way or another to evade or head off our response or to reduce its impact; or, in open societies, by prompting contentious national or international debate that may come to be seen as impairing the credibility of our avowed option and resolve. That is why the writer has argued elsewhere,[1] on prudential as well as ethical grounds, against the notion of declaratory policies that would purport to guarantee a nuclear response to use of biological or chemical weapons. We should, within the limits of any permanent international commitments we may have, avoid ruling any specific means either in or out in advance. The essence of our deterrent message, however communicated, should be that we will do whatever we find necessary to achieve our aim – perhaps the minimum necessary, but not less.

Proposition five is about probabilities. Ideal deterrence would deal in certainty; but amid life's complexities that is not always achievable. Where that is so we need to work with probabilities and possibilities. Figures as diverse as Charles de Gaulle and Henry Kissinger used, in their own styles, to remind us during the East/West confrontation that it was at best unprovable that the United States would risk embarking on processes that might lead to the sacrifice of its cities for European causes; but the converse was also unprovable for Soviet leaders. Even a modest chance of a huge penalty can have great deterrent force. In different jargon, the 'expected value' of a disbenefit – the scale of the penalty factored with the perceived probability of its being levied – can outweigh even a high valuation and expectation of the benefit hoped for.

One further point of a slightly different kind – a semantic kind – before we move on from these abstractions. The root of the word 'deterrence' is that of 'terror'; it is about fear of costs; and clear discourse is helped by keeping it that way. What is sometimes called 'deterrence by denial' – preventing an adversary from gaining his objective by frustrating his attack – refers to a different concept, and to present this as a subset of deterrence is a misuse of language. If we want a term broad enough to embrace it, 'dissuasion' would be more accurate. French strategic analysts customarily used this as a virtual synonym for 'deterrence', but it properly reaches more widely.

A valuable linguistic usage, observable latterly with increasing frequency, classes as 'dissuasion' such concepts as the maintenance of United States military capability (whether offensive or defensive) so evidently weighty and sophisticated that potential adversaries are led to conclude – before any question arises of direct operational deterrence – that the effort to compete is not worth the political and economic costs.

Let us turn to deterrence in the world as it is now, altered by the ending of the Cold War and, still more recently, by the outrage of 11 September 2001.

As the 1990s progressed it became uncomfortably evident that history had not come to any sort of end; that there remained a significant number of actors ready to use illegitimate force to pursue objectives inimical to international order and peace; that the demise of the Cold War had indeed loosened constraints on some of these actors; and that we could not immediately count on holding them within structures as solid, well-understood and accepted as the central East/West standoff had become. A few commentators seemed even to despair of deterrence – how could we, they asked, deter people with different value-systems and less to lose?

Any agonizing of this kind was, however, overblown. Only the truly insane have no sense of weighing consequences; and to have a different value-system does not mean having none, no currency in which the risk of unacceptable disadvantage can be posed. One may narrow the point down further: it is hard to think of any instance in history of a state or similar power grouping that had no assets which it wished to retain, no collective concern for the lives of its members and no interest in the survival of its ruling regime. Where potential leverages of this kind exist – that is, everywhere – it must in principle be possible to construct penalty systems constraining the behaviour of states. The most vivid recent example of that is perhaps that of Iraq in 1991. Few regimes have been more careless of human decencies and of the lives of its individual citizens than Saddam Hussein's; yet though of its nature successful deterrence can hardly ever be formally proved – since it involves comparison between actual and alternative history – there is much reason to believe that Saddam's abstention from using his biological and chemical weapons was not unconnected with the facts of many-sided United States military power and Israel's possession of nuclear weapons. We may well need in future to build some deterrence frameworks in different and more varied ways – more broadly based, perhaps more multi-faceted – than we were accustomed to during the Cold War, in order to display prospective costs that bite credibly upon the values of particular adversaries about whose behaviour we are mistrustful. It may be, too, that some of what happened in the late 1990s has been unhelpful for the future building of such frameworks. This category includes the refusal of France, Russia and China – a refusal that subsequently came to carry heavy costs – to accept the costs and inconveniences of standing by their responsibilities in respect of Iraq's possession of weapons plainly prohibited to it by United Nations Security Council resolution. But the concept of deterrence is nowhere foredoomed to failure or irrelevance. There is no such thing as an undeterrable state.

But what about terrorists, who have no regime to be toppled, and may have no substantial infrastructure or armouries visible and available to be destroyed? It is by no means the case that non-state organisations engaged in international terrorism never have vulnerable assets, human or other, which they need or value highly; but the direct leverage of this kind is almost always far more limited than in respect of states.

In practice, however, few terrorist organisations of a type and size capable of doing massive damage outside their own homelands are truly and wholly independent of states, receiving neither conscious shelter nor support. To the extent that such aid is provided or condoned, the states responsible place themselves at risk of penalty; the experience of the Taleban government in the autumn of 2001 transmitted that message vividly. Sustaining, spreading and legitimating it for settings beyond Afghanistan can play an important part in deterring the terrorist threat, especially at higher levels of outrage such as the 11 September atrocity and the possible use of the kinds of instrument customarily aggregated as 'weapons of mass destruction'.

It is true that states supporting terrorism usually seek to conceal the fact, and that particular outrages may not always be immediately or conclusively traceable back to a harbouring state. But proposition five, about probabilities and risks, comes into play. A guilty state may not be sure of being found out; but equally it cannot be sure of not being found out. The graver the terrorist crime, the more determined the effort is likely to be to explore involvement, and the more severe the eventual penalty for complicity unmasked.

There is naturally now, in the wake of 11 September, a further strand of concern about the willingness (increasingly evident also in the Israeli/Palestinian context) of individuals to give their lives – give them, not merely risk them – in order to carry out terrorist attacks. What can deterrence, in the strict sense, do about these? In immediate terms, nothing. But they scarcely ever, if indeed ever, exist and operate in isolation from organisations, and these organisations rarely in isolation from states; and deterrence can be brought to bear by that route. We should, moreover, not write off entirely the idea of achieving something, in the long term, rather more directly. These individuals, whether regarded as tragic or awful, are not simply insane; they have their value-systems. They prize the respect of their families, their communities and their co-religionists; they often cherish the hope of a hereafter. The expectation of changing any of this may be distant and uncertain, and change cannot be imposed from outside the communities, especially if within them there is, as in the Middle East, a profound and shared sense of beleaguered grievance. But this dimension should not be abandoned. Islam – it is fair to focus there, because as a matter of plain fact the phenomenon of suicidal immolation is to be found above all in that environment – is a religion of moral teaching, and that teaching (at least in most of its explicit and established forms) does not commend acts like that of 11 September. If that be so, it is legitimate to wonder whether disapproval might come to be voiced more trenchantly and mobilized more effectively. That could make a genuine contribution to deterrence, through converting the reactions of families, friends and peers into costs rather than rewards. It would need, as a practical matter, to be partnered by a more resolute tackling of perceived grievance; and one must recognize the human difficulty often faced by moral teachers within settings where historic resentment is deeply ingrained. (It may be suspected – to invoke a parallel close to the writer personally – that in at least the initial stages of the Northern Ireland 'troubles' of the later twentieth century the Roman Catholic clergy there were not all as immediate, as outspoken, as unequivocal and as unanimous in their condemnation of Republican terrorism as Christian ethics truly required and as they themselves mostly later became; but significant change did take place, and progressively played a part in making community attitudes less tolerant of terrorism.) In brief, this is a relevant dimension of the terrorist problem; and there are opportunities and responsibilities capable of being exercised.

If that be thought a rather unusual aspect of deterrence, we might look next at another and more familiar instrument: the pursuit of criminals by international judicial process. The trial of Slobodan Milosevic and others from the wreck of Yugoslavia is another vehicle for the transmission of a warning message. Mechanisms of this kind ought to be viewed, and further developed, as part of the armoury of deterrence. For that among other reasons it is to be hoped, if perhaps without high near-term expectation, that United States leaders will come to reconsider their attitude to the concept of the International Criminal Court, where any real dangers – and these seem anyway remote – are surely outweighed by the benefits that could in time accumulate.

To illustrate some of what has been said above about deterrence in the twenty-first century, we might consider a more concrete idea. The international effort against the threat of biological weapons lost some impetus, following the decision of the United States Administration to walk away from the protracted collective endeavour to devise a verification protocol to underpin the comprehensive but largely toothless prohibitions in the 1972 Convention. At least one component in a fresh strategy – to complement whatever renewed steps are essayed to constrain BW possession – could be a more explicit and international deterrent to actual BW use, which is what matters in the end. The concept would be to build the largest possible coalition around a declaration of commitment, preferably centred on a Security Council

Resolution, that would engage all participating countries to treat any use of BW, regardless of attempted excuse, as a crime against humanity; to regard as having forfeited legitimacy any state committing the crime or helping its perpetrators; to pursue individual leaders responsible as international criminals; and to reverse any advantage secured by the crime.

To propound and examine this idea in full depth would need more extended treatment than is appropriate here; it is sketched just as exemplifying various features which could valuably play an increasing part in deterrent structures more generally. It would offer a broad basis of international support and legitimacy; it would focus upon posing risk to the continuance of guilty regimes, and to the freedom of guilty individuals; and it would stress the principle of not allowing improperly won benefits to stand.

The illustration can reach further. It is undoubtedly a problem with a possible BW threat that (unlike, say, nuclear assault by ballistic missiles) the very fact of external attack may not be swiftly apparent; and even thereafter the perpetrator may not be obvious. A state implicated in the offence might be tempted to gamble on that, and perhaps also on the possibility that international signatories would not hold solidly to their commitment, or might find difficulty in identifying and agreeing upon effective action to fulfil it. Once more, however, the converse is true: the wrongdoer would have to reckon, in advance, with the risk that involvement would be detected, and that the declared consequences would indeed flow from that.

This is no more than an example. The prime general contention of the present article is that though the world has moved on from the centrality of the Cold War and its nuclear-concentrated bilateral perceptions of deterrence, the underlying concept of deterrence remains valid and relevant. We need to exploit it more flexibly, with a wider range of instruments, a more finely calibrated bearing on the nature of particular actors, and wherever possible a broader base of international legitimacy and backing. It will continue to need to be viewed as just one among an array of potential approaches to protecting international security alongside, for example, allaying grievance, improving mechanisms for peaceful conflict resolution, creating positive incentives for desired behaviour, preventing the acquisition of pernicious capabilities, and improving ability to ward off attacks and lighten their effects. The salience of deterrence within a policy mix of such approaches will vary with situation, and will often not attain the centrality ascribed to it during the Cold War But there is no adequate reason to fear that there are large sectors of threat so entirely beyond the reach of deterrence that it can play no part.

NOTE

1. *Survival*, Vol. 37, No.4 (Winter 1995/96) pp. 187–91.

The Emergence of Stability: Deterrence-in-Motion and Deterrence Reconstructed

DARRYL HOWLETT

Deterrence has been a perennial feature of human relations throughout history: as a subject for theoretical and empirical investigation, it has spawned numerous conceptual models and case studies; and, as a debating topic concerned with the propensities for war in the nuclear age, it has generated intense reflection about the content of such strategies.[1]

In the period after 1945, and until the end of the 1980s, discussion about the theory and practice of nuclear deterrence dominated the agenda of the East–West Cold War. In those four-plus decades, the formulation of nuclear deterrence strategies in the West involved analysts and policy-makers from a wide range of backgrounds and academic disciplines.[2] It also embraced recurrent themes and concerns, which, in turn, produced diverse viewpoints and policy responses. Strategies of nuclear deterrence thus underwent several modifications, not only in response to developments in the East–West relationship, but also because technological innovation itself was a significant generator of new possibilities and challenges.[3]

Throughout the Cold War, a major preoccupation concerned the question of what if conflict broke out. It was generally assumed that, if the worst came to pass, nuclear weapons would be used (although strategies were not always explicit about the timing at which this would happen). As we are now aware, this scenario never occurred: for although the Cold War precipitated several crises, none led to overt conflict and nuclear weapons were never used.[4]

It is noteworthy, also, when assessing the history of ideas about deterrence, that leading writers on the subject have drawn similar conclusions concerning how this history has unfolded. Rather than viewing the history of theorizing about nuclear deterrence as an evolution in thinking, these writers suggest it is more appropriate to characterize this history in terms of cyclical debates in which key themes recurred.[5] Among these themes were: the arrival of the nuclear age and its impact on the nature of war; fear of pre-emption, surprise attack and the vulnerability of societies and bases; the consequences if nuclear deterrence failed and whether a nuclear conflict could be kept limited; what factors bolstered or undermined extended deterrence relationships; concerns about an upward spiralling nuclear arms race and its effects on precipitating an overt war; the consequences of nuclear proliferation and the prospects for conflict in a world of many nuclear possessors; concerns about rationality and whether this notion was universally shared between states; and, what was strategic stability and did arms control and disarmament agreements contribute to it.[6]

Much has been written previously on these themes and it is beyond the scope of this article to address them all in detail. For the purposes here, they will be considered under four broad headings: understanding the nuclear past; the notion of an 'absolute weapon' in human conflict; did differences in 'strategic culture' matter; and the nature of strategic stability and the contribution of arms control.

This article will conclude by making the following observations on the 1945–1990 period. First, nuclear knowledge is a complex area, but the end of the Cold War has allowed a more composite appreciation to emerge regarding the ideas surrounding nuclear deterrence and the strategies designed to implement them. Second, while judgements inevitably will vary, there are grounds for suggesting that a form of 'nuclear learning' occurred and this assisted in institutionalizing the East–West strategic relationship over time. Third, although a form of learning occurred, caution surrounds whether deterrence operated as expected at all times, as the period witnessed recurrent crises. Fourth, while the role of arms control may at times have been overstated, it did provide an important conduit for generating greater understanding between the adversaries about the nature of their strategic competition, and for codifying the mutually accepted rules and norms of this competition via agreements and arms limitation. Fifth, concerns about surprise attack and pre-emption precipitated moves towards diverse basing modes for delivery vehicles and heightened alert readiness strategies, but such fears could not be eliminated entirely. Sixth, misperception of intentions was also a recurrent theme, as unintended events and actions occurred which generated uncertainty on both sides. Seventh, both within and outside the East–West strategic relationship other aspects gained significance, as security guarantees and extended deterrent relationships were an important aspect of alliance arrangements. Finally, while the division of Europe may have contributed to stability in the context of the emerging post-Second World War environment, over time the desire for accommodation and change was a powerful factor in bridging, and eventually removing, this division.

Understanding the Nuclear Past

What constitutes knowledge of the nuclear past is a complex question, especially when dealing with a topic like deterrence. At one level, it can be viewed in terms of information and data. There is now a burgeoning empirical record of the events that dominated the East–West nuclear confrontation and, with the benefit of hindsight, an appraisal, or re-appraisal, can be made in light of the new information. Yet, this abundance of information can create its own problems, as the analyst may be, 'overwhelmed by the sheer volume of the material that has been generated'.[7] Even then, aspects of the nuclear past remain conjectural. This is because either the information is unavailable or incomplete, or simply that it is not possible to provide a full account of the different contexts in which nuclear deterrence strategies were formulated.

One development, which has reduced this limitation, is that contemporary studies have been able to include new information from archival sources and oral histories from the policy-makers involved. New insights have therefore been gleaned on issues such as the Soviet Union's view of conflict, deterrence and strategy in the nuclear age.[8] Such insights have complemented texts written during the Cold War and allowed for a greater understanding of the factors that shaped the East–West strategic relationship.[9]

At another level, it is possible to consider the nuclear past in terms of whether a form of 'learning' occurred. As the Cold War drew to a close, the proposition was advanced that a collective institutional memory concerning the theory and practice of deterrence had evolved since 1945. This process was referred to as 'nuclear learning', an experience derived largely from the East–West, primarily United States–Soviet Union, competition.[10] It was suggested that 'learning', to varying degrees, occurred in areas, such as: nuclear weapons and their effects; command and control procedures to reduce the risks of inadvertent conflict and the dangers of escalation; the spread of nuclear weapons; 'force and the volatility of the arms race'; the practice of arms control negotiations (which also involved disagreements about its value); and the force structures needed for deterrence.[11]

Concomitantly, this position acknowledged the limitations in evaluating whether any such learning had occurred, due to problems associated with what is known about deterrence and how it operated. Consequently, the following caveat was introduced:

> much of what passes for nuclear knowledge rests upon elaborate counterfactual arguments, abstractions based on assumptions about rational actors, assumptions about the other nation's known intentions, and simple intuitions.[12]

Some authors have also considered the period 1945–1990 as a nuclear order issue.[13] Associated with the notion of any order are a range of questions: is the order based solely on power relations, or on a combination of power, co-operative rules, norms and reciprocity; what are the institutions (both formal and informal), which contribute to the establishment of an order; and, is the order considered legitimate by all participants?[14] It is noteworthy that judgements have subsequently differed on the issue of nuclear order: from those who have questioned the legitimacy and power relations inherent in the formation of a post-war nuclear order; to those who consider the emerging order from 1945 to 1990 as an important element of East–West and global nuclear stability.

Was This the Era of the 'Absolute Weapon'?

In a volume that appeared in 1946, Bernard Brodie and other writers characterized the atomic bomb as a unique or 'Absolute Weapon', which had revolutionary ramifications.[15] These writers all agreed that the new weapon transformed the nature of conflict due to its destructive capability and the vulnerability of societies in the face of this capability: atomic weapons were qualitatively different.[16]

Brodie noted that gunpowder had once been thought of as the absolute weapon when it first appeared (as was the crossbow and the tank); but he judged atomic weapons to be fundamentally different from even these military innovations. Moreover, a little more than a decade later, when new technological developments were gripping the strategic imagination, Brodie would reiterate his earlier assessment of the impact of the atomic bomb:

> In an age that had grown used to taking rapid advances in military technology for granted, how remarkable was this immediate and almost universal consensus that the atomic bomb was different and epochal![17]

Coincidentally, in the same year that the Brodie volume appeared, Aldous Huxley issued a new foreword to *Brave New World*, a book initially published in 1932. Huxley admitted he had not foreseen the impact of the new atomic energy source and the revolution in human life it would engender. Interestingly, also, he considered that the advent of atomic energy marked:

> a great revolution in human history, but not (unless we blow ourselves to bits and so put an end to history) the final and most searching revolution ... This really revolutionary revolution is to be achieved, not in the external world, but in the souls and flesh of human beings.[18]

Similarly instructive of this immediate post-1945 period is that the newly formed United Nations (UN) began its institutional existence by making a distinction between conventional weapons and what, thereafter, would be termed weapons of mass destruction.[19] This set a categorical precedent that would later resonate in UN debates on disarmament and form the basis for multilateral agreements negotiated in that forum.

Experience of past conflicts often produced different appraisals of the impact of the 'new power'for those involved in operational matters. Some did view it in revolutionary terms, but others saw the atomic bomb as just another weapon in a long line of such weapons. Hence, they saw little difference between the destructive effects of conventional and atomic ordnance.[20] Experiential knowledge may thus have been the guide for this group, as this was a generation that had suffered two world wars in relatively quick succession and seen different types of weaponry used in both.

After 1945, technological and strategic innovation continued and some analysts point to the advent of hydrogen weapons and ballistic missiles as the key militarily significant developments of the Cold War.[21] As Joseph Nye has characterized it:

> The increased destructiveness of hydrogen bombs also dramatized the consequences of nuclear war. No longer could warfare be considered merely an extension of politics by other means. Karl von Clausewitz ... said war is a political act, and therefore absolute war is an absurdity. The enormous destructive power of nuclear weapons meant there was now a disproportion between the military means and most of the political ends that a country might seek.[22]

On 1 November 1952, the United States detonated the world's first thermonuclear device in the Pacific, an event that transformed the potential destructive power of the nuclear age from the kiloton to the megaton range.[23] Nine years later, in 1961, the Soviet Union exploded its biggest bomb, a hydrogen weapon measured at approximately 50 megatons.[24] This development, coupled with the announcement in 1957 that the Soviet Union had successfully tested an Inter-Continental Ballistic Missile, would have a profound effect on the strategic consciousness of the United States. Not only did it provoke concerns in the West (later found to be overstated), that the Soviet Union had a lead over the United States in ballistic missile technology, it also meant that the United States homeland was increasingly vulnerable to a surprise attack by such missiles.[25]

Writing during this period, Brodie considered that historical experience with war offered little guidance for dealing with the challenges posed by the new forms of weaponry.[26] However, he was not an advocate of nuclear elimination as a means for overcoming these challenges.[27] Conversely, neither was he a supporter of what he described as the 'bitter, relentless race in nuclear weapons and missiles'that had been the predominant feature of the East–West rivalry since 1945.[28] This, he argued, had, 'its own intrinsic dangers'.[29] In his view, the answer lay in devising a credible strategy of nuclear deterrence that would induce stability, reduce 'drastically the advantage that the enemy can derive from hitting first by surprise attack', and ensure the 'survival of the retaliatory force under attack'.[30]

John Herz's writings are also instructive of the zeitgeist of this period. Writing in 1959, Herz considered that the state was becoming increasingly 'permeable' and was losing one of its classical characteristics, the notion of territoriality. Although he would later revisit his position on the future role of the territorial state, Herz still believed that the rapidity of technological change was creating a new era for humans to contend with:

> there was now occurring...the most radical change in the nature of power and the characteristics of power units since the beginning of the modern state system or, perhaps, since the beginning of mankind.[31]

This contextual discussion of the themes of the period is intentional because it indicates the complexity surrounding early post-war debates about the revolutionary or otherwise nature of nuclear weapons. It also highlights the impact the weapon had on emerging concerns over surprise attack, vulnerability and technological change. These themes and concerns provided the prelude to a discussion that would resonate in later decades over the requirements for stable mutual deterrence and the force structures to support it.

Did Differences in Strategic Culture Matter?

In recent years there has been a resurgence of interest in the strategic culture approach.[32] Advocates of this approach consider that factors such as historical experience, geographical location, cultural identity and ideational influences matter when it comes to understanding why states pursue certain strategic policies in contrast to others. In the 1970s and early 1980s, these considerations led some writers to ask whether there were meaningful differences between the way the East and West formulated nuclear strategies. These analysts pointed to the different historical, geographical and cultural factors, which were deemed significant when it came to questions of strategy in the nuclear age: in effect, the United States and the Soviet Union had different 'national styles in strategy', or strategic cultures.[33]

In the West, deterrence theory relied on certain assumptions about rationality and how actors respond in different strategic situations.[34] In the discussion over strategic culture, a key aspect concerned the issue of rationality and whether it could be understood similarly in all states and regions. One position, for example, discerned that deterrence might not always operate as predicted by traditional deterrence theory because of the varied cultural understandings of what constituted a rational or irrational act. The converse position was that the traditional notion of rationality did apply in all cultural contexts, especially where nuclear decision-making was concerned.

This debate had implications for other elements of deterrence theory. One concerned the question of whether deterrence should be viewed as 'easy' or 'difficult'. Whereas the 'easy' school emphasizes that the costs and risks involved in any nuclear exchange are so high that any deterree will not seriously contemplate initiating such an outcome, the 'difficult' school attaches 'less weight to the impact of infinite costs and more weight to the possibility of highly motivated deterrees'.[35]

Where this had direct applicability was in discussions over the credibility of threats, as a threat could not be effective unless an adversary believed that it would be implemented.[36] Thomas Schelling provided one of the first pronouncements on this in 1961 when he wrote that, 'Making a credible threat involves proving that one would have to carry out the threat, or creating incentives for oneself or incurring penalties that would make one evidently want to'.[37]

The issue of credibility was an important feature of another form of deterrent arrangement, those involving third parties.[38] The nature of these arrangements raised a complex question: was deterrence more difficult in situations where third parties were covered by a nuclear umbrella of another state than in contexts associated with direct state-to-state deterrence between nuclear-armed adversaries?[39] Resolve and a willingness on the part of a nuclear-armed ally to make particular commitments to a third party subsequently came to be viewed as a crucial element of extended deterrence. In practical terms, this took the form of the stationing of forces on an ally's territory, bilateral security guarantees, and formal alliance arrangements for collective defence.

The notion of appropriate capability was also a part of theoretical discussion, as this involved a judgement concerning what sort of force structure would be required to deter an adversary. This force structure ultimately came to be defined not only as the ability to deliver nuclear weapons to designated targets, but also required the possession of a sufficiently survivable force capable of retaliating after an initial attack.

In terms of the effective communication of threat, the key aspect related to the channels and language of communication. It was considered necessary to communicate an intended threat effectively to an adversary, as any miscommunication, misunderstanding, or misperception could lead to confusion about what responses would follow a particular action.

The theory of deterrence thus involved judgements about what kinds of threats deter, what forces are required to accomplish such an outcome, and the means by which deterrent threats can be communicated between adversaries.[40] For the early writers on strategic culture, these considerations were not straightforward due to the historical and other culturally contingent experiences that had led each side to adopt different force structures and postures. From this position, these differences mattered in times of confrontation and in the day-to-day responses that each side made to the doctrines, deployments and arms control initiatives of the other.

The Nature of Strategic Stability and the Contribution of Arms Control

What constituted strategic stability was a perennial theme throughout the period 1945–1990. It has been suggested that underpinning traditional deterrence are, 'two distinct, yet compatible, strands of the theory... *structural... deterrence theory*... (and) *decision-theoretic deterrence theory*...'.[41] While the former theory considers that the key to international stability resides in the structure and distribution of power in the international system, the other, 'focuses on the interplay of outcomes, preferences, and choices in determining interstate conflict behavior'.[42]

Some have consequently viewed strategic stability in terms of achieving a central or strategic balance, which could be attained via specific force deployments and the negotiation of formal arms control measures. Others saw stability as a more complex phenomenon involving a range of factors (economic, political and military), all of which needed to be addressed if the prospects for war were to be reduced. The issue of how to define strategic stability was thus a significant one, as Soviet analyst, Mikhail Milstein, observed in the mid-1980s:

> Though the problem of strategic stability is not a new one, we do not have a common and comprehensive definition of it. Partially this is due to the fact that we are dealing with a very complex and, to a certain extent, broad and even controversial issue that touches upon the most important aspect of the relations between the two sides.[43]

Lawrence Freedman has observed that studies written in the early 1960s highlighted many of the issues associated with stability. In these studies, concerns were expressed about the difficulties of stabilizing the strategic environment and that the, 'greatest instability would be the coincidence of an international crisis with "the reciprocal fear of surprise attack"'.[44] It was therefore argued that efforts should be directed towards reducing the possibilities for pre-emption by arms control in order to create a stable mutual deterrent arrangement.[45]

This debate gathered momentum during the 1960s, propelled by evolving ideas about arms control and the desire to reduce crisis, proliferation and arms race instabilities.[46] By the mid-1960s, arms control, as a means for dealing with a dynamic strategic situation, was becoming a mainstay of US thinking. Many would view this change in orientation as a move away from disarmament. Advocates of arms control argued that this policy represented the most effective way to enhance strategic stability and to prevent war in the nuclear age.[47]

As indicated above, crisis instability represented one of the most complex areas for analysts to deal with. Crisis situations were said to present possibilities for both 'danger and opportunity'.[48] As Phil Williams has indicated:

> it has to be recognized that crises lie at the crucial juncture between peace and war. Crisis interactions can result either in the outbreak of war between the protagonists or in the peaceful resolution of the crisis in terms that are at least sufficiently satisfactory to the participants as to make the option of the resorting to force seem unattractive.[49]

The historical record suggests that dealing with such situations was not straightforward and this has led some writers to question whether nuclear weapons consistently made a difference during confrontations.[50]

For many, the Cuban missile crisis in October 1962 represented a key turning point in the 'nuclear learning' curve of the early Cold War.[51] This is considered to have been the closest the East and West came to an overt conflict, although both earlier and later events have been viewed as equally, if not more, significant. John Newhouse, for example, has commented that tensions over Berlin were also very high:

> The danger of nuclear war may have been most acute during the Cuban missile crisis... The crisis, however, was never as threatening to peace and stability as the frightening, uniquely volatile situation in Berlin during the summer and fall of 1961, perhaps the time of greatest peril in the nuclear age.[52]

Similarly, Scott Sagan and Jeremi Suri have pointed to crises that occurred after 1962 in which potentially dangerous consequences may have arisen from the dynamic interplay of decisions and events.[53]

The issue of interpreting intentions, both in crisis situations and in general relations, was therefore an important element in East–West strategic practice.[54] For writers like Derek Leebaert, one of the most important aspects was to get the balance right between capabilities and intentions:

> Policy recommendations founded entirely on opinions of enemy intentions are as fraught with peril as are those resting just on capabilities.

THE EMERGENCE OF STABILITY

But besides the volatility of intentions, their study is a far more esoteric, subjective, and fault-prone exercise than that of capabilities. An over-reliance on capabilities or intentions can be hazardous.[55]

Added to this were concerns that a nuclear conflagration might break out by accident or, as Daniel Frei put it, by 'false assumptions, i.e. on misjudgement or miscalculation by the persons legitimately authorized to decide on the use of nuclear weapons'.[56] As Matthew Woods has observed, at the heart of this position is a claim of human fallibility and that errors, whether motivated or unmotivated, are a routine feature of human actions.[57]

The issue of strategic stability was made more complex by debates over whether a strategic nuclear arms race existed and, if so, what factors contributed to it.[58] A central feature of this debate concerned the impact of quantitative and qualitative technological changes, and whether one side might gain a strategic advantage and become capable of launching a pre-emptive first strike with impunity. In an assessment of how particular analysts have considered this issue, James DeNardo writes that the key to much thinking about stable deterrence is the assumption concerning the requirement for an assured second strike:

> What deters a nuclear *first strike*, they assumed, is the compelling prospect of a retaliatory *second strike*. When both sides can marshal a devastating second strike, neither has any incentive to strike first – even in a crisis. Moreover, neither requires more or different nuclear forces to deter the other side. In this way, secure second strikes provide both *crisis stability* and *arms race stability*.[59]

In the East–West context, much attention focused on the relationship between the offence and the defence, and the contribution that arms control could make in reducing instability. The gradual acceptance, during the 1960s and early 1970s, of the notion of mutual strategic vulnerability and the requirement for an assured second-strike capability, eventually led to limitations on anti-ballistic missile (ABM) systems.[60] Nevertheless, although missile defences came to be viewed as destabilizing in the context of mutual vulnerability, vigorous debate about their utility – and whether particular weapon systems should be seen as either stabilizing or destabilizing – recurred throughout the Cold War.

Debates over proliferation stability were equally complex, as the question here was what impact would more states possessing nuclear weapons have on the prospects for international conflict? The issue of proliferation stability, or what initially was referred to as the 'nth country problem', would thus become one of the major factors in the overall consideration of strategic stability.[61]

In the 1960s, this issue was part of the debate over the stability of a bipolar in contrast to a multi-polar world.[62] In policymaking circles, it found expression in attempts to reduce complexity by limiting the number of potential nuclear decision-making centres and nuclear-possessor states. This was done via the negotiation of specific alliance arrangements and security guarantees, which incorporated pledges of commitment to the defence of particular territories or states and allowed for greater consultations over nuclear decision-making.

It was also pursued through international legal agreements, such as the Treaty on the Non-Proliferation of Nuclear Weapons (NPT). The NPT involved a complex and delicate compromise, based on a distinction between a Nuclear Weapon State (NWS) and a Non-Nuclear Weapon State (NNWS).[63] Although this compromise developed into an acceptable arrangement, not just for the main protagonists in the East–West relationship but for other parties as well, there were always tensions inherent in the assumptions underpinning it. The NPT therefore rested on an understanding of reciprocity and the ability of all parties to fulfil their obligations under the Treaty. This and other issues became perennial debating topics at the NPT's five-yearly review conferences in 1975, 1980, 1985 and 1990.

Conclusion

John Lewis Gaddis, writing in the early 1990s, speculated that the end of the Cold War was likely to become a key turning point, equally as significant as previous epochal changes. 'Historians', he wrote, 'will certainly regard the years 1989–1991 as a turning point comparable in importance to the years 1789–1794, or 1917–1918, or 1945–1947'.[64] More than a decade on, those observations still resonate.

The years 1989–1991 also coincided with the ending of what has been termed, the 'first nuclear age'.[65] This age had been characterized by an intense ideological and nuclear confrontation, yet the Cold War was concluded without overt conflict or any nuclear weapons being used. As John Orme has put it, 'the cold war never escalated from a clash of ideas to a clash of arms'.[66]

Assessments of the role of deterrent strategies in securing what Gaddis, originally in 1986, referred to as 'the long peace', range from those who consider that these strategies were a primary cause of insecurity between East and West, to those who view the absence of war, in the 1945–1990 period, as a direct consequence of such strategies.[67] Some also consider that the 'long peace' was attributable to the specific combination of the advent of nuclear weapons, acceptance, over time, of the post-World War Two *status quo* in Europe, and the bipolar configuration of power relations between East and West.[68] In contrast, others view nuclear weapons as 'essentially irrelevant' to post-1945 history because factors, such as industrial, economic and institutional changes, were already rendering major war obsolete.[69]

Good leadership has also been identified as an important factor in securing the 'long peace', especially in times of confrontation. Evaluating the extent to which stability and accommodation between East and West rested on the qualities of leadership is not straightforward as other factors, such as institutions, ideas, structural constraints, may have been equally, if not more, significant.[70] Biographical techniques to discern how the respective leaders viewed the first nuclear age have been used in one study to ask the question: 'Did the advent of the nuclear bomb prevent the Third World War?'[71] In the Introduction to that volume, however, one of the editors says the evidence concerning the leaders addressed by their authors is inconclusive.[72] Elsewhere, Gaddis has written that nuclear weapons had:

> a remarkably *theatrical* effect upon the course of the Cold War. They created the mood of dark foreboding that transfixed the world... They required statesmen to become actors: success or failure depended, or so it seemed, not on what one was really doing, but on what one *appeared* to be doing.[73]

Besides the role of any individual leader, did any collective institutional memory, or 'nuclear learning', occur? A word of caution must still be sounded on what can be said about whether there was any development of common nuclear knowledge between the two sides. Yet, there are grounds for suggesting that a form of learning did occur, which, over time, served to regulate and institutionalize the East–West competition. It was not always an upward learning curve, but both sides did initiate measures to: avoid, where possible, a direct clash of military forces; keep communication channels open at all times, especially during crises; negotiate limitations on nuclear forces; and, formalize confidence and security building measures to reduce concerns of surprise attack (for both conventional and nuclear forces).[74]

It can also be argued that an evolving nuclear order did emerge in the post-1945 environment, although it was always under strain from questions of legitimacy, political change and technological innovation. In historical terms, this order moved from being based, in the early Cold War years, on military power relations primarily (and where conflict was considered imminent); to a situation, by the latter 1980s, more akin to a nuclear order of reciprocal accommodation based on common rules, norms, and bilateral and multilateral arms control arrangements (and where conflict was deemed a latent and less pressing element).

Many in the East–West context may therefore look back on this latter period especially, as a time when they could rely on an element of certainty (although not predictability) in planning, as the strategic competitor for both sides was known and policies could be devised accordingly. Conversely, others will reflect with a less sanguine outlook and judge that this was an era when nuclear weapons were not only produced in large numbers, these weapons were on high alert and occupied a far too prominent position in East–West strategic relations. Some will also view this particular nuclear order as lacking legitimacy because it produced both a divisive hierarchy of nuclear possessors and non-possessors, and a set of arrangements that were not conducive to an enduring peace.[75] Yet, there was no war between the main protagonists and by any estimation this was an extraordinary outcome given past experience of major conflict in human affairs: what remains unknowable is whether the context in which this particular nuclear environment evolved was unique and what the consequences would be if it was.

NOTES

The title of this paper has been adapted from Ernest Yanarella, '"Reconstructed Logic" and "Logic-in-use" in decision-making analysis: Graham Allison', *Policy*, Vol.8, (1975) quoted in Steve Smith, 'Allison and the Cuban Missile Crisis', *Millenium*, Vol.9, No.1 (1980), pp.21–40.

1. See Keith B. Payne and C. Dale Walton, 'Deterrence in the Post-Cold War World', in John Baylis, James Wirtz, Eliot Cohen and Colin S. Gray (eds), *Strategy in the Contemporary World. An Introduction to Strategic Studies* (Oxford: Oxford University Press, 2002); Stephen J. Cimbala, *The Past and Future of Nuclear Deterrence* (Westport, CT: Praeger, 1998); Max G. Mainwaring (ed.), *Deterrence in the 21st Century* (London: Frank Cass, 2001); and George Quester, *Deterrence before Hiroshima* (New York: 1966).
2. Payne and Walton, 'Deterrence in the Post-Cold War World', p.165; and John Garnett, 'Introduction', in John Garnett (ed.), *Theories of Peace and Security. A Reader in Contemporary Strategic Thought* (London: Macmillan, 1970), p.19.
3. See Lawrence Freedman, *The Evolution of Nuclear Strategy*, 2nd edition (Basingstoke: Macmillan in association with the International Institute for Strategic Studies, 1989); John S. Duffield, 'The Evolution of NATO's Strategy of Flexible Response: A Reinterpretation', *Security Studies*, Vol.1, No.1 (Autumn 1991), pp.132–56; David N. Schwartz, *NATO's Nuclear Dilemmas* (Washington, DC: Brookings Institution, 1983); Shaun R. Gregory, *Nuclear Weapons Operations and the Strategy of Flexible Response Nuclear Command and Control in NATO* (Basingstoke: Macmillan, 1996); Fred C. Ikle, 'Can Nuclear Deterrence last out the Century', *Foreign Affairs*, Vol.51, No.2 (Jan. 1973), pp.267–85; and Helga Haftendorf, *NATO and the Nuclear Revolution: A Crisis of Credibility, 1966–1967* (Oxford: Clarendon Press, 1996).
4. Richard J. Harknett, James J. Wirtz and T.V. Paul, 'Introduction: Understanding Nuclear Weapons in a Transforming World', in T.V. Paul, Richard J. Harknett and James J. Wirtz (eds), *The Absolute Weapon Revisited. Nuclear Arms and the Emerging International Order* (Ann Arbor, MI: University of Michigan Press, 1998), p.1.
5. Freedman, *The Evolution of Nuclear Strategy*, p.xviii; and Richard K. Betts, 'The Concept of Deterrence in the Postwar Era', *Security Studies*, Vol.1, No.1, (Autumn 1991), p.27.

6. It has been noted by several authors that many themes associated with deterrence, including critical commentaries, originated in key texts largely produced in a period from 1957 to 1966. Among these were: Henry Kissinger, *Nuclear Weapons and Foreign Policy* (New York: Harper, 1957); Albert Wohlstetter, 'The Delicate Balance of Terror', *Foreign Affairs*, Vol.37, No.2 (Jan. 1959), pp.211–34; Anatol Rapoport, *Fights, Games and Debates* (Ann Arbor, MI: Michigan University Press, 1960); Thomas Schelling, *The Strategy of Conflict* (New York: Oxford University Press, 1960); Pierre Gallois, *The Balance of Terror: Strategy for the Nuclear Age*, translated from French by Richard Howard (Boston: Houghton Mifflin, 1961); Glenn Snyder, *Deterrence and Defense* (Princeton, NJ: Princeton University Press, 1961); Herman Kahn, *Thinking About the Unthinkable* (New York: Horizon Press, 1962); Alastair Buchan and Philip Windsor, *Arms and Stability in Europe* (London: Chatto and Windus, 1963); Morton Halperin, *Limited War in the Nuclear Age* (New York: John Wiley and Sons, 1963); Philip Green, *Deadly Logic: The Theory of Nuclear Deterrence* (Columbus, OH: Ohio State University Press, 1966); Klaus Knorr, *On the Uses of Military Power in the Nuclear Age* (Princeton, NJ: Princeton University Press, 1966); and Thomas Schelling, *Arms and Influence* (New Haven, CT: Yale University Press, 1966).
7. Freedman, *The Evolution of Nuclear Strategy*, p.xviii.
8. Nikolai Sokov, review of Pavel Podvig (ed.), *Russian Strategic Forces* (Cambridge, MA: MIT Press, 2001), *The Nonproliferation Review*, Vol.9, No.1 (Spring 2002), p.172 and endnote 2. See also David Holloway, *Stalin and the Bomb: The Soviet Union and Atomic Energy, 1939–1956* (New Haven: Yale University Press, 1994); Murray Feshbach (ed.), *National Security Issues of the USSR* (Dordrecht, Boston and Lancaster: Martinus Nijhoff, 1987); John Baylis and Gerald Segal (eds), *Soviet Strategy* (London: Croom Helm, 1981); Jennifer G. Mathers, *The Russian Nuclear Shield From Stalin to Yeltsin* (Basingstoke: Macmillan in association with St Antony's College, Oxford, 2000); Margot Light, *The Soviet Theory of International Relations* (Brighton: Wheatsheaf Books, 1988), esp. pp.215–26; Mary Kaldor, *The Imaginary War. Understanding the East–West Conflict* (Oxford: Basil Blackwell, 1990), ch.11; and Derek Leebaert (ed.), *Soviet Military Thinking* (London: Allen and Unwin, 1981).
9. David Holloway, 'Soviet Nuclear History. Sources for Stalin and the Bomb', *Cold War International History Project Bulletin*, No.4 (Fall 1994), pp.1–9.
10. See Joseph S. Nye, 'Nuclear Learning and U.S.–Soviet Security Regimes', *International Organization*, Vol.41, No.3 (Summer 1987), pp.371–402.
11. Ibid. pp.382–3.
12. Ibid. p.382.
13. In the Western context, this began with the publication of Bernard Brodie's edited volume, *The Absolute Weapon: Atomic Power and World Order* (New York: Harcourt, Brace) in 1946 and continued throughout the Cold War. See Hedley Bull, *The Control of the Arms Race* (London: International Institute for Strategic Studies, 1961); John J. Weltman, 'Nuclear Devolution and World Order', *World Politics*, Vol.32 (Jan. 1980), pp.169–93; Lawrence Scheinman, *The International Atomic Energy Agency and World Nuclear Order* (Washington, DC: John Hopkins University Press, 1987); Jorn Gjelstad and Olav Njolstad (eds), *Nuclear Rivalry and International Order* (London: Sage, 1996); and William Walker, 'Nuclear order and disorder', *International Affairs*, Vol.76, No.4 (Oct. 2000), pp.703–24.
14. For an overview of the Western literature on world order ideas see Hidemi Suganami, *The Domestic Analogy and World Order Proposals* (Cambridge: Cambridge University Press, 1989). On the notion of international order see Ian Clark, *Reform and Resistance in the International Order* (Cambridge: Cambrige University Press, 1980); and Nicholas J. Rengger, *International Relations, Political Theory and the Problem of Order* (London: Routledge, 2000).
15. See also Bernard Brodie and Eilene Galloway, *The Atomic Bomb and the Armed Services* (Washington, DC.: Library of Congress Legislative Reference Service, Public Affairs Bulletin No.55, May 1947). For background on the thinking of Brodie and others during

this early nuclear period see Fred Kaplan, *The Wizards of Armageddon* (Stanford: Stanford University Press, 1983). On the idea of revolutionary change in military technology see Barry Buzan and Eric Herring, *The Arms Dynamic in World Politics* (London: Lynne Rienner, 1998), ch.2; Martin van Creveld, *Technology and War: From 2000 B.C. to the Present* (New York: The Free Press, 1989); and Theo Farrell and Terry Terriff (eds), *The Sources of Military Change. Culture, Politics, Technology* (London: Lynne Rienner, 2002).

16. Harknett, Wirtz and Paul (eds), 'Introduction: Understanding Nuclear Weapons in a Transforming World', pp.5–6.
17. Bernard Brodie, *Strategy in the Missile Age* (Princeton, NJ: Princeton University Press, 1971 [1959]), p.151.
18. Aldous Huxley, *Brave New World* (London: Chatto and Windus, 1946), foreword.
19. John Simpson, 'The UN's Role in Disarmament: Retrospect and Prospect', *Contemporary Security Policy*, Vol.15, No.1 (April 1994), pp.55–67.
20. George H. Quester, *Nuclear Diplomacy. The First Twenty Five Years* (New York: The Dunellen Company, 1970), pp.36–7; Joseph S. Nye, *Understanding International Conflicts. An Introduction to Theory and History* (New York: HarperCollins, 1993), p.120; and Michael Mandelbaum, *The Nuclear Revolution: International Politics before and after Hiroshima* (Cambridge: Cambridge University Press, 1981).
21. John Lewis Gaddis, 'Conclusion', in John Lewis Gaddis, Philip H. Gordon, Ernest R. May and Jonathon Rosenberg (eds), *Cold War Statesmen Confront the Bomb. Nuclear Diplomacy Since 1945* (Oxford: Clarendon Press, 1999), pp.260–71. For background see John Lewis Gaddis, *We Now Know. Rethinking Cold War History* (Oxford: Clarendon Press, 1997), ch.8.
22. Nye, *Understanding International Conflicts*, p.121.
23. Richard Rhodes, *Dark Sun. The Making of the Hydrogen Bomb*, (New York: Simon and Schuster, 1995).
24. Viktor Adamsky and Yuri Smirnov, 'Moscow's Biggest Bomb: The 50-Megaton Test of October 1961', *Cold War International History Project*, No.4, pp.3, 19–21.
25. John W. Spanier and Joseph L. Nogee, *The Politics of Disarmament: A Study in Soviet-American Gamesmanship* (New York: Praeger, 1962), pp.100–101; Paul Kennedy, *The Rise and Fall of the Great Powers* (London: Unwin Hyman, 1988), p.388; and Kaplan, *The Wizards of Armageddon*, pp.294–5.
26. Brodie, *Strategy in the Missile Age*, p.390.
27. Ibid. p.300.
28. Ibid.
29. Ibid.
30. Ibid. p.394.
31. John H. Herz, *International Politics in the Atomic Age* (New York and London: Columbia University Press, 1959), p.22.
32. For discussion of this approach see Alastair Iain Johnston, 'Thinking About Strategic Culture', *International Security*, Vol.19, No.4 (Spring 1995), pp.32–64; Peter J. Katzenstein (ed.), *The Culture of National Security: Norms and Identity in World Politics* (New York: Columbia University Press, 1996); Michael C. Desch, 'Culture Clash: Assessing the Importance of Ideas in Security Studies', *International Security*, Vol.23, No.1 (Summer 1998), pp.141–70; Colin S. Gray, 'Strategic Culture as Context: The First Generation of Theory Strikes Back', *Review of International Studies*, Vol.25, No.1 (Jan. 1999), pp.49–70; Theo Farrell, 'Culture and Military Power', *Review of International Studies*, Vol.24, No.3 (July 1998), pp.407–16; and Beatrice Heuser, *Nuclear Mentalities, Strategies and Beliefs in Britain, France and the FRG* (Basingstoke: Macmillan, 1998).
33. See Jack Snyder, *The Soviet Strategic Culture: Implications for Nuclear Options*, Rand R-2154-AF (Santa Monica, CA: Rand Corporation, 1977); Ken Booth, *Strategy and Ethnocentrism* (New York: Holmes and Meier, 1979); Ken Booth, 'The Concept of Strategic Culture Affirmed', in Carl C. Jacobsen (ed.), *Strategic Power USA/USSR* (Basingstoke: Macmillan, 1990), pp.121–30; Colin S. Gray, *Nuclear Strategy and National Style* (London: Hamilton

Press, 1986); John Erickson, 'The Soviet View of Deterrence', *Survival*, Vol.14, No.6 (1982), pp.242–51; Gerald Segal, 'Strategy and Ethnic Chic', *International Affairs*, Vol.60 (1984), pp.15–30; and David T. Twining, 'Soviet Strategic Culture', *Intelligence and National Security*, Vol.4 (1989), pp.169–88.
34. For a discussion of the issues surrounding rationality see Patrick M. Morgan, *Deterrence: A Conceptual Analysis* (New York: Sage, 1977); John Garnett, 'Strategic Studies and Its Assumptions', in John Baylis, Ken Booth, John Garnett and Phil Williams, *Contemporary Strategy. Theories and Policies* (London: Croom Helm, 1975), pp.16–19; Booth, *Strategy and Ethnocentrism*; John Steinbrunner, 'Beyond Rational Deterrence: The Struggle for New Conceptions', *World Politics*, Vol.28 (1976), pp.223–45; Frank C. Zagare and D. Marc Kilgour, *Perfect Deterrence* (Cambridge: Cambridge University Press, 2000); and James G. Blight and David A. Welch, 'Risking "The Destruction of Nations": Lessons of the Cuban Missile Crisis for New and Aspiring Nuclear States', *Security Studies*, Vol. 4, No. 4 (Summer 1995), pp.811–50.
35. Buzan and Herring, *The Arms Dynamic in World Politics*, p.170.
36. See Snyder, *Deterrence and Defense*; Schelling, *Arms and Influence*; Phil Williams, 'Deterrence', in Baylis, Booth, Garnett and Williams, pp.75–6; and Stephen J. Cimbala, 'Deterrence and Friction: Implications for Missile Defense', *Defense and Security Analysis*, Vol.18, No.3 (2002), p.203.
37. Schelling, *The Strategy of Conflict*, p.187.
38. Bruce M. Russett, 'The Calculus of Deterrence', in James N. Rosenau (ed.), *International Politics and Foreign Policy* (New York: The Free Press, 1969), pp.359–69.
39. Richard Betts indicates that this issue emerged in the 1950s and concerned two types of deterrence: 'at one level was "basic," "central," or "passive," or "Type I" deterrence, meaning the prevention of enemy nuclear attack on the homeland by the threat of second-strike retaliation. At another level was "extended," "active" or "Type II" deterrence, meaning the prevention of enemy attack on allies. The great debate which has persisted ever since has been whether both sorts of deterrence could or could not be accomplished with reliance on nuclear threats.' Betts, 'The Concept of Deterrence in the Postwar Era', p.29.
40. For a discussion see Buzan and Herring, *The Arms Dynamic in World Politics*, ch.10.
41. Zagare and Kilgour, *Perfect Deterrence*, p.8
42. Ibid. p.16.
43. Mikhail Milstein, 'The Problem of Strategic Stability', in Joseph Rotblat and Sven Hellman (eds), *Nuclear Strategy and World Security*, Annals of Pugwash 1984 (Basingstoke: Macmillan, 1985), p.14.
44. Freedman, *The Evolution of Nuclear Strategy*, p.199.
45. Ibid. See also, Robert Ayson, 'Bargaining With Nuclear Weapons: Thomas Schelling's "General" Concept of Stability', *Journal of Strategic Studies*, Vol.23, No.2 (June 2000), pp.48–71.
46. See Thomas C. Schelling and Morton H. Halperin, *Strategy and Arms Control* (New York: The 20th Century Fund, 1961); Donald G. Brennan (ed.), *Arms Control, Disarmament, and National Security* (New York: George Brazilier, 1961); Bull, *The Control of the Arms Race*; Roger K. Smith, 'The Marginalization of Superpower Arms Control', *Security Studies*, Vol.1, No.1 (Autumn 1991), pp.37–53; Emmanuel Adler, 'The Emergence of Cooperation: National Epistemic Communities and the International Evolution of the Idea of Nuclear Arms Control', *International Organization*, Vol.50, No.1 (Winter 1996), pp.101–45; Stuart Croft, *Strategies of Arms Control: A History and Typology* (Manchester: Manchester University Press, 1969), pp.33–40; John Baylis, 'Arms Control and Disarmament' in Baylis, Wirtz, Cohen and Gray (eds), *Strategy in the Contemporary World*, pp.191–7; and Robert Hunt Sprinkle, 'Two Cold Wars and Why they Ended Differently', *Review of International Studies*, Vol.25, No.4 (October 1999), pp. 637–9.
47. A number of these themes are outlined in John Garnett, ed., *Theories of Peace and Security: A Reader in Contemporary Strategic Thought* (London: MacMillan, 1970).
48. Eric Herring, *Danger and Opportunity: Explaining International Crisis Outcomes* (Manchester: Manchester University Press, 1995).

49. Phil Williams, 'Crisis Management', in Baylis, Booth, Garnett and Williams, *Contemporary Strategy: Theories and Policies*, p.153.
50. See: Richard Ned Lebow, *Nuclear Crisis Management. A Dangerous Illusion* (Ithaca, NY: Cornell University Press, 1987); Paul Bracken, *The Command and Control of Nuclear Weapons* (New Haven, CT: Yale University Press, 1983); Robert Jervis, Richard Ned Lebow and Janice Gross Stein, *Psychology and Deterrence* (Baltimore, MD: John Hopkins University Press, 1985); Richard Ned Lebow and Janice Gross Stein, *When Does Deterrence Succeed and How Do We Know?*, Occasional Papers 8 (Ottawa: Canadian Institute for International Peace and Security, Feb. 1990); and Christoph Bluth, *The Nuclear Challenge. US–Russian strategic relations after the Cold War* (Aldershot: Ashgate, 2000), p.14.
51. Samuel Wells, for example, considers that the 'Cuban missile crisis had a generally sobering effect on both sides'; Samuel Wells, 'Nuclear Weapons and European Security during the Cold War', in Michael J. Hogan (ed.), *The End of the Cold War. Its Meaning and Implications* (Cambridge: Cambridge University Press, 1992), p.71. The October 1962 crisis is probably the most documented of all such crises that occurred during the Cold War. Among the many commentaries on this event are: Robert F. Kennedy, *Thirteen Days: A Memoir of the Cuban Missile Crisis* (New York: Norton, 1971); Graham T. Allison, *Essence of Decision: Explaining the Cuban Missile Crisis* (Boston: Little, Brown and Co., 1971); Lawrence Freedman, 'Logic, Politics and Foreign Policy', *International Affairs*, Vol.52 (1976), pp.434–49; Amos Perlmutter, 'The Presidential Political Center and Foreign Policy', *World Politics*, Vol.27 (1974), pp.87–106; Steve Smith, 'Allison and the Cuban Missile Crisis'; James G. Blight and David A. Welch, *On the Brink: Americans and Soviets Reexamine the Cuban Missile Crisis* (New York: Noonday, 1990); and Graham T. Allison and Philip D. Zelikow, *Essence of Decision: Explaining The Cuban Missile Crisis*, 2nd edition (New York: Longman, 1999).
52. John Newhouse, *The Nuclear Age. From Hiroshima to Star Wars* (London: Michael Joseph, 1989), pp.13, 150–60. Taliaferro also notes the seriousness of the Berlin crisis in 1961. See Jeffrey W. Taliaferro, 'Realism, Power Shifts, and Major War', *Security Studies*, Vol.10, No.4 (Summer 2001), pp.167–70 especially.
53. Scott D. Sagan and Jeremi Suri, 'The Madman Nuclear Alert. Secrecy, Signaling, and Safety in October 1969', *International Security*, Vol.27, No.4 (Spring 2003), pp.150–83.
54. Raymond L. Garhoff, 'On Estimating and Imputing Intentions', *International Security*, Vol.2 (Winter 1978), pp.22–32.
55. Derek Leebaert, 'The Context of Soviet Military Thinking', in Leebaert, *Soviet Military Thinking*, p.13.
56. Daniel Frei (with Christian Catrina), *Risks of Unintentional Nuclear War*, UNIDIR, Geneva, 1982, p.ix. See also Bruce Blair, *The Logic of Accidental Nuclear War* (Washington, DC: The Brookings Institution, 1993). For a discussion of crisis control initiatives see Richard Smoke, 'Crisis Control Measures', in Rotblat and Hellman, *Nuclear Strategy and World Security*, pp.28–39.
57. Matthew Woods, 'Invisible Weapons, Visible Choices: Unpacking the New Deterrence', *Contemporary Security Policy*, Vol.18, No.3 (Dec. 1997), pp.1–37.
58. Colin S. Gray, 'The Arms Race Phenomenon', *World Politics*, Vol.24, No.1 (Oct. 1971), pp.39–79; Albert Wohlstetter, 'Is There a Strategic Arms Race', *Foreign Policy*, No.15 (Summer 1974), pp.3–20; Marek Thee, *Military Technology, Military Strategy and the Arms Race* (London: Croom Helm, 1986); Lewis F. Richardson, *Arms and Insecurity* (Pittsburgh: Boxwood Press, 1960); and Deborah Shapley, 'Technology Creep and the Arms Race', *Science*, 201, pp.1102–5, 1192–6.
59. James DeNardo, 'Complexity, Formal Methods, and Ideology in International Studies', in Michael W. Doyle and G. John Ikenberry (eds), *New Thinking in International Relations Theory* (Boulder, CO: Westview, 1997), p.127.
60. John H. Barton and Lawrence D. Weiler (eds), *International Arms Control. Issues and Agreements* (Stanford: Stanford University Press, 1976).
61. For an early discussion of how the 'nth country problem' was viewed, see Bull, *The Control of the Arms Race*.

62. See Karl W. Deutsch and J. David Singer, 'Multipolar Power Systems and International Stability', *World Politics*, Vol.16 (1964), pp.390–404; Waltz, 'The Stability of the Bipolar World'; and Richard N. Rosecrance, 'Bipolarity, Multipolarity, and the Future', *The Journal of Conflict Resolution*, Vol.10 (1966), pp.314–27.
63. The NPT defined a NWS as a state that had exploded a nuclear weapon or other explosive nuclear device prior to 1 January 1967. All other states that ratified the Treaty had to do so as NNWS. This raised questions thereafter about how to engage with states that produced a nuclear weapon or nuclear device after that date. See John Simpson and Tony McGrew (eds), *The International Nuclear Non-proliferation System: Challenges and Choices* (Basingstoke: Macmillan, 1984). See also George Bunn, *Arms Control by Committee: Managing Negotiations with the Russians* (Stanford, CA: Stanford University Press, 1992); William Epstein, *The Last Chance, Nuclear Proliferation and Arms Control* (New York: The Free Press, 1976); Stephen Lee, 'Nuclear Proliferation and Nuclear Entitlement', *Ethics and International Affairs*, Vol.9 (1995), pp.101–31; Caroline Thomas, *In Search of Security* (Brighton: Wheatsheaf, 1987), ch.6; David A.V. Fischer, *Stopping the Spread of Nuclear Weapons: The Past and the Prospects* (New York and London: Routledge, 1992); and Mohamed I. Shaker, *The Nuclear Non-Proliferation Treaty*, Vols 1 and 2 (London: Oceana, 1980).
64. John Lewis Gaddis, 'The Cold War, the Long Peace, and the Future', in Hogan, *The End of the Cold War*, p.22.
65. Colin S. Gray, *The Second Nuclear Age* (Boulder, CO and London: Lynne Rienner, 1999).
66. John D. Orme, 'The War That Never Happened: Structure, Statesmanship, and the Origins of the Long Peace', *Security Studies*, Vol.10, No.4 (Summer 2001), p.124.
67. John Lewis Gaddis, 'The Long Peace: Elements of Stability in the Postwar International System', *International Security*, Vol.10, No.4 (Spring 1986), pp.99–142. See also John Lewis Gaddis, *The Long Peace: Inquiries into the History of the Cold War* (Oxford: Oxford University Press, 1987).
68. Charles Kegley, *The Long Postwar Peace: Contending Explanations and Projections* (New York: HarperCollins, 1991). While Orme acknowledges the contribution made by authors such as Gaddis on the reasons for the 'long peace', he considers that the argument indicating that this outcome was due to bipolarity and nuclear weapons has been overstated. Rather, the absence of overt war between East and West 'rested not solely on the strength of deterrence, but also on the weakness of any motive to alter the *status quo*'. He argues that both the United States and the Soviet Union had no pressing desire to overturn the post-Second World War settlement on the division of Europe. This provided the basis for what he terms, 'divisible security', a situation that satisfied the minimal security objectives of the two states. Orme also suggests that there were 'four potential sources of instability: Germany, Eastern Europe, the shifting nuclear balance, and the problem of Berlin'. Orme, 'The War That Never Happened'.
69. John E. Mueller, *Retreat from Doomsday: The Obsolescence of Major War* (New York: Basic Books, 1989). Elsewhere, Mueller has made a distinction between 'essential' and 'complete' irrelevance in the context of nuclear weapons. As he explains, 'while I maintain that nuclear weapons have been *essentially* irrelevant to the course of post-World War II history, I do not maintain that they have been *completely* irrelevant. The question in all this is not whether nuclear weapons have made any difference whatever, but whether they have been a crucial – determining – influence in keeping leaders cautious and the world free from major war.' John Mueller, 'Epilogue', in John Lewis Gaddis, Philip H. Gordon, Ernest R. May and Jonathon Rosenberg (eds), *Cold War Statesmen Confront the Bomb: Nuclear Diplomacy Since 1945* (Oxford: Oxford University Press, 1999), p.278. For a discussion of these themes see: Robert Jervis, 'The Political Effects of Nuclear Weapons. A Comment', *International Security*, Vol.13, No.2 (Fall 1988), pp.80–90; and John Vasquez, *The Power of Power Politics: From Classical Realism to Neotraditionalism* (Cambridge: Cambridge University Press, 1998), pp.311–12.
70. See Richard Ned Lebow, 'The Rise and Fall of the Cold War', *Review of International Studies*, Vol.25, Special Issue (Dec. 1999), pp.21–39.

71. Gaddis, Gordon, May and Rosenberg (eds), *Cold War Statesmen Confront the Bomb*.
72. Ernest R. May, 'Introduction', in Gaddis, Gordon, May and Rosenberg (eds), *Cold War Statesmen Confront The Bomb*.
73. Gaddis, *We Now Know*, p.258.
74. For a discussion and details of the agreements see Lewis A. Dunn, *Controlling the Bomb. Nuclear Proliferation in the 1990s* (New Haven and London: Yale University Press, 1982), pp.18–21; Scott D. Sagan, 'Rules of Engagement', *Security Studies*, Vol.1, No.1 (Autumn 1991), pp.78–108; Kurt M. Cambell, 'The U.S.–Soviet Agreement on the Prevention of Dangerous Military Activities', *Security Studies*, Vol.1 No.1 (Autumn 1991), pp.109–31; Robert E. Osgood and Jonathon Tucker, *Force, Order and Justice* (Baltimore, MD: The John Hopkins University Press, 1967); Alexander L. George, Philip J. Farley and Alexander Dallin (eds), *U.S.–Soviet Security Cooperation* (Oxford: Oxford University Press, 1988); Robert Axelrod, *The Evolution of Cooperation* (New York: Basic Books, 1984); David Dewitt and Hans Rattinger (eds), *East–West Arms Control. Challenges for the Western Alliance* (London: Routledge, 1992); and Jozef Goldblat, *Arms Control. A Guide to Negotiations and Agreements*, (London: Sage, 1994).
75. For a discussion of these positions see Regina Cowen Karp (ed.), *Security with Nuclear Weapons? Different Perspectives on National Security* (Oxford: Oxford University Press for SIPRI, 1991); Regina Cowen Karp (ed.), *Security Without Nuclear Weapons. Different Perspectives on Non-Nuclear Security* (Oxford: Oxford University Press for SIPRI, 1992); and John Baylis and Robert O'Neill (eds), *Alternative Nuclear Futures. The Role of Nuclear Weapons in the Post-Cold War World* (Oxford: Oxford University Press, 2000).

Deterrence Asymmetry and Other Challenges to Small Nuclear Forces

P.K. GHOSH

Even though nuclear weapons have been around since 1945 the methodology of the maintenance of stable nuclear deterrence is still debated endlessly. The strategy to evolve a stable nuclear deterrence in a world in which nuclear weapons are synonymous with their deterrence capability, rather than their true war-fighting ability, is a continuous process and has been so for the last five decades. To many it would seem that since the large available nuclear weaponry in the world has never been used in any form of war-fighting after 1945, despite severe provocation (Cuban Missile crisis), umpteen threats (Kargil Conflict) and blackmails, this is proof enough that the deterrence philosophy has been successful to a large degree.[1] Thus the use of nuclear weapons in their 'political weapon' manifestation rather than as 'military weaponry' has always been more acceptable to the world.

In the Cold War era voluminous material was written on various aspects of nuclear deterrence. The entire nuclear debate revolved around the two superpower arsenals and their Massive Retaliation and MAD (Mutually Assured Destruction) philosophies. The context of the deterrence asymmetry that was deemed to have existed at that time was seen entirely through stockpile levels of the two superpowers. The problems of deterrence asymmetry of the other Nuclear Weapon States (NWS) with respect to the superpowers was often glossed over.[2] However, with the dissipation of the Cold War, challenges of the NWS in maintenance of deterrence stability became more acute as most of these states (except the United States and Russia) adopted a 'minimalist' or 'near minimalist' posture.[3] The 'eternal question' of 'how much will provide credible strategic deterrence?' loomed large over the nuclear debate once again. This problem became complex with the rise of Nuclear Weapon Capable States like India that adopted the minimalist 'minimum credible deterrence' posture, and others like Pakistan and Israel, who were forced to keep their arsenals small due to numerous reasons. Thus the challenge for all these smaller nuclear forces essentially became one of managing a credible deterrence with their relatively small arsenals against a background of deterrence asymmetry between themselves and larger powers. The aim of this paper is to explore the numerous challenges that small nuclear forces (SNFs) face in maintenance of credible deterrence against a background challenge of asymmetry.

Small Nuclear Forces

The proliferation of nuclear weapons has led to a number of emerging nations that are currently in possession or on the 'threshold' of possession of 'small' nuclear arsenals. In the meanwhile, nuclear arsenals of the established NWS have also seen a steady decline. While the nuclear arsenals of both Russia and the United States are still 'large' by any standard, the arsenals of countries like France and the United Kingdom have undergone dramatic reductions.[4] Not only have their stockpiles seen a steady decline but the number and type of delivery platforms have also seen considerable downsizing. The United Kingdom has reduced its arsenal by 70 per cent since the Cold War and currently is dependent on a single sea leg of the triad, while France is dependent on its air force and the sea leg of the dyad.

China, the last to join the 'established' NWS with its first nuclear tests in 1964 has not been known to have a very extensive arsenal stockpile despite its dependence on the entire triad for their delivery. India and Pakistan, the new overt nuclear weapons capable states have very limited stockpiles and delivery platforms. The case of Israel as a covert *de facto* nuclear power is no different in that it is unlikely to have an extensive range of delivery platforms or stockpile, keeping in view the ambiguous nature of their nuclear programme.[5] Hence the basic question that arises out of this background is: what should be the defining factor of an identifiable SNF? Should one only consider the weapons in the stockpile and the number of warheads as a primary classification aid or should the number and types of delivery platforms be the prime criterion? Or should similarity in the types of challenges being faced by these states in addition to the 'small' characteristics of the weapons in their arsenals along with the restricted number of delivery platforms be the overall deciding factor?

Prior to determining the applicability of these factors to various candidate states it is essential to understand the views of other scholars on the issue. Rodney Jones while writing on SNFs has distinguished between the dwarfs and the giants of nuclear arsenals. Though he agrees that the French, British and Chinese arsenals are far smaller than those of the Soviet Union/Russia and the United States however, he defines 'small arsenals' as other than those of the 'established nuclear weapon powers'.[6] Thus according to his classification the weapons in its arsenal have become the defining factor of an SNF. Rajesh Rajgopalan on the other hand has defined SNFs as all other nations with nuclear arsenals other than Russia and the United States, without elaborating the prime criterion for drawing such a perimeter.[7]

Coming back to the question of the deciding factor for an SNF, the French *Force de Frappe*, with nearly 350 warheads in its stockpile, would be a candidate for classification as an SNF if only the numerical strength of the stockpile was to be considered. The United Kingdom with about 200 would also be a strong candidate for the group while China with a debatable number of 290 strategic and 120 low yield tactical warheads would manage to squeeze itself into the group.[8] The number of warheads in the stockpiles of India, Pakistan, Israel and North Korea are highly debatable but are expected to be small (less than 100) and hence are clear candidates for the grouping. Consideration of only delivery platforms for strategic weapons gives a slightly different picture. Britain with the Trident II armed Vanguard class SSBNs would have the minimum number but technologically the most advanced strategic delivery platform. France with its numerically superior dyad would come a close second. The term 'strategic' would become indistinguishable from 'sub-strategic' in the cases of the nuclear weapon capable states with their technologically inferior delivery platforms whose numbers are debatable. Out of the considered group, China would probably end up with the maximum number of strategic delivery platforms in their triad format, though much of it would be technologically inferior. Thus in this case it becomes evident that it is difficult to classify SNFs only according to the strategic/sub strategic delivery platforms.

Consideration of the challenges of the 'smaller' nuclear states would be interesting. India, Pakistan and Israel would face similar challenges as they are 'growing or modernizing' nuclear weapons powers apart from being Third World countries. Britain and France, on the other hand, are 'reducing'[9] nuclear powers that, after having reached a high threshold of technological and numerical advantage in the Cold War era, consider it prudent to prune down their arsenals in view of the changed threat perceptions and to reduce the economic burden. China's case is unique in that it is an established NWS and yet faces the other challenges faced by the 'smaller and growing nuclear states of the Third World' due to its limited all-round capability.

Thus, if one was to take all three parameters, SNFs could be classified as states with less nuclear weapon capability, both in terms of stockpile arsenal and in terms of delivery platforms, that face similar challenges.[10] Hence the accent is not only restricted to the mere numbers of warheads in the stockpile or delivery platforms but also on the similarity of challenges that these states face.

Deterrence Asymmetry

In reality there exists no credible defence against nuclear weapons. Since the level of destruction in any nuclear exchange is expected to be horrendously high, the best defence that can be achieved is through various forms of deterrence. The problem of how much is good enough to provide credible deterrence is an acute problem for all SNFs. Deterrence *per se* does not require the creation of an arsenal superior or even equal to that of the potential adversary, as the mere threat (implied or otherwise) is good enough for deterring the adversary.[11] Bundy has repeatedly argued from the Cuban Missile crisis experience that nuclear superiority was and is inconsequential in ensuring nuclear deterrence. 'Mutual deterrence, has been steady through more than three decades of dramatic variations in the relative numbers of warheads, in delivery systems and in the vulnerability of particular systems on each side'.[12]

However for an SNF the problem is compounded as, when aiming to deter, the acquisition of more weapons may be unnecessary or wasteful while less may seemingly diminish the capability to deter.[13] Hence nuclear asymmetry is the core problem and a challenge that continues to affect the conduct of the SNFs, their foreign policy and military equations.[14] It is this asymmetry that exposes them to 'coercion', blackmail and pre-emptive strikes against their nuclear installations. Against actual use of two bombs in 1945 there have been over 46 identifiable threats that were held out in ways that were more explicit than the implicit threat of mere possession of such weapons. All these cases occurred when the threatening power enjoyed a favourable asymmetry in nuclear weaponry.[15]

Coercion

NWS have often resorted to nuclear coercion in pursuit of their national interest and that has been a stark reality. This coercion has occurred not only been between nuclear weapons capable and non-nuclear weapons capable states but also between states that possess these weapons. This is where there exists a thread of dichotomy over how nuclear coercion or blackmail could work if both sides would be able to deter one another? Opposing schools of thought on nuclear deterrence fundamentally agree that nuclear weapons are essentially deterrence weapons. Few would disagree that to achieve a credible deterrence it is not necessary to equal (or outnumber) the arsenal of the adversary. As Kenneth Waltz, a proliferation optimist states, while writing on the stable deterrence relationship between the growing number of nuclear states 'whatever be the number of nuclear states, a nuclear world is tolerable if those states are able to send convincing deterrence messages: it is useless to attempt to conquer because you will be severely punished'.[16] Thus the underlying thought is that, if a nuclear state can send a deterrence message effectively (as the presence of nuclear weapons usually does), then a nuclear skirmish is fruitless as it is bound to effect both sides. If this is true then how is it that, in a process of coercion (or blackmail) between two nuclear states, one side coerces and the other side 'agrees' to be coerced.

The reason for this may lie in the conventional weapons psychological mindset that associates sizes of nuclear arsenals to various 'levels' of deterrence. Hence a state with a larger nuclear weapon arsenal may at times succeed in politically coercing another nuclear capable state with a smaller arsenal but a survivable credible deterrent, due to the typical conventional weapon psyche that is difficult to obliterate. Thus this is a major challenge for SNFs that are restricted due to their inherent smaller arsenals. In this context it is interesting to note that China had acquired nuclear weapons (and is modernizing them) mainly to safeguard against nuclear 'blackmail'.[17]

Another aspect that is important with regards to the 'success' of any coercion is that the message that is to be sent must be understood along with its proper nuances. Often this does not happen, leading to ambiguous results in the end. The best example of this is the sending of the United States nuclear armed task force, led by USS *Enterprise*, into the Indian Ocean in 1971 by President Nixon. While the reason was essentially to pressurize India (that was in conflict with Pakistan at that time) the force was never sighted by any of the Indian Naval forces operating in the region. Hence, the message sent was so ambiguous that it had no effect on the course of the conflict whatsoever.[18]

Pre-emptive Strikes

The SNFs and the emerging nuclear powers face the challenge of 'forcible' counter-proliferation in the form of pre-emptive strikes or preventive war. However there are numerous practical difficulties in carrying out pre-emptive strikes. The school of thought maintained by the proliferation optimists uses the argument that the costs of aggression may be so high and unsure that it will not be profitable to engage in it. As Kenneth Waltz writes

> Prevention and pre-emption are difficult games because the costs are so high if the games are not perfectly played ... Ultimately, the inhibitions (against such attacks) lie in the impossibility of knowing for sure that a disarming strike will totally destroy an opposing force and in the immense destruction even a few warheads can wreak.[19]

It is not only the response of the victim that has to be taken into account but, in the case of non-nuclear states, the reaction of other nuclear capable states also needs to be considered. The proliferation pessimists on the other hand are doubtful if the new nuclear powers will remain immune to preventive war temptations. This is especially so when Cold War history is replete with examples.[20] The attempt of the super powers to prevent the Chinese nuclear weapons programme in the 1960s; Egypt's desire to thwart Israel's nuclear development after the Middle East War of 1967; and the Clinton Administration's threat to strike North Korean nuclear facilities are all examples where pre-emptive strikes were seriously considered. In the case of South Asia, the United States, thought of sabotaging Pakistani nuclear capability is another striking example.[21] However, it was the United States' determination to eliminate the Iraqi capability for WMD manufacture and their nuclear infrastructure by bombing it during the Gulf War that proved that the results of such strikes at best can be ambiguous. As one senior George Bush Administration official was quoted saying 'one still has uncertainty as to whether or not the capacity to possess a small number of nuclear weapons has been eliminated'.[22] In fact it is commonly believed that some of the Iraqi nuclear testing facility escaped without damage despite all the bombing from a position of nearly complete air superiority.

Analysts feel that many factors and nuances influence the 'urge' for pre-emptive strikes or attack against newer nuclear forces. For example Sagan contends that civil–military relationships have a large bearing on carrying out preventive wars or strikes. Since military officers often tend to see war as inevitable and necessary, the thinking causes them to proceed with the 'better now than later' logic and in favour of offensive doctrines.[23] However, as Feaver writes, preventive wars are more likely if there is a catalyst that lowers the cost – as when Saddam Hussain handed the United States the *casus belli* – and such catalysts are more important than the civil–military relationship.[24] Thus we see that SNFs face this serious challenge of pre-emptive strikes though the consequences of such an attack may be high and the results ambiguous at best.

Technological

The continual availability of high-end technology is a serious constraint for the development and expansion of weaponry by the SNFs. Some analysts fear that the technological and financial weaknesses of such nuclear powers would result in small arsenals, vulnerable to first-strike operations. These, operating under rudimentary command and control infrastructures, would create greater pressures on crisis stability and increase the chances of accidents and unauthorized seizure.[25] On the other hand, others believe that, although the lack of capabilities (and resources) may be a bane from the stability point of view, in practice it may prove a blessing in disguise. While constraints limit arsenal size and, in theory, create inviting targets for offensive action, they also restrict the weapons available for counterforce attacks unless they were delivered with improbable accuracy. Thus it inhibits sparse arsenals from being used against each other.[26] However, this argument forecloses the fact that these nuclear powers would not necessarily be averse to having a targeting philosophy consisting of a majority of counter-value targets, as they can create a larger fear psychosis. In addition it would not necessarily be such a 'blessing' as it would still expose them to coercion and blackmail from states with bigger nuclear arsenals.

Hence SNFs, when faced with continual technological challenges, may follow the undermentioned response strategies in trying to overcome them:

- utilization of low technology options;
- development of equivalent or alternative technologies;
- acquisition through covert means; or
- acquisition through other NWS.

Utilization of Low-Technological Options

The SNFs with lesser technological reach and ability are known to often resort to innovative 'low-tech' options in an effort to solve the problems of a higher degree. As Jordan Seng argues, since the arsenals tend to be small and 'simple' in composition their delivery systems too will not be greatly varied or highly sophisticated. Such states make their arsenal survivable by simple concealment strategies that may camouflage their weapons from the pre-emptive strikes of their adversaries.[27] The Chinese, for example, have deployed their missiles in as few as two missiles per unit. Their missiles are stored in tunnels, caves and other camouflaged sites.[28] The Israelis, too, have reportedly stored their Jericho missiles in the caves at Zekhareyh.[29] India's attempt at concealing and camouflaging its May 1998 nuclear tests from satellites in the sky, using technologically simple but elaborate methods, is another example. This entire operation had the multi-billion dollar US satellites fooled and the United States came to know of the tests only after the event, despite the fact that these tests were conducted after a prolonged period of preparation.

Often the requirement of technology itself is 'low' for the SNFs as the arsenals themselves are small. In this context a lot has already been written on the requirement and importance of advanced command and control structures in SNFs. There is a considered view that compared to advanced nuclear states, states with smaller arsenals (so-called minor proliferators) have fewer resources for developing sophisticated command and control systems as they neither have the resources to develop them nor do they need them. Thus in effect their means are in proportion to their needs.[30] Taking the example of India, there has been an ongoing debate on the required level and importance of command and control infrastructure for its nuclear arsenal. According to some analysts its professed 'no first use' (NFU) posture[31] has made the task of having a command and control system simpler.[32] This is because there exists the expensive 'luxury' of waiting for the first attack to take place rather than carry out a 'launch on warning' or a first strike. This view has its detractors. Gurmeet Kanwal, for example, feels that such an economics driven approach is patently flawed and technically unsound. He argues for a more elaborate structure that is transparent and is able to fulfil the two conflicting aspects of 'positive' and 'negative' control apart from being inherently survivable.[33] While this logic cannot be faulted, the fact remains that with a lesser number of weapons to 'manage' (that need not necessarily be 'ready to use'), the SNFs have a big advantage. Elaborately complicated systems reminiscent of the Cold War period are no longer necessary for the SNFs, though the basic requirements of such a system would remain the same. The task is further simplified with the NFU posture of states like India and China.

Development of Equivalent/Alternative Technologies

The other option that SNFs often resort to in case of unavailability of a particular technology is to try themselves to develop the same level of technological expertise. This is not an easy path to choose but inevitable if access to that particular technology is difficult to obtain. The Chinese developed the final stages of the fission (atom) bomb themselves after waiting expectantly for the Soviets to deliver it. The design was refused at the last very minute by the Soviets.[34] The Indians developed the cryogenic engine technology to be used in their space programmes (mainly the Geostationary Satellite Launch Vehicle programme) after the Russians, under severe United States pressure, backed out of the technology transfer clause that accompanied the transfer of the seven cryogenic engines.[35] The development of the Param series of super computers with massive parallel computing abilities by C-DAC Pune is another example in this context. This technology was developed after India was denied the Cray X-MP super computer by the United States[36] as there was an anxiety in the United States about their super computer being used for nuclear weaponization programmes. Thus restraining critical technologies to SNFs may, at times, lead to further anxieties.

Acquisition through Covert Means

The use of covert means to gain access to 'high-end' technology by states that are in the process of developing nuclear arsenals is almost as old as nuclear history itself. Since denial of critical technologies is a part of non-proliferation activities the requirement of such is often met through either covert means or through the use of 'dual use' technologies (unless the state can develop it by itself). While there have been numerous examples of such actions, two famous fairly recent incidents that caught the media glare have been mentioned. Both expose China's efforts in either proliferating sensitive nuclear technologies or trying to gain access towards it.

CHALLENGES TO SMALL NUCLEAR FORCES 37

China has been covertly transferring sensitive nuclear technology, as well as infrastructural equipment including missiles, to Pakistan for a long time. Done in direct contravention to arms control and non-proliferation treaties like the NPT and the MTCR,[37] this has been a source of constant worry not only for adversarial neighbours, like India, but also for most Western powers and the United States. There have been numerous occasions when these violations have come to the fore, like the issue of supply of 5,000 ring magnets to Pakistan for its centrifuges. These tailor-made magnets were made by the China Nuclear Energy Industry Corporation (CNEIC) and their supply to the Pakistani nuclear establishment was a breach of Article III(2) of the NPT.[38]

The Chinese themselves have very often tried to gain access to restricted technology from the United States by covert means, including espionage. They supposedly had 'surreptitiously taken' the design of the neutron bomb from the Lawrence Livermore Laboratories and in an equally sensational exposure managed to 'steal' the design of the sophisticated W88 nuclear warhead. This technology was expected to give them a quantum leap in their MIRV capability. The Chinese were struggling to master this technology for a long time and until then had access only to the simpler MRV technology.[39]

Acquisition through other NWS

With the non-proliferation regimes getting stricter the chances of substantial overt cooperation on nuclear weapons technology between SNFs and other NWS or technologically advanced states has receded considerably, leading to many covert alignments (a minuscule amount of which have been mentioned above as examples.) The Soviet help to the Chinese in acquiring nuclear bomb technology in the 1950s is only one example amongst many others in which the NWS have collaborated for technology transfers on weapon issues. However there have been numerous such technology cooperative transfers on the issue of utilization of nuclear energy for peaceful purposes. There have been umpteen countries, including NWS, that have built nuclear reactors in SNFs and other countries. While undoubtedly many of these states have 'misused' the spent fuel and also have covertly built up their reserves of weapons-grade fissionable material, the topic remains debatable and is considered outside the purview of this paper.

Economic

It is normally assumed that one of the primary challenges that almost all SNFs (that are mostly within developing nations) face is the lack of economic resources when funding vastly expensive nuclear arsenals. It has also been argued that since these countries are too poor to invest in advanced command and control systems, they will be too poor to build large arsenals.[40]

However, this entire argument regarding lack of financial resources is only partially true. While it cannot be denied that costs of building the 'bomb' are not very high,[41] the infrastructural and maintenance costs are simply exorbitant. However, the fact remains that many of these poorer states are quite willing to spend large amounts of money on nuclear weapons programmes that have come to be associated with 'national prestige'. With the estimate of the amount of money being spent on nuclear-related programmes always being either classified or most likely shrouded in a veil of secrecy[42] the argument of financial constraints stands moderated to an extent. It does not however preclude the fact that nuclear programmes involve huge expenditures that are a big drain on any economy. Both financial and technological constraints combine to restrict the attainment of the 'bomb' or enlarging of the arsenal beyond a certain point. As an example, costs overruns figured highly in Brazil and Argentina's abandonment of nuclear weapons programmes.[43] Similarly Iraq is expected to have spent billions of dollars in its largely unsuccessful attempt to build the bomb.

In a related aspect economic constraints restrict the ability of the SNFs to engage in counter-force targeting philosophy. The reason for this being that counter-force nuclear-use doctrines require a much larger number of highly accurate and technically advanced delivery platforms than would be required for counter-value targeting. Thus with the need to avoid unnecessary expenditure on massive build-ups, the choice of counter-force strategies will be a function of the technological capability and economic constraints with the likelihood of SNFs choosing a mixture of counter-force and counter-value strategies. The economic and technological constraints not only restrict the choice of targeting strategies but also the choice of delivery platforms. An SNF is more likely to have an arsenal of nuclear bombs delivered by nuclear capable aircraft, not necessarily long-range strategic bombers as they are expensive and difficult to procure. Nuclear tipped land-based missiles form the other leg of the triad that is the arsenal of choice for all SNFs. This is because they are relatively inexpensive and technologically they are easier to procure or manufacture. On the other hand the sea-based leg of the triad is not only exorbitantly expensive to procure and maintain but the required level of technological expertise is much higher than the other two legs. Given the advantage that it is the most survivable leg of the triad, it is also the most coveted leg, currently only possessed by China.[44]

Material Resources

Material resources are the other major challenge that is faced by SNFs. While the resources for infrastructural build up have been mentioned earlier, with the substitution of 'low-tech' options being a response option, in this section the lack of weapons-grade fissile material needs to be mentioned. The lack of weapons-grade fissile material is what restricts the manufacture of additional weaponry and hence is a serious constraint for the SNFs in increasing their arsenals. The amount of material available within a particular country is often the best and most accurate way to get an indication of the capability or number of weapons of the 'arsenal in being', especially since SNFs will keep it a closely guarded secret. Unfortunately, just as the exact number of weapons is shrouded in secrecy, so the availability of the amount of weapons-grade fissile material is never accurately known. It is precisely this 'opaque' situation that leads to various guestimates being forwarded. For example, there has been considerable conjecture as to the precise number of weapons in the Indian and Pakistani nuclear arsenals, especially in the aftermath of the 1998 nuclear explosions. On 7 June 2000, a sensational news report by NBC, quoting US intelligence sources, stated that Pakistan had five times more warheads than India (around 25 to 100) along with highly accurate delivery platforms, all built or procured with Chinese help. Other reports of similar estimates flowed in. Bharat Kanad, quoting the US Congressional Research Service, stated that by 2000 India, with an annual production of 127 kg of unsafeguarded fissile material, would have accrued about 1607 kg, enough to make 400 bombs.[45] Studies by the International Institute of Strategic Studies (IISS) credited India with 65 warheads as against 39 for Pakistan by 1999.[46] Thus we see that the available amount of weapons grade fissile material is directly related to the capability or the size of the nuclear arsenal and hence is a challenge for the SNFs.

Accidental War

In the last two decades a number of arguments have been forwarded on the enhanced threat of accidental war that exists due to nuclear proliferation with the 'minor proliferators' having rudimentary command and control systems with indistinct processes of decision-making. Whatever be the merits or demerits of the case, the fact remains that this debate is more acute for the Western scholars than the SNFs themselves. This is not to discount the importance of the topic but place it equally along with other challenges. One of the main advantages that SNFs have in this regard is their small nuclear arsenal and hence, as Jordan Seng argues, that they have two main advantages in terms of command and control over the super powers. First, the greater organizational simplicity that stems from the small size and simple composition of the arsenals. This helps in alleviating fears concerning rigid operating procedures; launch delegation; and lack of use-control technologies. Thus operational and organizational dangers are minimized. Second they are able to protect their smaller arsenals using weapon survival strategies of concealment. This in turn eliminates the need for hair triggered 'launch on warning' procedures and the time pressures that they generate.[47]

Thus the pessimistic view that nuclear weapons have made deliberate war less likely and have simultaneously made accidental war more likely[48] is unlikely to be completely true, at least in the South Asian context. The presence of nuclear weapons did not prevent the Kargil conflict from taking place while to date there have been no instances of an accidental war with nuclear weapons. There is no doubt that all the SNFs do possesses command and control structures that need considerable technical upgrading but, again, due to the smaller arsenal size, lesser dispersion of weapons and control and operational tasks imposed upon a selected and restricted number of personnel, the chances of organizational lapses and accidental wars are reduced. This is not to suggest that the SNFs do not require higher technologies, because they do. With the availability of higher end command and control and weapon use technologies including a later generation of Permissive Action Links (PALs) and Permissive Enable Systems (PESs)[49] within the SNFs the chances of accidental war are likely to recede further.

International Pressure from Arms Control and Counter-Proliferation Lobbies

Whatever be the nuances of the academic debate on the effects of nuclear proliferation on strategic deterrence, the fact remains that the NWS have always vehemently supported proliferation control and have restricted other states from acquiring nuclear weapons capabilities. This had been done indirectly by restricting technology out-flow or more directly through non-proliferation treaties. There are presently numerous technological controls that keep sensitive technologies expensive and difficult to obtain. This 'helps' in restricting the magnitude and complexity of the nuclear programme of those states that already have the capability unless they are able somehow to develop them on their own or they resort to covert methods of acquisition. The more direct methods of restricting the sizes of the arsenals of the SNFs and other nuclear threshold nations involve non-proliferation treaties. (The CTBT, that had aimed at control of testing, is in limbo due to the refusal of the US Senate to ratify it.) The proposed FMCT (Fissile Material Cutoff Treaty) on the other hand, which aims at freezing the stockpile of unsafeguarded nuclear fuel, would be successful in restricting the numbers of arsenal weapons though it is unlikely to be successful in preventing states from developing the nuclear bomb.

The Clinton Administration had also been following the 'capping and rollback strategy', especially with regard to proliferation in South Asia. The idea was floated in spring 1993 and it first sought an agreement from India and Pakistan for verifiable fissile material cut-offs and emphasized the limiting of nuclear proliferation in the region, hoping to achieve a total roll-back at some point of time in future. The efforts failed as the negotiations faltered.[50] The final nail in the coffin was provided by the nuclear tests of 1998 by both India and Pakistan. These were followed by a momentary renewed interest in this strategy by the United States that refused to be convinced of its utter failure. Fortunately with respect to India, this was followed by the Strobe Talbot and Jaswant Singh series of talks. These were path-breaking and provided an opportunity to understand each other's perspectives. The cap/ roll-back strategy received a quiet burial. Thus, irrespective of the moral implications of nuclear proliferation, the SNFs continue to face challenges from arms control and proliferation lobbies that not only seek to deny them access to advanced technologies but also restrict the sizes of the arsenals by 'limiting and safeguarding' the amount of available fissile material.

Conclusion

The methodology of the maintenance of stable nuclear deterrence is still being endlessly debated despite the passage of more than five decades. The strategy is to evolve a stable nuclear deterrence in a world in which nuclear weapons are used for their deterrence capability rather than their war-fighting potential. During the Cold War the entire nuclear debate revolved around the two superpower arsenals, but with its dissipation and altered threat perceptions the problem of 'how much will provide credible strategic deterrence?' became complex with the rise of Nuclear Weapon Capable States like India that adopted the 'minimum credible deterrence' posture, and others like Pakistan and Israel who were forced to keep their arsenals small. Thus the challenge was in managing a credible deterrence with their small arsenals against a background of deterrence asymmetry between themselves and with larger powers.

Deterrence *per se* does not require the creation of an arsenal superior or even equal to that of that of the potential adversary. Despite this and a conventional weapon mindset, nuclear asymmetry is perceived as the core problem and a challenge that continues to affect the conduct of the SNFs, and their military equations. It is this asymmetry that exposes them to 'coercion', blackmail and pre-emptive strikes against their nuclear installations. Thus NWS have often resorted to nuclear coercion and/or attempts at pre-emptive strikes in pursuit of their national interest but the consequences are not only dangerous but ambiguous at best. The continual availability of high-end technology is a serious constraint for the development and expansion of weaponry by the SNFs. When faced with such a challenge the states, in trying to overcome them, opt for response strategies like utilizing low technology options; developing equivalent or alternative technologies; acquiring them through covert means; or, finally, by overt means through other NWS.

It is normally assumed that one of the primary challenges that almost all SNFs (that are mostly within developing nations) face is lack of economic resources to fund vastly expensive nuclear arsenals. However, the fact remains that many of these poorer states are quite willing to spend large amounts of money on nuclear weapons programmes that have come to be associated with 'national prestige'. Invariably with all SNFs (or even with other NWS for that matter) the estimated amount of money being spent on nuclear-related programmes is always shrouded in a veil of secrecy. At the other end of the spectrum cost overruns figured highly in Brazil and Argentina's abandonment of nuclear weapons programmes. Economic and technological constraints restrict these states' ability to engage in counter-force targeting as this would require larger and highly accurate weapon platforms, also constraining the choice of delivery platforms in the arsenal. This is because different triad legs are associated with differing levels of technology and economic costs.

Material resources in the form of lack of weapons-grade fissile material are one aspect that restricts the manufacture of additional weaponry and hence are a serious constraint for the SNFs in increasing their arsenal. In addition, the capability or the size of the nuclear arsenal is directly related to the available amount of weapons-grade fissile material.

The chance of accidental war is another challenge that affects Western minds more than the SNFs themselves. The simplicity and the size of the arsenals coupled with a No First Use (NFU) posture by some SNFs helps in eliminating the requirement of complex command and control systems. However this does not preclude the requirement of advanced weapon use technologies.

International pressure from arms control and counter proliferation policies in the form of various treaties is another challenge to the SNFs. These are either applied directly and restrain the transfer of critical technologies or try to stop nuclear testing while freezing the amount of available weapons grade material.

Thus we see that the SNFs are handicapped and face serious challenges in maintenance of a credible deterrence with their smaller nuclear arsenals. However the fact remains that despite these constraints nuclear weapons have been proliferating and the number of threshold nuclear states is on the increase with the dream of a nuclear free world becoming dim.

NOTES

The views expressed in this article are the personal views of the author. They do not represent the views of any organization whatsoever.

1. Some, like John Mueller, however have argued that nuclear weapons were irrelevant in preventing major wars after the World Wars. 'The Essential Irrelevance of Nuclear Weapons: Stability in the Post War World', *International Security* (Fall 1989), pp.55–79. It is unlikely that it holds good for SNFs due to their numerous wars.

2. One of the reasons for this could be alignment of the other NWS (except China) with the superpowers leading to an envelopment of the individual identities within the bloc under the overpowering presence of the superpower. Hence it could be said that NATO, to an extent, led to a loss of the individual identities of France and Britain.
3. See P.K. Ghosh, 'Emerging Trends In Nuclear Triad', *Strategic Analysis*, Vol.25, No.2 (May 2001) pp.265–7.
4. For details see ibid. pp.247–51.
5. Though they are estimated to have around 200 warheads in their stockpile and according to a report a complete triad of delivery platforms. For details of the Israeli nuclear arsenal see Hans M. Kristensen and Joshua M. Handler, *Tables for Nuclear Forces*, SIPRI Year Book 2001 (Oxford: Oxford University Press, 2001) p.483.
6. Rodney W. Jones, 'Small Nuclear Forces', in Rodney W. Jones (ed.), *Small Nuclear Forces and US Security Policy* (Lexington, MA: Lexington Books, 1984), p.1.
7. Rajesh Rajgopalan, 'Nuclear Strategy and Small Nuclear Forces: The Conceptual Requirements', *Strategic Analysis* Vol.22, No.7 (Oct. 1999), footnote 2, p.1128.
8. For details of nuclear arsenals and their associated delivery platforms see Ghosh, 'Emerging Trends In Nuclear Triad', pp.247–55, 262–4. Also see Kristensen and Handler, *Tables for Nuclear Forces*, pp.469–71, 475–8.
9. The term 'reducing' has been used in the sense of a reduction in nuclear arsenal capability and not necessarily deterrence capability, which in itself is a debatable topic. These countries have adopted a 'minimalist' posture as it has been felt that it can provide them with adequate 'credible' deterrence even with this dramatic reduction in their nuclear weaponry.
10. This would effectively rule out possession of crude 'nuclear weapons' by non-state actors from this definition.
11. Cold War history is replete with such examples as the Cuban missile crisis wherein the United States had reconciled themselves to a negotiated settlement despite their ability to totally annihilate the USSR. The fear of some Soviet nuclear weapons getting through and destroying a few American cities was probably the major factor that led to this decision.
12. See McGeorge Bundy, *Danger and Survival: Choices About the Bomb in the First Fifty Years* (New Delhi, Affiliated East West Press/in co-operation with Random House, New York, 1989) p.592. He has expressed similar views in his other essays.
13. Rajgopalan, 'Nuclear Strategy and Small Nuclear Forces' p.1117.
14. See Jasjit Singh, 'Challenges of Strategic Defence', *Frontline*, April 11–24 1998.
15. Ibid.
16. Kenneth Waltz, *The Spread of Nuclear Weapons: More may be Better*, Adelphi Paper 171 (London IISS, Autumn 1981) pp.5, 7.
17. Singh, 'Challenges of Strategic Defence'.
18. P.K. Ghosh, 'Revisiting Gunboat Diplomacy: An Instrument of Threat or Use of Limited Naval Force', *Strategic Analysis*, Vol.23, No.11 (Feb. 2001), pp.2013–14.
19. Waltz, 'The Spread of Nuclear Weapons', p.17.
20. David J. Karl, 'Proliferation Pessimism and Emerging Nuclear Powers', *International Security*, Vol.21, No.3 (Winter 1996), p.96.
21. Karl, 'Proliferation Pessimism' pp.96–7.
22. Ronald F. Lehman, 'A North Korean Nuclear Weapons Program; International Implications', *Security Dialogue*, Vol.24 (Sept. 1993), p.270.
23. Scott D. Sagan, 'The Perils of Proliferation: Organisation Theory, Deterrence Theory and the Spread of Nuclear Weapons', *International Security*, Vol.18, No.4 (Spring 1995), pp.74–85.
24. Peter D. Feaver, 'Proliferation Pessimism and Emerging Nuclear Powers', *International Security*, Vol.22, No.2 (Fall 1997), p.188.
25. Karl Kaiser, 'Non Proliferation and Nuclear Deterrence', *Survival*, Vol.31 (March/April 1989), pp.126–7; Lewis A. Dunn, *Controlling the Bomb; Nuclear Proliferation in 1980s* (New Haven, CT: Yale University Press, 1982), pp.71–5.
26. Karl, 'Proliferation Pessimism, pp.104–5.
27. Jordan Seng, 'Less is More: Command and Control Advantages of Minor Nuclear States', *Security Studies*, Vol.6, No.4 (Summer 1997), p.63.

28. Robert S. Norris, Andrew S. Burrows and Richard W. Fieldhouse, *Nuclear Weapons Data Book* Vol.5, *British French and Chinese Nuclear Weapons*, (Boulder, CO: Westview Press, 1994), p.374.
29. Kristensen and Handler, *Tables for Nuclear Forces*, p.483.
30. Seng, 'Less is More', p.89.
31. As stated in Art. 2 of the Draft Indian Nuclear Doctrine presented by the NSAB on 17 Aug 1999, available at <http://www.meadev.gov.in/govt/indnucld.htm>.
32. This view has been propounded by many, including K. Subramanyum in his 'Nuclear Force Design and Minimum Deterrence Strategy', in Bharat Karnad (ed.), *Future Imperiled: Indian Security in the 1990s and Beyond* (New Delhi: Viking Penguin India, 1994), pp.191–4.
33. Gurmeet Kanwal, *Nuclear Defence: Shaping the Arsenal*, (New Delhi: Knowledge World, 2001), pp.143–7. Positive control concerns the proper authorization of nuclear operations while negative control seeks to prevent the accidental or unauthorized use or possible theft of these weapons.
34. For a detailed view of the numerous events associated with this see John Wilson and Xue Litai, *China Builds the Bomb* (Stanford: Stanford University Press, 1988), pp.60–72, 137–50.
35. See S. Srinivasan, 'India Developing Launch Engine', <http://www.space.com>, 23 Oct. 2001 and 'HAL Developing Indigenous Cryo-engine for GSLV', *The BusinessLine* (internet edition) (24 Jan. 2001) and 'Indigenous Cryogenic Engine to be Ready by 2004', *Times of India* (8 Dec. 2001). The impression that the development of this technology would give India the ability to develop ICBMs is only partially true as these cryo-engines are rarely if ever used in ICBMs. However, the basic technology for putting a geostationary satellite into orbit and that of an intercontinental ballistic missile is essentially the same. Hence, theoretically, India is capable of developing an ICBM. Also see Raj Chengappa, 'India is Now A Space Power', *India Today*, 30 April 2001.
36. See 'India's Param 10000 Super Computer' at <http://www.webspawner.com>.
37. The Missile Technology Control Regime is not a 'treaty' in the truest sense of the word, it is more of an alliance. In 1991, China had agreed to support the MTCR conditionally and in February 1992 provided a commitment in writing to the US that it would adhere to the clauses of the MTCR. This led the US to lift missile-related sanctions against China in June 1992. However, despite this and in complete violation of the MTCR, the Chinese have transferred missiles and missile-related technology to Pakistan. For a more detailed treatment see Savita Pandey, 'Missile Technology Control Regime: Impact Assessment', *Strategic Analysis*, Vol.22, No.6 (Sept. 1999), pp.923–45.
38. For a more detailed view see Congressional Record, 'Chinese Nuclear Exports to Pakistan' (Senate, 7 Feb. 1996), pp.S1070, S1071, S1072 (this includes Bill Gertz, 'China Nuclear Transfer Exposed: Hill Expected to Urge Sanctions' *Washington Times*, 5 Feb. 1996; and R. Jeffery Smith, 'China Aids Pakistan Nuclear Program', *Washington Post*, 7 Feb. 1996) available at <http://www.fas.org/irp/congress/1996-cr/s960207b.htm>. Also see K. Subramanyam, 'The China Factor', *Economic Times*, 22 Jan.1999.
39. For details see Stephen I. Schwartz, 'A Very Convenient Scandal', *Bulletin of the Atomic Scientists*, Vol.55, No.3 (May/June 1999), and Jeffrey Richelson, 'Perspective: Uncertain Damage', *Bulletin of the Atomic Scientists*, Vol.55, No.5 (Sept./Oct. 1999), pp.17–19.
40. See Leonard S. Spector, 'Repentant Nuclear Proliferators', *Foreign Policy*, No.88 (Fall 1992), pp.3–20.
41. According to Stephen I. Schwartz, who, along with his team, carried out a four-year study into nuclear related costs estimates in US and published his major findings, *Atomic Audit: The Cost and Consequences of US Nuclear Weapons Since 1940* (Washington DC: Brookings Institution Press, 1998) p.3. In the US out of the total $5.5 trillion spent on nuclear related projects since 1940 only 7 per cent or $409.4 billion was spent on building nuclear weapons.
42. For more detailed treatment of costs of nuclear delivery systems and unavailability of estimated nuclear cost expenditures of most states see P.K. Ghosh, 'Economic Dimension of the Strategic Nuclear Triad', *Strategic Analysis*, Vol.26, No.2 (Apr–Jun 2002), pp.227–93.

43. See Itty Abraham, *Pakistan–India and Argentina–Brazil: Stepping Back from the Nuclear Threshold*, Occasional Paper No. 15 (Washington, DC: Henry L. Stimson Institute, 1993) as cited in Seng, 'Less is More', p.67.
44. For detailed approach to the triad legs see Ghosh, 'Economic Dimension of the Strategic Nuclear Triad'.
45. Bharat Karnad, 'Going Thermonuclear: Why, With What Forces, at What Cost', *U.S.I. Journal*, Vol.128, No.3 (1998), p.315. For a more detailed approach see P.K. Ghosh, 'India Pakistan Nuclear Parity: Is it Feasible or Necessary', *Strategic Analysis*, Vol.25, No.4 (July 2001) pp.524–5.
46. As stated in 'Pakistan retains failed N-state image', *The Times of India*, 19 May 2001.
47. Seng, 'Less is More', pp.63, 72.
48. Scott D. Sagan, *Limits of Safety: Organizations, Accidents and Nuclear Weapons* (Princeton, NJ: Princeton University Press, 1994) p.264.
49. PALs are essentially interlocks. Electronic later generation PALs ensure that weapons cannot be launched without codes being directly transmitted from central authorities. PESs ensure that individual launch operators cannot launch weapons without concurrence of other operators in the same command. For a more detailed description of PALs and associated devices see Peter Stein and Peter D. Feaver, *Assuring Control of Nuclear Weapons: The Evolution of Permissive Action Links*, CSIA Occasional Paper, No.2, (Cambridge, MA: Harvard University, 1987).
50. Seng 'Less is More', p.90.

Deterrence and Asymmetry: Non-State Actors and Mass Casualty Terrorism

WYN Q. BOWEN

> *The attacks against the US homeland in September 2001 demonstrate that terrorist groups possess both the motivations and capabilities to conduct devastating attacks on US territory, citizens and infrastructure. Often these groups have the support of state sponsors or enjoy sanctuary and protection of states but some have the resources and capabilities to operate without state sponsorship. In addition, the rapid proliferation of CBRNE technology gives rise to the danger that future terrorist attacks might involve such weapons.*
> Quadrennial Defense Review, US DOD, 30 September 2001[1]

At first glance it is difficult to perceive a significant role for deterrence strategies in preventing non-state actors – such as the Al Qaeda network – from perpetrating 'mass casualty' events as epitomized by the terrorist attacks in the United States on 11 September 2001. The main reason being that the motives of those non-state actors willing and potentially capable of perpetrating such events – whether using chemical, biological, radiological, nuclear or enhanced explosive (CBRNE) weapons – are likely to be so extreme, and their level of resolve so high, that deterrence may simply not be applicable. More realistic preventive options would appear to involve strategies that focus on disrupting and destroying terrorist organizations of concern including their capabilities. The on-going military campaign in Afghanistan against Al Qaeda is supportive of this viewpoint. Nevertheless, this paper will demonstrate that deterrence probably will retain some utility as one element of a broader and comprehensive strategy for confronting the threat of mass casualty terrorism. It has been suggested that such a strategy would need to include the following policy imperatives within three identifiable phases: (1) 'Pre-event': deter, protect, prepare; (2) 'Trans-event': deter, attribute, interdict; and (3) 'Post-event': investigate, prosecute, retaliate, investigate and recover.[2]

The aim of this paper is not to forecast the likelihood of mass casualty terrorism, nor is it to advocate deterrence over other approaches. Rather, the aim is to explore the difficulties likely to be involved when applying the concept in such an asymmetric context as the global war on terror. The paper begins by outlining the dimensions of 'asymmetry' likely to influence deterrence relationships between fundamentally dissimilar opponents – for example as characterized by the United States and its allies on one hand and Al Qaeda on the other. This is followed by a re-cap on the basics of deterrence. The paper then considers the inherent complexities associated with developing deterrence strategies designed to prevent non-state actors from perpetrating mass casualty events. Key findings are identified at the end.

Dimensions of Asymmetry

In recent years the concept of 'asymmetry' has received growing attention in Western security circles. It has been used to describe and analyse how current and future conflicts involving industrially advanced Western states – or coalitions/alliances thereof – are likely to be characterized by significant dissimilarities between them and their adversaries; whether these are state actors (e.g. Iraq, Serbia), non-state actors (e.g. Al Qaeda) or some form of hybrid (e.g. Al Qaeda–Taleban). At least three dimensions of asymmetry can be identified. Each is pertinent to evaluating the complexities associated with developing deterrence strategies *vis-à-vis* non-state actors.

Asymmetry 1

An initial dimension involves the relative balance of interests at stake between adversaries. The stakes involved in any conflict scenario will determine the resolve of all parties to pay the human and financial price to realise desired objectives, whether stated or otherwise. The greater the interests an actor perceives to be at stake, the greater the resolve to prevail over an adversary, and vice versa. Significant dissimilarities between opponents on this level can have a profound impact on the nature and duration of a conflict. One only has to recall the United States' failed humanitarian involvement in Somalia in 1993/94 as evidence of how a lack of vital interests can undermine resolve. More recently it could be argued that prior to 11 September 2001 the balance of resolve between Al Qaeda and the United States was not tilted in the latter's favour. Al Qaeda certainly posed a direct threat to US security interests in the Middle East and Africa, but it was not deemed sufficient to warrant an all-out military, economic and diplomatic campaign – the global war on terror – to eradicate this terrorist network. The devastating and unprecedented attacks against New York and Washington radically altered this balance by fundamentally strengthening American resolve to secure vital US interests. It could be argued, then, that the events of 11 September served to balance out somewhat the interest/resolve relationship between the United States (along with its Western allies) and Al Qaeda. This relationship looks set to remain relatively symmetrical for the foreseeable future and this should bolster at least one key variable (intent/resolve) of any Western deterrence formula aimed at preventing mass casualty attacks. However, this will not be sufficient by itself to achieve successful deterrence. Indeed, the second and third dimensions of asymmetry are directly relevant to understanding other key deterrence variables.

Asymmetry 2

The second dimension involves the potential existence of political, economic, social and cultural dissimilarities between opponents. Significant differences in these areas will result in key decision makers on opposing sides possessing divergent value-systems and mind-sets. Hence, their perceptions of reality are likely to differ and such differences will likely translate into divergent constraints on action. For Western democratic states political and legal constraints can have a profound effect in terms of their behaviour in conflict situations, especially if an adversary is not similarly constrained. For example, the controversy over the treatment of Al Qaeda detainees at Guantanamo Bay has been demonstrative of such a divergence in constraints; it is unlikely that Al Qaeda would be similarly influenced by international opinion as the United States has been with regard to defending its behaviour in this area. In addition, Al Qaeda's willingness to attack civilian targets with the aim of generating mass casualties is illustrative of an absence of political and moral constraints; or at least it appears that way from a Western viewpoint. The upshot is that any attempt to deter non-state actors will require the deterring party to be aware of the 'lens' through which such actors are likely to perceive a deterrent message. Such awareness will inform assessments of the potential susceptibility of real and potential non-state adversaries to deterrence logic.

Asymmetry 3

Most frequently in recent years the concept of asymmetry has been applied to the growing technological gap in conventional military capabilities between Western states (with the United States occupying a pre-eminent position) and non-Western adversaries (state, non-state, hybrid). Most writing on asymmetry has focused on the means through which adversaries could attempt to circumvent the West's conventional superiority in order to avoid a force-on-force military confrontation. In a briefing to Congress in February 2002, Director of Central Intelligence George Tenet said the inability of 'real or potential adversaries' to match American military power is forcing some to 'invest in "asymmetric" niche capabilities'.[3] Indeed, the term 'asymmetric strategies' is often used to label approaches that underdogs might employ to avoid direct military confrontation; and to focus instead on exploiting key political and military vulnerabilities such as the perceived Western sensitivity to casualties and collateral damage. Examples of approaches cited throughout the literature on asymmetry include the threat or use of CBRNE weapons and information (cyber) attacks against military and civilian computer systems and networks. In terms of the threat posed by non-state actors, Tenet noted the following:

> Although the September 11 attacks suggest that Al Qaeda and other terrorists will continue to use conventional weapons, one of our highest concerns is their stated readiness to attempt unconventional attacks against us. As early as 1998, Osama bin Laden publicly declared that acquiring unconventional weapons was 'a religious duty'. Terrorist groups worldwide have ready access to information on chemical, biological, and even nuclear weapons via the Internet, and we know that Al Qaeda was working to acquire some of the most dangerous chemical agents and toxins. Documents recovered from Al Qaeda facilities in Afghanistan show that bin Laden was pursuing a sophisticated biological weapons research program ... We also believe that bin Laden was seeking to acquire or develop a nuclear device. Al Qaeda may be pursuing a radioactive dispersal device; what some call a 'dirty bomb'.[4]

Given the level of destruction achieved in New York using 'conventional' means, the term 'weapon of mass effect' has entered the strategic lexicon. According to one analysis, 'between the jets, the fuel, and the kinetic force of the collapsing World Trade Center buildings, the southwestern tip of Manhattan had been struck with a force estimated at twice the size of the smallest US tactical nuclear weapon'.[5] Tenet referred to other methods of perpetrating mass effects:

> Alternatively, Al Qaeda or other terrorist groups might also try to launch conventional attacks against the chemical or nuclear industrial infrastructure of the United States to cause widespread toxic or radiological damage. We are also alert to the possibility of cyber warfare attack by terrorists. September 11 demonstrated our dependence on critical infrastructure systems that rely on electronic and computer networks. Attacks of this nature will become an increasingly viable option for terrorists as they and other foreign adversaries become more familiar with these targets, and the technologies required to attack them.[6]

What role, then, might deterrence play in preventing non-state actors like Al Qaeda from resorting to asymmetric strategies designed to perpetrate mass casualties and effects? Before addressing this question it is necessary to re-cap briefly on the concept of deterrence.

Deterrence

The aim of deterrence is to preserve the *status quo*; to prevent a real or potential adversary from initiating a course of action. The concept is related to, but different from, what is sometimes referred to as 'compellence' but more often as 'coercion'. The focus in this latter case is on altering the *status quo* – the aim is to get the target 'to do' something (to cease or to initiate an action).[7] For example, US air strikes against Libya in 1986 were designed in part to compel the Qaddafi regime to stop sponsoring terrorist activity against American targets in Western Europe. The aim was to alter Libyan policy and not to preserve the *status quo* under which the regime in Tripoli was sponsoring terrorist activities. The proximity of the two concepts often causes confusion in application and this will be addressed later.

Mechanisms

There are two principal deterrence mechanisms. The first involves the dissuasive effect sought by threatening an opponent with an unacceptable level of 'punishment', the impact of which would significantly outweigh the potential gains associated with pursuing a particular course of action. Traditionally, this approach is seen to involve threats to target civilian assets. The second mechanism focuses on 'denial' where the possession and development of certain types of capabilities could potentially deter an opponent from pursuing a given objective or conflict strategy. The aim is to sow the seed of doubt in an opponent's mind by undermining confidence in his capability to achieve the desired outcome. Obviously, a comprehensive deterrent strategy could combine aspects of retaliation and denial. For example, the current Bush administration appears to favour such an approach for deterring unconventional weapons use by regimes of concern through combining denial capabilities – based in part on the development of missile defences – with the threat of punishment.[8] It will be shown shortly that both mechanisms are also applicable in terms of deterring mass casualty terrorism.

It is straightforward to determine whether a deterrence strategy has failed because the action the deterrer is seeking to prevent takes place. However, if the action does not occur it is not so easy to determine the extent to which a deterrent strategy succeeded as there will be no obvious evidence to scrutinize because nothing would have happened. Indeed, it can never be 100 per cent clear whether one's actions were 'crucial or irrelevant' to why an opponent chooses not to do something.[9] This issue is likely to have important implications for evaluating the success of any deterrent strategy aimed at non-state actors.

Key Variables

Deterrence is an inherently psychological exercise because the aim is to convince an opponent not to pursue a course of action by influencing calculations of the possible and probable costs and gains. Achieving this necessitates understanding what motivates the target, how it perceives the world, the target's likely resolve to pursue objectives in the face of significant obstacles, and its offensive capabilities including conflict strategies and techniques. It will also involve identifying an opponent's vulnerabilities, or pressure points that, if targeted successfully, could potentially induce inaction.

A credible deterrence strategy will also need to include the following components on behalf of the deterrer: (1) possession of the requisite 'capability' to fulfil on the deterrent message, or at least the appearance of this; (2) possession of the requisite 'intent' and 'resolve' to fulfil on the deterrent message, or at least the appearance of this; and (3) the effective communication of the deterrent message to either specific or generic opponents (including the 'red lines', or thresholds, not to be crossed). On this last point, it is possible to differentiate between strategies that focus on specific adversaries and those designed to have a preventive effect against generic opponents. In the former case, a targeted strategy will require specific contextual knowledge related to the actor's motives, resolve, conflict strategies and constraints on action. It will also involve knowledge of the target's decision-making processes and command and control structures.

As the communication process is pivotal to successful deterrence the prospects for success will be undermined if the message being transmitted is misunderstood. According to Gerald Steinberg, the communication process can be complicated by ethnic, national, religious and linguistic differences.[10] Indeed, this could evidently be the case in an asymmetric scenario such as the war on terrorism. Linked to communication is the issue of rationality; deterrence assumes that the target will be a cost–benefit calculator. Rationality can be defined as 'the ability to weigh options on the basis of potential costs and benefits, as well as consideration of the likely reaction to each move'.[11] However, what is rational to one actor will not necessarily be the same for another. Rationality will be influenced significantly by culture, value systems and the processes through which decisions are reached. Consequently, a priority must be placed on getting inside an opponent's 'black-box' to understand what is rational in the target's mind-set. According to Herbert Simon, one needs to understand 'where the frame of reference for the actor's thinking comes from', 'how it is evoked', and the 'set of alternatives' considered by an opponent in the 'choice process'.[12] This will be a pivotal issue when evaluating the susceptibility of non-state actors to deterrence.

This section has offered only a brief generalization on the concept of deterrence. However, it is sufficient to draw out issues that need addressing when assessing the potential utility of deterrence in preventing non-state actors perpetrating mass casualty attacks. Contextual information would need to be inserted within this framework to make it pertinent to specific scenarios; what works in one situation is far from guaranteed to work in another. Consequently, an emphasis needs to be placed on situational awareness – knowing your opponent as well as yourself, and recognizing that conflict relationships evolve over time. The concept of asymmetry has obvious uses in this respect because it helps identify the dissimilarities between opponents that can influence deterrence outcomes.

Deterrence, Non-state Actors and Mass Casualty Terrorism

The application of deterrence in this context can be examined at several different levels. The focus could be on: the mechanisms and targets of deterrence; the aim and role of deterrence as one element of a broader counter-terrorist strategy; or key variables likely to influence the prospects for success. This section explores these and other related issues with the goal of illustrating the complexities of deterrence in such an asymmetric context.

Role and Aim of Deterrence

The first issue is determining the role and aim of deterrence as part of wider counter-terrorist efforts designed to prevent mass casualty attacks. Several questions stand out in this respect:

- Is the focus on preventing all actions that could generate mass casualties or just preventing specific types of activity?
- Is the aim to prevent the escalation of an asymmetric conflict above a given threshold? If so, is the threshold defined by weapon type, geography or something else?
- Is the aim to buy time for other approaches to take effect, which may ultimately be designed to defeat a non-state actor?
- How significant is deterrence within the overall approach to the problem?
- To what extent will deterrence be based on military, diplomatic, economic or law enforcement capabilities and activities?

The answers to these questions will determine the choice of target(s), the mechanisms adopted and the overall character of a deterrent strategy. In *Deterrence and Influence in Counter-Terrorism*, Davis and Jenkins break down the actors, or targets, in a 'terrorist system' into the following categories: top leaders, lieutenants, foot soldiers, recruiters, external suppliers and facilitators and heads of supportive states.[13] The most direct approach would involve targeting the leaders and members of organizations like Al Qaeda.

Targeting Terrorists (I): Deterrence by Denial

A denial-based approach would involve demonstrating that the capability existed to ward off, or to minimize damage in the event of, attack thereby mitigating the desired effects. For example, in terms of chemical and biological threats against non-military targets comprehensive preparations for consequence management could have a dissuasive effect. Important capabilities would include the demonstrated readiness of first responders – such as the Fire, Police and Ambulance Services – to cope effectively with, and hence to mitigate the effects of, chemical or biological incidents. Among other things, this would involve the possession of suitable vaccines and knowledge of how specific agents work. Project BioShield announced by US President George W. Bush in his State of the Union address in January 2003 is a pertinent example in this context. The project represents 'a comprehensive effort to develop and make available modern, effective drugs and vaccines to protect against attack by biological and chemical weapons or other dangerous pathogens'.[14] On a different level, a deterrent effect could be sought by demonstrating a robust capability for preventing, or limiting, the proliferation of materials, technology and expertise required by non-state actors to manufacture CBRN weapons. Applicable capabilities here could include robust export controls and the proven ability to detect – through intelligence gathering and analysis – and interdict suspect shipments; the aim being to convince an opponent that the acquisition of CBRN capabilities is fraught with difficulty and not worth the expenditure of the necessary time, resources and effort. The US-led and interdiction-focused Proliferation Security Initiative (PSI) launched in 2003 is a good example of how international cooperation, coordination and intelligence sharing can help to disrupt proliferation networks. There would also appear to be some scope for deterring non-state actors by developing forensic (nuclear and biological) 'attribution' capabilities to underline the threat of retribution. Jay Davis contends that if an actor knows an event can be traced back to the planner and implementer this can create 'strong inhibitions in those that are not personally suicidal'. He adds that such a threat would be bolstered now that the United States has shown willing to get in harm's way to pursue its enemies following 11 September.[15]

In terms of deterrence by denial *vis-à-vis* 'conventional' attacks, developing, bolstering and refining the core elements of counter-terrorist strategies could have a deterrent effect. The findings of the commission charged by the US Department of Defense to investigate the USS *Cole* attack of October 2000 are informative in this respect. The report refers to the role that force protection assets and techniques, as well as anti-terrorism measures, could play in deterring terrorist attacks. For example, this would include a demonstrated capability to locate and interdict non-state actors (and their capabilities) before they can act. The commission concluded that, 'we must develop and resource credible deterrence standards; deterrence specific tactics, techniques and procedures; and defensive equipment packages'.[16]

It is evident that military, intelligence, diplomatic and law enforcement capabilities – among others – all have a role to play in strengthening deterrence by denial. However, a potential drawback with this mechanism could involve deterrence becoming a double-edged sword; where success in deterring one avenue of attack prompts an opponent to shift focus and to strike at less protected areas, or vulnerabilities, using different means – the 'balloon effect'.[17] (Were 11 September, Bali and Madrid examples of such a shift?) Alternative approaches could be less predictable and potentially more dangerous. If the goal is to buy time – for example, to frustrate an adversary who is strongly motivated to change the *status quo* – George and Smoke argue that the consequences of succeeding are not always predictable and favourable to the deterring party.[18] They argue that deterrence success in the short term may not always result in long-term success because an adversary may become increasingly desperate to mount a challenge and may proceed to acquire greater resources to do so.[19] However, this is not to say that developing specific denial capabilities should be avoided. Rather, it is important to remain aware of the interactive nature of strategy and the potentially negative consequences of developing a specific posture.

Targeting Terrorists (II): Deterrence by Threat of Punishment

What about deterrence based on threats of punishment against the leadership and members of terrorist groups? Are there punishment strategies that might deter in this context? Gerald Steinberg has referred to 'the mistaken belief that terrorists such as bin Laden and members of groups such as Hamas, Hizbullah, and Islamic Jihad are suicidal and cannot be deterred'. According to Steinberg, it is possible to identify 'high value targets' including family and supporters that would cause even the most radical leaders to calculate the possible and probable costs and benefits of particular courses of action. Steinberg argues that unlike suicide bombers, terrorist leaders are not so quick to sacrifice their own lives and to risk the destruction of their supporters and the end of any legacy. As a result, he says attention needs to be focused on examining the extent to which such leaders, and their supporters and lieutenants, will respond to retaliatory threats. Moreover, Steinberg raises the question of whether there are symbols of central importance to specific terrorists that could be identified and threatened as part of a deterrent strategy.[20] (What would be the equivalent of the World Trade Center to bin Laden?) From a Western standpoint, however, political, legal and ethical constraints would make such approaches difficult if not impossible to legitimize if pursued overtly by democratic governments. Even if such threats were made covertly, the target would certainly question their credibility because of the knowledge that the deterrer would be operating under such constraints. Moreover, such threats would need to be squared off against the broader goal of reducing the danger posed by non-state actors such as Al Qaeda. Arguably, these types of threats would increase rather than reduce the terrorist danger by alienating the deterrer even further from the target's existing and 'potential' support base.

Targeting Terrorists (III): Susceptibility to Deterrence Logic

> *September 11 creates a new level of destruction toward which other terrorists will strive.*[21]

> *The September 11 attacks underscored a final long-term trend. Power – the power to kill, destroy, disrupt, alarm, and force nations to divert vast resources to protection against attacks – is descending to smaller and smaller groups, whose grievances, real or imaginary, it will not always be possible to satisfy.*[22]

Brian Jenkins, 15 November 2001

The key issue when targeting non-state actors is their susceptibility to the logic of deterrence. As stated earlier, deterrence assumes a level of rationality on behalf of the target. It was also noted that different actors will calculate possible and probable costs and gains differently, and this will be influenced by context specific variables such as the target's value system, mind-set and decision-making processes. Understanding these variables will be pivotal to determining whether a target is deterrable and, if so, how best to formulate a suitable deterrence strategy.

As cost–benefit calculators, for example, 'traditional' terrorist groups are unlikely to contemplate perpetrating mass casualty events. Groups motivated by nationalist goals such as the IRA and ETA have tended to employ violence against places or people associated with a political objective. As Brian Jenkins famously once said, their goal has been 'a lot of people watching, not a lot of people dead'.[23] Consequently, such groups tend to self-impose restraint and calibrate their actions to avoid damaging any perceived underlying sympathy and support for their cause. In this respect they can be said to behave as rational cost–benefit calculators. Thus, traditional groups tend to be open to negotiation and susceptible to inducements. As a result they will tend to 'self-deter' when it comes to mass casualty terrorism.

The non-state actors most likely to contemplate mass casualty terrorism, whether through suicide operations or otherwise, are those that espouse extreme views derived from religious radicalism (for example, radical

Islam) or apocalyptic beliefs. The fanaticism of such actors is usually reflected in their harbouring of unrealisable goals and insusceptibility to negotiation and inducements. Aum Shinrikyo and Al Qaeda are pertinent examples as both have already demonstrated a willingness to perpetrate mass fatalities and destruction through indiscriminate attacks against civilian targets. The Aum Shinrikyo sect was motivated to use chemical and biological agents in order to cause death, terror and disruption on such a large scale that the resultant disorder and instability would destroy the existing social structure. According to John Parachini, Aum imagined a world 'they sought to create that was not constrained by the world in which they lived. To bring this imaginary world into being, they sought weapons they believed might trigger an apocalypse from which they emerged as a dominant power'.[24] Moreover, the group was characterized by fanatically obedient followers and a charismatic leader in Shoko Asahara.[25] Osama bin Laden and the Al Qaeda network are other key examples because of their claims to be religiously motivated and acting in the name of Islam when espousing objectives such as 'eliminating Israel', 'destroying America' and 'killing all Americans'.

As deterrence is about preserving the *status quo* it follows that for it to work successfully the target must believe, or be made to believe, that the *status quo* is preferable to the costs of acting; at least in the short-term if the goal of deterrence is to buy time for other approaches to take effect. However, if an opponent is sufficiently determined to alter the *status quo* this could make deterrence unworkable – as Achen and Snidal note, 'not all conceivable opponents are deterrable'.[26] The more fanatical a terrorist organization's motives, the stronger the resolve of its members is likely to be and the less susceptible to deterrence; this will be particularly true if members of the target group think in suicidal terms, which numerous members of Al Qaeda evidently do. Indeed, it appears that many members of Al Qaeda are willing to endure significant costs and destruction in pursuit of their goals. As a consequence, deterrence is likely to constitute a short-term delaying option at best in this context to buy time for other approaches (physical disruption and destruction) to work.

To assess as accurately as possible the susceptibility of non-state actors to deterrence logic will take a concerted and targeted intelligence collection and analysis effort. In part this could focus on how specific groups, or individuals within those groups, calculate costs and benefits: are they 'risk prone' or 'risk averse', and do they think in terms of 'minimizing losses' or 'maximizing gains'? To what extent are they motivated by survival, security, recognition, wealth, power or accomplishment? According to Robert Jervis, 'in almost no interactions do two adversaries understand each other's goals, fears, means-ends beliefs, and perceptions'.[27] An additional avenue for inquiry would be evaluating the processes through which suspect groups make decisions. It will also be important to avoid viewing the capabilities and intentions of such actors in the same way as one views one's own role and situation. As Jervis argues, while the commitments of the deterrer may appear 'objectively clear and credible' to a disinterested third party, they may not be perceived that way by the target.[28]

Targeting Regimes: Deterrence by Punishment

Alternative targets for deterrence are the regimes on and from whose territory terrorist groups might attempt to organize and to operate. Deterrence in this context would involve threats to punish regimes if they are found to be assisting suspect non-state actors by sponsoring, harbouring or merely tolerating them. The US-led campaign against the Taleban in Afghanistan is informative here because it sent a message signalling that the United States and its allies possess the intent, the resolve and the capability to punish and unseat regimes that contemplate supporting, harbouring or tolerating the likes of Osama bin Laden and Al Qaeda. On this point, Gerald Steinberg wonders that if the costs of hosting Al Qaeda had been made clear to Taleban leaders in the months and years prior to 11 September then this could have resulted in the eviction of Osama bin Laden from Afghanistan.[29] However, strictly speaking such an approach would have been an example of coercion and not deterrence because the aim would have been to induce the Taleban to alter rather than preserve the *status quo*. For example, the highly asymmetric cruise missile strikes against Al Qaeda training camps in Afghanistan in response to the African embassy bombings in 1998 were coercive rather than deterrent in nature. Moreover, the high-profile but relatively low-grade nature of this response by the Clinton administration did not send a concrete and credible message of American resolve to defeat Al Qaeda. However, it should be remembered that the administration's missile attacks on Afghanistan, as well as Sudan, were not in response to strikes against the economic and political power centres of the United States. Thus, at that time the intent/resolve balance between the United States and Al Qaeda was asymmetrical and tipped in the latter's favour.

Philip Heymann has identified several questions to address when targeting regimes for deterrent purposes:

- To what extent does a regime have control over a terrorist group?
- What degree of support is a regime giving to a group?
- Is territory being made freely available?
- Is it providing resources such as money and weapons?
- Is a regime merely providing sanctuary and nothing else?[30]

These are all important questions when formulating a strategy to influence a regime's behaviour. However, Heymann's focus is on regimes that are already involved with terrorist entities in one way or another. Strictly speaking any threats in this context would be coercive in nature because the aim would be to change the *status quo*. Nevertheless, Heymann makes several important points relevant to both coercion and deterrence. To begin with he raises the potentiality that a terrorist-supporting regime may perceive retaliatory action, or the threat of it, by an external power as preferable to the potentially negative domestic effects that could ensue if an attempt was made to act against the interests of specific non-state actors. Moreover, Heymann notes that a supporting regime may believe that retaliatory strikes could have a beneficial effect.[31] For example, this could include justification to clamp down on domestic opponents in a siege-type atmosphere or the generation of international sympathy and support. Finally, Heymann draws attention to the question of legality under international law. Specifically, he raises the issue of proof and responsibility, and makes the point that the only response deemed legal under international law would be actions designed as a specific deterrent – acting in self-defence under article 2(4) of the UN Charter.[32] On this point, the issue of proof could potentially be used to strengthen deterrence *vis-à-vis* regimes. A proven attribution capability designed to generate evidence of complicity – through focused intelligence collection and analysis – could strengthen deterrence by demonstrating an ability to rapidly bring international law and support to bear, thereby legitimizing action against a suspect regime.

The war in 2003 to unseat Saddam Hussein in Iraq was partially justified by the Bush administration, although not the Blair government, on Baghdad's alleged connections to international terrorism and specifically to Al Qaeda. Although it has since emerged that no such links existed, the controversial military campaign to impose regime change could strengthen deterrence vis-à-vis other governments that contemplate sponsoring terrorists in the future. The Bush administration certainly viewed toppling Saddam as a means through which to shape the evolving strategic landscape and to send a message of intent and resolve to potential opponents at the state actor level. However, while deterrence may well have been strengthened in this respect, the invasion of Iraq and the volatile post-war security environment has arguably undermined the overall war on terror and increased the short- and long-term threat of mass casualty terrorism. First, the war and its aftermath appear to have increased support throughout the Arab and Muslim worlds for radical Islamic movements like Al Qaeda by further alienating from the United States the actual and potential support base for such organizations. Second, because Coalition forces have been tied down fighting a counter-insurgency campaign in Iraq they have effectively been prevented from contributing elsewhere in the war on terror.

Deterrence Versus Coercion

As stated earlier a subtle conceptual difference exists between deterrence and coercion. In the case of the Taleban and Qaddafi regimes – both of which have been implicated in acts of international terrorism – any threats and actions against them have been designed to induce altered behaviour; to change the *status quo* by ending their support for terrorism. In the Libyan case, United States attempts to punish and coerce the Qaddafi regime in 1986 for its sponsorship of international terrorism involved the limited application of military force against leadership targets in Tripoli. This ultimately failed given Libya's subsequent implication in the bombing of a Pan Am passenger plane over Lockerbie in 1988. In the Taleban case, initial American attempts at coercion failed and the US-dominated coalition was forced to use brute force (forcible offence) to impose regime change in Afghanistan – the Taleban was not induced through coercion to comply with United States' demands to give up bin Laden and other Al Qaeda suspects. In short, if a regime is already involved in some form of terrorist-associated activity, any threats to influence behaviour will be coercive and not deterrent because the aim will be altering the *status quo*; to change the regime's behaviour. Deterrence is about preserving the *status quo*; keeping things as they are. Consequently, a strictly deterrent strategy would only be relevant to regimes not currently implicated in any form of terrorist support but which might contemplate becoming involved in the future. The upshot from this is that in conceptual terms coercion (changing the *status quo*) needs to be considered as related to but different from deterrence (preserving the *status quo*) in the context of responding to the threat of mass casualty terrorism.

Conclusions

Several findings can be derived from the foregoing analysis.

'Denial' and 'punishment' mechanisms both seem to be applicable *vis-à-vis* deterring mass casualty terrorism. Deterrence by denial appears most applicable when the target is a non-state actor, and deterrence by threat of punishment when the target is a regime contemplating whether or how to support a terrorist group.

Deterrence by denial aimed at non-state actors will realistically only be a delaying option at best – for other approaches to take effect – given the extreme motives and high level of resolve associated with the members and leaders of those groups likely to contemplate mass casualty terrorism.

Western democratic states are subject to radically different constraints – political, legal and ethical – from those of non-state actors and these will shape significantly the types of messages that Western states can credibly and legitimately send as part of any deterrence strategy.

A potential drawback with deterrence by denial is that such an approach could become a double-edged sword; where success in one dimension prompts a non-state adversary to shift focus and to strike at less protected areas, or vulnerabilities, using different means. This does not mean that developing specific denial capabilities should be avoided. However, it is important to remain aware that because strategy is an interactive contest there could well be some negative consequences associated with developing a specific posture.

The key to countering CBRNE terrorism will be the 'accurate' and 'timely' collection and analysis of intelligence – primarily human intelligence (HUMINT) – on the individuals, groups, networks and states of greatest concern in this area. Admittedly, this is easier said than done because of the inherent difficulties associated with monitoring such actors. If it was straightforward we would not have seen such incidents as the World Trade Center and the anthrax attacks in the United States, the Bali nightclub bombing and the Madrid attacks. In terms of non-state actors, intelligence collection and analysis needs to focus on the three dimensions of asymmetry outlined earlier: (1) interest/resolve; (2) value systems, mind-sets and perceptions (rationality); and (3) conflict strategies, techniques and capabilities. Such an approach should generate greater access to and understanding of those organizations that might consider employing CBRNE. It should also generate knowledge of the CBRNE-related activities of such entities and how best to disrupt them.

In terms of deterrence, a specific priority should be placed on collecting and analysing intelligence to evaluate the susceptibility of non-state organizations – their members and leaders – to deterrence logic. A priority should be placed on getting inside an opponent's 'black-box' to understand what is rational in the target's mind-set. To re-cap from earlier, one needs to understand 'where the frame of reference for the actor's thinking comes from', 'how it is evoked', and the 'set of alternatives' considered by an opponent in the 'choice process'.[33] Humint will be key here in order to generate the necessary understanding of a real or potential adversary's motives, resolve, culture, internal workings and decision processes, resources, capabilities, locations and conflict techniques.

US and allied action in the war on terrorism should hopefully in the long run strengthen both deterrence and coercion *vis-à-vis* regimes that contemplate supporting terrorist-related activities because it sends a message of resolve. The stakes involved for the United States and its allies are currently perceived to be very high and this should ensure that the intent/resolve dimension of any deterrent strategy would remain solid for the foreseeable future. However, while the war in Iraq may well strengthen deterrence at the state actor level, it has arguably undermined broader counter-terrorism goals by increasing the support for radical Islamic groups throughout the Arab and Muslim worlds.

Deterrence can realistically be only one element of a much broader counter-terrorist effort. However, the preparations and activities associated with other approaches should serve to strengthen the deterrence aspect. For example, preparations for consequence management could potentially have a dissuasive effect.

There is a subtle conceptual difference between deterrence and coercion. If a regime is already involved in some form of terrorist-associated activity, any threats to influence behaviour will be coercive and not deterrent because the aim will be altering the *status quo*; to put an end to the regime's terrorist-associated activity. However, deterrence is about preserving the *status quo*; keeping things as they are.

NOTES

This chapter was originally drafted in 2002.
The analysis, opinions and conclusions expressed or implied in this article are those of the author and do not necessarily represent the views of the JSCSC, the UK MoD or any other government agency.

1. CBRNE = chemical, biological, radiological, nuclear and enhanced explosive. Quote taken from 'Part I: America's Security in the Twenty-First Century', *Quadrenial Defense Review Report (QDR)* (US Department of Defense, 30 September 2001) p.5.
2. Seminar presentation by Mike Wermuth, Executive Director of the US 'Gilmore Commission' (Centre for Defence Studies, King's College, London, 25 Oct. 2001). The Gilmore Commission is the congressionally mandated Advisory Panel to Assess Domestic Response Capabilities for Terrorism Involving Weapons of Mass Destruction.
3. DCI Worldwide Threat Briefing 2002: Converging Dangers in a Post 9/11 World, Testimony of Director of Central Intelligence, George J. Tenet, Before The Select Committee on Intelligence, Senate, US Congress, 6 Feb. 2002 < http://www.odci.gov/cia/public_affairs/speeches/dci_speech_02062002.html >.
4. DCI Worldwide Threat Briefing 2002. See also: *Responsibility for the Terrorist Atrocities in the United States, 11 September 2001: An Updated Account*, document released by Her Majesty's Government, 10 Downing Street, London (Nov. 2001); Statement on 'Terrorism: Current and Long Term Threats', Brian Michael Jenkins, Senior Advisor to the President of the RAND Corporation, before the Senate Armed Services Subcommittee on Emerging Threats, 15 Nov. 2001, p.7. It became evident during the 1990s that certain groups were interested in acquiring some form of CBRN capability. In July 1999, the 'Deutch Commission' reported that at least a dozen terrorist groups had expressed an interest in or had actively sought to acquire CBRN. See *Combating Proliferation of Weapons of Mass Destruction* (Report of the Commission to Assess the Organization of the Federal Government to Combat the Proliferation of Weapons of Mass Destruction, 14 July 1999), p.1.
5. Linda Rothstein, 'After September 11', *Bulletin of the Atomic Scientists*, Vol.57, No.6 (Nov./Dec. 2001), pp.44–8, available at: < http://www.bullatomsci.org/issues/2001/nd01/nd01rothstein.html/ >.
6. DCI Worldwide Threat Briefing 2002.
7. See for example: Thomas Schelling, *Arms and Influence* (New Haven: Yale University Press, 1966).

8. See for example: *Fact Sheet on Missile Defense and Deterrence*, Bureau of Arms Control, US Department of State (1 Sept. 2001), available at: < http://www.state.gov/t/ac/rls/fs/2001/4891.htm > .
9. Robert T. Art, 'To What Ends Military Power?', *International Security* Vol.4 (Spring 1980), p.8.
10. Gerald M. Steinberg, 'Rediscovering Deterrence After September 11, 2001', *Jerusalem Letter*/Viewpoints, No.467 (2 Dec. 2001), Jerusalem Center for Public Affairs, available at < http://www.jcpa.org/jl/vp467.htm > .
11. Steinberg, 'Rediscovering Deterrence After September 11, 2001'.
12. Herbert Simon, quoted in Richard Lebow and Janice Stein, 'Rational Deterrence Theory: I Think, Therefore I Deter', *World Politics*, Vol.42. No.2 (Jan. 1989), p.215.
13. Paul K. Davis and Brian Michael Jenkins, *Deterrence and Influence in Counter-Terrorism* (Santa Monica, CA: RAND, 2002), p.15.
14. 'President Details Project BioShield', Office of the Press Secretary, White House, 3 February 2003, available at ⟨http://www.whitehouse.gov/news/releases/2003/02/20030203.html⟩.
15. Jay Davis, *The Grand Challenges of Counter-Terrorism* (Center for Global Security Research, Lawrence Livermore National Laboratory, 2001), available at < http://cgsr.llnl.gov/future2001/davis.html > .
16. *USS Cole Commission Report* US Department of Defense (9 Jan. 2001), Executive Summary available at: ⟨http://www.fas.org/irp/threat/cole.htm⟩.
17. See Anthony H. Cordesman, *Asymmetric Warfare Versus Counterterrorism: Rethinking CBRN and CIP Defense and Response* (Washington, DC: Center for Strategic and International Studies, Dec. 2000), p.14.
18. Alexander George and Richard Smoke, 'Deterrence and Foreign Policy', *World Politics*, Vol.41, No.2 (Jan. 1989), p.182.
19. Ibid. p.173.
20. Steinberg, 'Rediscovering Deterrence After September 11'.
21. Statement on 'Terrorism: Current and Long Term Threats', Brian Michael Jenkins, Senior Advisor to the President of the RAND Corporation, before the Senate Armed Services Subcommittee on Emerging Threats (15 Nov. 2001), p.4.
22. Ibid. p.9.
23. Ibid. p.8.
24. Statement on 'Anthrax Attacks, Biological Terrorism and Preventive Responses', John Parachini, Policy Analyst, RAND Washington Office, before the Subcommittee on Technology, Terrorism and Government Information, Nov. 2001, p.8. See RAND Testimony, CT-186, Nov. 2001 < http://www.rand.org/ > .
25. Jenkins 'Terrorism: Current and Long Term Threats', p.6.
26. Christopher H. Achen and Duncan Snidal, 'Rational Deterrence Theory and Comparative Case Studies', *World Politics*, Vol.41, No.2 (Jan. 1989) p.153.
27. Robert Jervis, 'Rational Deterrence: Theory and Evidence', *World Politics*, Vol.41, No.2 (Jan. 1989) p.196.
28. Jervis, 'Rational Deterrence', p.196.
29. Steinberg, 'Rediscovering Deterrence After September 11, 2001'.
30. Philip B. Heymann, *Terrorism and America: A Commonsense Strategy for a Democratic Society* (Cambridge, MA: MIT Press, 1998) p.67.
31. Heymann, *Terrorism and America*, p.73.
32. Ibid. p.70.
33. Lebow and Stein, 'Rational Deterrence Theory', p.215.

The New Indeterminacy of Deterrence and Missile Defence

AARON KARP

Missile defence, as everyone knows, is the conceptual opposite of deterrence. Or is it? Widely anticipated as either the most decisive or the most destabilizing step in security policy, the American withdrawal from the Anti-Ballistic Missile (ABM) Treaty on 13 June 2002 came and went with surprisingly little comment. Instead of revolutionizing global security, death of the ABM Treaty, erasing the foundation of Cold War stability, has had only the most ambiguous impact. Instead of ushering a new era of defence dominance, the shift from exclusive reliance on strategic deterrence seems to be perpetuating the uncertainty of the recent past.

Although the ABM Treaty is dead, and the United States has begun deployment of theatre missile defences and initiated construction of strategic missile defences, the riddles of international security remain much as before. What happened? Why did the mighty roar of missile defence yield to an increasingly mousy squeak? It is argued here that this surprising turn of events is due to changes in the nature of deterrence. As a result, deterrence and missile defence have ceased to be polar opposites. As their individual roles have become less decisive and more enigmatic, the relationship between the two is being redefined. With no going back to the easy categories of the Cold War era, deterrence and defence are just two more parts of twenty-first century strategic indeterminance. Since neither alone offers a sufficient basis for strategic security, ways must be found to make them compatible.

Several factors were responsible for the mutual transformation of deterrence and defence. Above all, though, is the changing nature of global threats and the credibility of retaliation. The appearance of new strategic threats has undermined the overwhelming salience of deterrence. As understood by commentators like Robert Jervis, deterrence was a universal concept, technologically determined by nuclear weapons and the certainty of retaliation.[1] There remains a strong element of truth to this perspective. But deterrence now faces unprecedented limits to its effectiveness. In place of erstwhile universality, deterrence has become discrete. Sometimes it almost certainly works, but other times it very well might not. Similarly, missile defence has lost its universal impact. Before it was of minimal value and potentially dangerous, threatening to undermine stability based on the ability to retaliate. It still remains counterproductive or irrelevant in situations where deterrence is strong. But it has found a new mission reinforcing stability where deterrence is questionable.

To deal with these differences, the universal theory of deterrence needs to be replaced by a more nuanced understanding of security problems, an outlook that acknowledges these differences. In the place of the simple East–West balance, we now face a variety of strategic balances, each with their own dynamics. The role of deterrence and its relationship to defence can only be fully appreciated by considering these problems of context.

Strategic problems can be divided into three groups with their own implications for deterrence and defence.[2] *Type I* deterrence describes the situation among stable nuclear powers, where deterrent relationships remain much as before. Here the reduction in global tensions has simply strengthened stability, creating minimal need for missile defence. *Type II* deterrence is a looser phenomenon involving strategic conflict with less predictable nuclear powers. Against these actors threats of retaliation may or may not be effective. This type of deterrence is less reliable and urgently requires buttressing. These situations have emerged as the most common justification for missile defence. Finally there is *Type III* deterrence, involving terrorist actors against whom retaliation is all but impossible and the effectiveness of deterrence is highly questionable. Previously overlooked, these situations have emerged since 11 September 2001 as the most serious challenges to deterrence, creating unprecedented need for missile defences tailored to their unique circumstances.

To be sure, these categories are not absolute. Because strategic weapons, including missile defences, have capabilities that reach beyond their intended targets, different deterrent situations often overlap. One of the most important challenges of the new strategic environment will be reinforcing the walls separating these three categories. How, in other words, do we ensure that defences intended to deal with the uncertainty of Type-II and the inherent instability of Type-III situations do not weaken the strength of Type-I deterrence? A second major problem will be reorienting missile defence priorities to deal specifically with those situations where deterrence failures are most likely, above all stressing the terrorist challenges of Type-III deterrence failure.

Old Ideas in a New World

Since the mid-1960s, the debate over missile defence has not been about the future so much as it is about the past. For over thirty years missile defence was not a weapon but a symbol, given mythic characteristics by advocates and enemies. To its supporters missile defence was a virtual panacea to the painful dangers and political limits of nuclear deterrence.[3] More modest advocates still characterized it as an essential instrument to minimize the truly awful dangers of deterrence failure. To its opponents, missile defence would undermine mutual deterrence, eliminating the only reliable barrier to nuclear war.[4]

Emerging from such an overheated environment, it is no surprise that current positions on missile defence retain much of their old rigidity. Although the issues have changed almost beyond recognition, both the threats and responses, the positions of political parties and analysts remain much as before. The threat shifted from thousands of nuclear warheads from the Soviet Union to a handful from North Korea and other rogue actors as well as hundreds of conventionally armed missiles. The response evolved just as dramatically, from nuclear-armed interceptors to kinetic energy kill vehicles. Even so, positions today resemble nothing so much as positions yesterday.

Repelled by the polarization, some analysts have begun to search for a middle ground, arguing that the real need today is not for intellectual purity based on repetition of ageing shibboleths. More imagination is needed, rather, to adapt old ideas to the needs of a new geopolitical situation.[5] In this broader strategic environment, old certainties must yield to newer doubts. The impact of missile defences may be much smaller than either side imagines. There is growing reason to think that both their benefits and dangers have been greatly exaggerated. Far from revolutionizing strategic affairs, their main effect will be to reaffirm existing trends, whatever they may be. As a result, their impact on the relationship between deterrence and defence will remain ambiguous. Much the same can be said of their impact on other major strategic debates, such as offence versus defence stability and the riddles of extended deterrence. Rather than look for resolution of these disputes, observers would be better advised to anticipate them to remain highly politicized and controversial.

To some degree, this strategic indeterminacy is the result of the protracted introduction of missile defences. Transformation from deterrence to defence dominance can be abrupt only in the abstract. Missile defence remains an enormously demanding technology, one that cannot be unveiled fully grown. Although full-scale development of hit-to-kill, mid-course intercept technology began in 1996, initial deployment of American national missile defences only began in 2004. There is no consensus, even among the operational commands, when full operational capability will be achieved.[6] The slow process gives governments plenty of time to adjust their capabilities and expectations, offering a reassuring contrast to an abrupt transition, the kind that strategic thinkers always fear most. But, as argued here, time only facilitates what would be a gentle transition anyway.

Much of the confusion over the role of missile defence comes from the fallacy of examining its effects exclusively in terms of nuclear stability. It is the broader international political and strategic context, rather than any intrinsic capabilities of missile defences, that will most influence their impact. Contrary to much of what is commonly said, missile defences are far from the greatest force shaping the global security order. Despite the considerable attention they receive, it is factors completely outside most missile defence debates which will do the most to shape the role of these weapons. The strategic implications of missile defences will be determined by broader trends governing the nature of armed conflict and the use of force. Above all, it will be the decline of state-to-state warfare and the rise of the revolution in military affairs that will structure the environment in which missile defences operate.

The highly polarized debates of the past have left us unprepared to deal with the greatest significance of missile defence, which must be inherently ambiguous. Like virtually all major new military technologies, the place of missile defence will be determined not by their own particular characteristics so much as the strategic context in which they are deployed. Although particular threats clearly are getting worse, the over-all strategic environment for major powers is increasingly benign, especially regarding the threats from other countries which missile defence is intended to counter. The decline of state threats makes the technical job of missile defence much easier and less urgent. It also reduces their over-all impact on strategic stability.

For all the ink spilled contesting the role of missile defences for the United States, the real tests will come elsewhere. It is in regional contexts, where state-to-state warfare remains more likely, that missile defences will have the greatest impact on perceptions and expectations, and on actual war fighting. As for actual use, it is against a new class of missile threats from very short-range missiles that missile defences are most likely to be employed, against which they will be most severely tested.

The Mysterious Disappearance of Missile Defence

It was events of 1998, proliferation's *annus horribilis*, that finished off the last remaining artefacts of the Cold War security framework, ushering an early start to twenty-first century. Suddenly, proliferation no longer could be reassuringly assumed to be a gradual process, accompanied by luxurious warnings that lead only to ambiguous developments. Above all, this was the year of unexpected nuclear tests in India and Pakistan. Equally unpredicted was the series of long-range missile tests in India, Iran, Pakistan and above all in North Korea. The year ended with the complete collapse of the UN inspection system for Iraq, leading to the world's first non-proliferation war,

Operation Desert Fox, a four-day Anglo-American aerial attack on suspect sites in Iraq.

In the middle of these catastrophes came publication of the Rumsfeld Commission report on ballistic missile threats to the United States. While the findings of the commission were modest, concluding that long-range missile threats could emerge more rapidly than previously believed, the impact was much greater. Ballistic missile proliferation no longer could be portrayed as a predictable threat.[7] No less significant was the Commission's demonstration of broad political agreement. Partisan polarization was yielding to a new consensus on the nature of missile dangers.[8] In Washington it was becoming harder to resist the belief that long-range missile threats could emerge faster than responses could be improvised.[9]

Testifying to the overwhelming acceptance of nuclear deterrence, the primary issue ceased to be the acts of proliferators. Instead it was the planned response of the United States that caused greatest controversy. This twist of events lies in the fundamental importance of ideas over things.[10] While regional weapons created enormous problems, they did not shake basic assumptions about international conflict. In and of itself, there is nothing new in the sight of a country trying to perfect long-range offensive weapons. We had the whole Cold War to get accustomed to that. It was, rather, the growing American determination to deploy new defensive weapons that suggested a far greater transformation in the rules of global security.

By signing into law the 1999 American Missile Defense Act, President Clinton set the United States on a collision course with its rivals and allies alike. Other issues might temporarily assert greater immediate concern, but the overwhelming importance of missile defence has not been challenged since. Here alone was an issue which challenged the essential assumptions of international security since the end of the Second World War. Much more so than the missile proliferation to which it was a response, it was missile defence that emerged as the agent of doubt. Above, all, missile defence compelled security thinkers to reconsider the role of deterrence, the ability to prevent conflict through threat of retaliation, as opposed to overcoming enemies exclusively through the ability to defeat them. At stake was not just a choice of military strategies, but rival visions of world order and the possibilities for peace.

Other problems, serious though they are, do not force us to re-evaluate what we mean by security itself. Fighting in the Middle East or tensions with China disturb regional security, but mostly seem to reaffirm traditional beliefs about international stability and transformation. While the dilemmas of humanitarian intervention or the politics of tight military budgets and technical modernization might engage a broad spectrum of countries, they do not polarize the international community the same way either.

Even 11 September seems insufficient to rival its salience. Although it has assumed unprecedented importance, terrorism remains an oddity of international security, impervious to theoretical analysis and resistant to the policy process. Far from challenging old security priorities, terrorism has emerged as a completely separate category. Despite the broad consequences for homeland security, the newly exposed vulnerabilities only partially offset the mounting importance of missile proliferation among untrustworthy states. In the United States, Al Qaeda terrorism turned out to be more of a catalyst for defence spending than for defence thinking. In other countries it became important mostly because it was such a preoccupation for the Americans.

The round of consultations undertaken by the newly elected Bush administration in the spring of 2001 put the international community on notice that the new president had made up his mind. The consultations were a major diplomatic success, winning broad but grudging acceptance of American determination to press ahead with actual deployment. But they failed to resolve the underlying issues about the impact for international security. To the contrary, they mostly stirred up even greater consternation. 'Where are the Americans leading us?' governments and analysts seemed to ask.

When President Bush announced his intention to withdraw the United States from the 1972 ABM Treaty, there could be no doubt that a momentous process had truly begun.[11] Yet only a few months later the issue had mysteriously disappeared from international agendas. Angry scepticism and feelings of abandonment began to shift toward muted acceptance.[12] What had been an issue for cabinet ministers and heads of government reverted to something it had not been for years; the arcane business of specialists. At a May 2002 NATO conference on the future of international security the widely respected German Ambassador to Washington, Wolfgang Ischinger, articulated a thought on many minds when he asked 'Whatever happened to missile defence?'.[13]

Coming to Terms: Russia, Europe, China and America

Indeed, what happened? Only a few months earlier global opinion was lining up solidly against American plans. Even the self-consciously multilateralist, consensus-oriented Clinton Administration began to confront rising criticism against what was widely perceived as its unilateralist demeanour. In pursuit of unachievable notions of insular security, it was said, the United States was sacrificing alliance solidarity, abandoning arms control, and courting global opposition. Confrontation seemed unavoidable. With America determined to plough its own furrow, the biggest question was the reaction of other countries. All that remained to see was the severity of the inevitable diplomatic breakdown.

How bad would it be? Russian leaders left no doubt that they would demand a high price for an American withdrawal from the ABM Treaty. Cooperation, they insisted, was impossible.[14] Optimists thought Russia would be content to compensate by withdrawing from the START treaties and re-MIRVing its ballistic missiles. Or would Moscow insist on retribution, angrily opposing further NATO expansion, accelerating technical aid to Iran, and maybe even foment crisis with vulnerable neighbours like Latvia and Georgia?[15] In much of Europe, there was greater sympathy for the Russian position, which supported a comforting *status quo* against American disruption.[16] And as for China, there was less doubt. The prospect of an uninhibited Sino-American nuclear arms race seemed so inevitable that some Washington commentators almost seemed to take comfort in the possibility.[17]

Instead we now face rising acceptance of the American path and even quiet acknowledgement that it might serve global interests. Although they were seriously tested, relations between the United States and other major powers survived. The cause appears to be growing appreciation that American missile defence would not affect deterrence toward them. Partially as a result of American consultations, partially through their own political processes, the leaders of Russia, Europe and China seem to recognize that American missile defence will not revolutionize their own safety. In other words, they acknowledge that it does not replace or seriously threaten Type-I deterrence.

Whether it was based on interest or principle, dissent reflected convictions. Having made their opposition so stark, the leaders of Russia, Europe and China could not be expected to simply contradict themselves outright. Rather what gradually emerged, beginning in the autumn of 2001, was a gradual shift in their rhetoric and increasing willingness to cooperate with the United States. This trend cannot be separated from the shadow of 11 September. But nor can it be reduced to a simple reaction to the crimes of Al Qaeda, since it goes far beyond the needs of fighting terror. An American diplomatic offensive almost without contemporary precedent (the diplomacy of the 1999 Kosovo war comes closest) also was crucial, but this too was insufficient to explain the rapidity and thoroughness of the transformation.

The change was most explicit in Russia. As recently as June 2001, Vladimir Putin had signed an unprecedented mutual security treaty with China, implicitly designed to balance American global influence. Russia resisted change in its strategic arrangements because any change inherently reduced not just its brute military resources but, more importantly, any remaining appearance of superpower equality. Yet even this began to yield as Russia accommodated American determination.

In the summer and autumn of 2001, discussions on America's planned withdrawal from the ABM Treaty shifted from emphasizing Russian opposition to the character of its acceptance. Larger factors obviously were at work.

Only a more general shift can account for Russia's simultaneous acceptance – however grudging – of a major NATO expansion. To be sure, in exchange it was receiving a new relationship with NATO.[18] But even the most optimistic evaluation would struggle to present this as a fair quid pro quo. In addition to the impact of 11 September, and the offer of more institutional relations with NATO, must be added the flexibility of Vladimir Putin. His decision to tie Russia's future more firmly with the West undoubtedly contributed to his acceptance of a new strategic environment.[19] But Putin's willingness to accept a relationship with America without the previously essential ABM Treaty and the alternative only of a disappointing SORT agreement implied that the Kremlin was evaluating strategic problems completely differently.

The role of intervening factors is more subtle in Western Europe, where the acceptance of American determination to proceed with missile defence was, if anything, more hesitant than in Russia. While Russian opposition was based on its own self-interest, Europe's was based on principles. This made compromise more difficult; one can bargain interests since they tend to be relative, but that is not as true of principles. Hesitant to leave the familiarity of nuclear deterrence, unconvinced of the need for an alternative, many European leaders sought to convince their American allies of the folly of their ways.

Specific national perspectives also came into play. Britain, the least integrated of major European actors, could most easily afford to take an independent line, allowing it to be cautiously supportive of Washington. For Germany it was essential to avoid a disastrous confrontation between Washington and Moscow, which would force Europe miserably into the middle.[20] As Moscow's position began to ease, Germany's could also. France seemed to regard missile defence as just another issue with which to tar the Americans with the brush of irresponsibility.

Europe's attitudes toward missile defence cannot be separated from its reaction to a variety of American policies which rejected the consensus approach that increasingly distinguishes European initiatives. For the Clinton administration, missile defence was the first major unilateralist rift. Almost immediately after swearing in to office, though, it was President Bush who provided far more nationalist fodder, beginning with his rejection of the Kyoto Convention and continuing with his opposition to the institutionalization of the Biological Weapons Convention, the UN Small Arms process, and the International Criminal Court. Complaining about the poor state of trans-Atlantic relations grew into a small industry.[21]

But it would be a mistake to take European dissatisfaction at face value. Regardless of the abundant sincerity about discontent with America's determination to proceed with missile defence, it was difficult to distinguish the language of this critique from the European criticism of so many other things American. There is a revealing symmetry, for example, between European criticism of missile defence and globalization.[22] These alternate in the headlines, joined now and then by other issues like Kyoto and the ICC, ensuring that the anti-American theme never disappears entirely. Missile defence may be important, but it is not viewed in isolation. Rather it is part of a set of problems that mostly reflect Europe's discontent with its identity and global role.[23] It is highly revealing that at the same moment that European dissatisfaction with American missile defence planning began to diminish, other painful trans-Atlantic issues returned to the fore.[24]

The politics of missile defence in Europe have to do with a great many things, far more than the narrow issues of missile proliferation. In addition to the frustrations of European political identity, one must note the slow progress of forging an ESDP and the seemingly insurmountable problems of low defence spending and declining military relevance. After Russia made clear its acceptance of American missile defence plans, European opposition immediately diminished, as it had to. But it certainly did not disappear; the broader misgivings remain.

China had been even more outspoken in its opposition than Russia, convinced that American plans were aimed squarely at blocking its hopes of emerging as a 'peer competitor' or of taking control of Taiwan. The American expectation – which official spokesmen and analysts in Beijing did nothing to diminish – was that China would respond by rapidly expanding its own missile forces. Illustrated by crises like the May 1999 bombing of the Belgrade embassy and the March 2001 spy plane affair, the climate of distrust seemed certain to carry over to missile defences as well.

Yet China too has moderated its rhetoric toward the United States and shows no signs of preparing to dramatically develop its forces. Threats have become more vague and – with the vital exception of Taiwan – gradually disappeared.[25] Cooperation on anti-terrorism has been good, but analysts consistently maintain this is too little to sustain a cooperative relationship.[26] More salient is the apparent decision by Chinese leaders that American national missile defence is something they cannot stop, but probably can live with.[27] The Bush Administration has made this easier by offering what few incentives its suspicious attitudes permit. But this does not conceal the fact that the change was mostly made in Beijing.

Finally, it is important not to overlook the reaction of the United States to its own missile defence initiatives. Here at last is one area where America mostly resembles the rest of the world. Perhaps the greatest surprise of its missile defence planning is how little it has affected the rest of American defence planning. Despite withdrawing from the ABM Treaty and beginning construction on an interceptor facility in Alaska, the United States has done little else as a result. Unlike anti-terrorism or Iraq, missile defence has not made Washington more assertive. Nor has it led to calls for more aggressive use of force. It has no visible effect on planning to deal with contingencies like war with Iraq or North Korea. Conventional forces have not been cut, nor have nuclear forces become more prominent.[28] Like virtually everyone else, the United States seems to have taken missile defence in its stride.

Al Qaeda Versus Deterrence

The foregoing only confirms the decline of concern over missile defence. It leaves unresolved the mystery of where that concern went. While many particular factors have been mentioned, these cannot account for the remarkable continuity of global reactions.

It is contended here that broad explanations lie elsewhere; not in the special characteristics of national policy and bi-lateral diplomacy, but in the broader transformation of armed conflict. Three factors that contributed to the acceptance of missile defence stand out: the declining credibility of deterrence, the transformation of the purposes of warfare, and the revolution in military affairs. Uniting them all is the transference of concern from Type-I deterrent situations to less predictable Type-II and Type-III scenarios.

Of most recent vintage are the events of 11 September. Although the attacks demanded a radical adjustment of security priorities, one of the greatest effects was not what they changed but what they reaffirmed. In addition to the more tangible casualties, the credibility of nuclear deterrence acquired fresh and very deep scars.

The importance of 11 September illustrates the overwhelming importance of political context for missile defences. Although nothing that happened on that day directly engaged nuclear forces or long-range missiles, and even perfect missile defences would not have helped, the implicit meaning will continue to affect an ever wider part of security planning. At the most superficial level, it became much harder for public officials to resist major new defence programs. Raising the American defence budget ten per cent in 2001 and a planned increase of ten per cent more in 2002 eased procurement tensions. Tough decisions were resolved or at least postponed. Previously sick projects like the V-22 Osprey, the CVX Class aircraft carrier and even the F-22 fighter suddenly sprang back. The cancellation of the Crusader self-propelled howitzer six months later stands out as the exception that seemingly proves the rule.

That missile defence prospered under such a climate is no surprise. Even as deployment of interceptors begins in Alaska, it costs the United States a relatively small share of its total military spending.[29] Even if total program costs rise to the highest levels currently anticipated (the top estimate as of this writing is $238 billion through to the year 2025) the funds are there.[30]

But emergency support tends to be ephemeral. The depth and breadth of current advocacy in the United States, and new tolerance in Europe and elsewhere, belies something more fundamental.

How much did the traumatic attacks affect missile defence planning *per se*? To some leaders it was all but irrelevant. They stress the lack of a direct link and insist that the rush to missile defence is little more than misplaced and wasteful hysteria.[31] Homeland defence, oriented specifically to deal with WMD terrorism and intelligence reform, is said to be more appropriate. Multilateral consensus matters much more than before, and this should not be endangered by divisive projects that only address secondary threats.[32]

These critiques miss the most important long-term victim of 11 September, which was Type-II and especially Type-III deterrence. The temptation to believe otherwise is understandable. As the foundation of Western security throughout the Cold War, deterrence offered security on the cheap. In exchange for a moderate investment of treasure, acceptance of great risks and the assumption of human rationality, deterrence gave political and military stability. After witnessing the continuous failures of defence through the previous 300 years of the Westphalian era, what a pleasure it was to find a military tool that really worked! The pity is that it cannot be expected to work as effectively ever again, except in the narrow confines of Type-I environments.

Deterrence was already sick even before 11 September. Could it prevent nuclear, chemical or biological attacks by rogue states? Through the 1990s the answer increasingly came back 'maybe'. Would it prevent the use of long-range ballistic missiles? Here we already had ample evidence that it did not. Even if the World Trade Center and Pentagon attacks did not eliminate the credibility of deterrence, they showed how its relevance had declined. This attitude is articulated in the careful wording of the 2002 Nuclear Posture Review.[33] This document, the clearest statement of American strategic policy to emerge from the Bush Administration so far, is distinguished by its caution. As Jim Wirtz and James Russell note in the following article, the NPR does not reject deterrence or argue that it must be replaced by defence. Rather it shows how the balance has shifted. Where defence previously was an ancillary if deterrence should fail, now the two are roughly equal in American planning. Hopefully deterrence will work, the NPR seems to say, but gone is the absolute faith of the past.

While American opinion is most willing to question the contemporary relevance of deterrence, doubts have begun to emerge elsewhere too. In Russia, these doubts mostly address the relevance of nuclear weapons. With major reductions in its nuclear forces inevitable, probably lower than the ceilings of the May 2002 treaty on strategic nuclear forces, Russian analysts as well are more willing to acknowledge the declining relevance of deterrent forces.[34] The strongest reaffirmations of deterrent faith continue to come, not unexpectedly, from China, and especially from France, where it is necessary to persuade domestic audiences of its continuing relevance.[35] The more extensive reaffirmations of deterrence are themselves revealing. Deterrence remains essential, one French analyst maintains, not to deal with immediate dangers – there are no relevant ones, he concedes – but to be able to deal with unknown contingencies. Something strange, he appeals, could happen.[36] The point is well intended but impossible to take seriously; by the same standard the French need lancers and pikemen too.

It is Not About States Any More

In a sense, defenders of universal deterrence are right; it was not tested on 11 September. Indeed, that is the point. The events that day demonstrated not just the declining relevance of classical Type-I deterrence, but even more the essential weakness of Type-II and Type-III. Deterrence became a victim of its own success. Having made the dangers of state-to-state war unacceptable, Westphalian warfare became obsolete. It no longer made sense to risk warfare for territorial gain. The Cuban missile crisis showed that even the manipulation of deterrent threats was too risky to tolerate.

The reasons for the decline of state-to-state warfare have been widely discussed, but remain obscure and controversial. Explanations range from the rise of Kantian democratic peace to Fukuyama's Hegel-inspired end of Universal History. In between are empirically based observations of the obsolescence of major war. None of these ideas are completely satisfying, but they are on to something.

More sceptical authors believe that the change is far from complete. Instead the world is increasingly divided into zones of war and zones of peace. On the one hand are post-modern regions based on individualism and rejection of warfare. On the other are old-fashioned Westphalian regions where states matter most of all and still think very seriously about ripping away pieces of each other.[37] Even this residual notion of international threats reduces both the salience of deterrence and missile defence. No longer can they be dominant issues, since state-to-state war itself has ceased to be dominant. Rather, strategic problems are mostly about managing the risks of accidents and dealing with confrontations on strategic interstices, the boundaries between states who like to fight and those who prefer not to.

As the country most likely to find itself in conflict with rogue states and compelled to test the weaknesses of Type-II deterrence, the United States has the greatest need for deterrent forces and increasingly for missile defences. But even this need is not enormous. Since such forces are affordable (for the

United States, that is) procurement is fully justified. But this does not assure them a place at the centre even of American strategic planning.

The centre of state-to-state conflict, obviously, has moved elsewhere. Most revealing for contemporary concerns is the work of Edward Luttwak, who argued that the perverse logic of warfare works like Newtonian physics. In war, he notes, nothing fails like success.[38] Successful strategies, he maintains, automatically invite counter-strategies. As potential adversaries learn and adapt, repetition of a successful strategic formula is bound to fail. Having successfully controlled the threat of state-to-state war, governments left themselves open to more creative alternatives. As early as the end of the Cold War, prescient analysts acknowledged the decline of state-to-state warfare, and the rise of other dangers. Above all, they began cautioning against terrorism by non-state actors. This was the conclusion of Martin van Creveld. A more systematic argument was developed by William Lind, who noted that the essential openness of Western societies would emerge as their greatest weakness, allowing terrorism to evolve into the dominant systematic danger.[39]

Who Needs Missile Defences?

If missile defences are primarily an instrument for dealing with deterrence failure between states, their role is narrowed to very specific situations and circumstances. Above all, they matter in specific theatres of conflict. Far from being universal approaches to security, they are reserved almost exclusively for marginal regions.

The real tests of missile defence will not be for national missile defences deployed by the United States. That is long-term security against marginal threats. For the United States, the greatest advantage of national missile defences is not dealing with failure in its ability to deter others, but countering the ability of others to deter the United States. This is reassuring the American and possibly European public of their immunity or at least partial protection against missile threats from others, facilitating public support for intervention abroad, especially against adversaries who may be nuclear or biologically armed. Rather than de-coupling, as some fear, missile defences will tend to strengthen American willingness to uphold defence commitments.[40]

The rising acceptance of missile defence in Europe and Russia reflects recognition of this point; it probably does not directly affect them. Far from being an issue of East–West stability, missile defence for them remains almost too distant to be a proper North–South issue either. Assertions that Europe is simply more tolerant of living with threats and uncertainty are pompous and misleading. To the contrary, Europe has been exceptionally secure and is more likely than the United States to stay that way. For Europe and Russia, missile defence is increasingly tolerable because it is very nearly irrelevant. Only by placing their armed forces in harm's way in distant lands is it likely to become relevant. No wonder Europe has shown only the slightest interest in acquiring a system for the territorial defence of Europe.[41] Theatre defences, though, are potentially more worthwhile.

Instead, it is within specific regions that Type-II deterrence will face its greatest tests and missile defence will be most in demand. Not surprisingly, China is still the most sensitive of all major powers about missile defence. This is not because its security relies on the ability to annihilate the United States. Rather it is Taiwan that makes the use of missile and theatre defences more feasible. Similarly, missile defences have already become a permanent part of the strategic equation in the Middle East and in South Asia they are likely to join the forces of India in the not-so-distant future.

The global debate about American national missile defence has been a valuable exercise, creating a new consensus on the nature of deterrence and the risks of conflict in the post-modern world. What it has only begun to engage are regional scenarios where state-to-state warfare remains more feasible and the actual use of these weapons is more imaginable.

The Real Threat

If thinking about missile defences is to be guided by our expectations about missile use, ICBM attacks on the territory of the United States or other Western countries lose much of their urgency. Regional scenarios are where long-range missiles are much more likely to be used, and it makes sense to redirect the debate over the implications of missile defence to address those priorities instead. The ballistic missiles that are most likely to be used, however, are neither intercontinental nor long-range. It is short-range weapons, and extremely short-range weapons at that, which are used almost routinely in many conflicts around the world.

Because we are accustomed to thinking of missile defences as an expensive response to long-range threats, short-range threats have not received sufficient attention. Indeed, because they focus on ICBMs alone, even well-respected analysts have been dismissive of the link between missiles and terrorism.[42] The technical problems of shooting down short-range weapons are also more demanding, with little time for the basic problems of warning, tracking and interception. But the threat from such systems is growing and carries much of the same impact as proliferation from long-range ballistic missiles. Just as the nature of global conflict has shifted to emphasize terrorism and terrorist weapons, missile threats have changed as well. This is likely to emerge as the next great challenge for missile defence.

To be sure, individual small rockets are no weapon of mass destruction. But in large numbers their effects are devastating. In 1982 it was attacks by small artillery rockets that provoked Israel's invasion of Lebanon. In Afghanistan, small rockets were used by the *Hizbi-Islami* forces of Gulbuddin Hekmatyar to devastate much of Kabul in 1994, creating enormous swaths of destruction readily visible today. Identical rockets were fired regularly by Hizbollah guerrillas in Lebanon against Israeli forces and settlements in an attempt to win political and territorial concessions. Comparable attacks by Iraqi-based Iranian factions provoked periodic border skirmishes. In November 2001 Palestinian fighters in Gaza began to fire home-made rockets against Israeli territory as well. The Palestinian attacks did no damage, but created a major new symbol of national resistance.

As terrorism evolves into the predominant form of post-modern warfare, the incentives for terrorist use of short-range ballistic missiles will increase too. Ironically, the more successful efforts are at stopping traditional terror attacks, the more likely they are to seek stand-off weapons. Of course terrorists are more likely to use more readily available mortars and rocket-propelled grenades. But the same logic that makes ballistic missiles appealing for government armed forces – even when armed exclusively with conventional high explosives – will work for terrorists too. As much as any other political faction, they gain an image of impunity and technical virtuosity. Just as ballistic missiles have disproportionate advantages for states, they also will appeal in the same way to terrorists.

Against such challenges, deterrence is questionable at best. Non-state actors deprive deterrence of the one thing it needs most: a target for retaliation. Type-III deterrence, deterrence without a reasonable chance of retaliation, is the weakest form of all. Worse, such situations virtually ensure that retaliation will most grievously hurt those with no stake in the conflict, probably even other victims of terrorist activity. Against such threats, missile defences truly come into their own.

The difficulties of defence in such situations, though, are even worse than for more orthodox missile challenges. Israel and the United States are developing a defensive system to deal with this threat, although the technical problems are still serious.[43] This, at least, is familiar. It is the political problems of using such a system against terrorist missiles that are most disturbing. The most effective method always will be pre-emptive attack, but this only plays directly into the terrorist hopes, worsening the conflict and raising the costs of further engagements. Short-range defences, moreover, will tend to be short-range themselves, creating pressure for forward deployment. They raise all the familiar political problems of boost phase defences: escalating tension, exposing vulnerable defensive forces, inviting counter attack and arousing outside criticism.

The change in much of global opinion following the American withdrawal from the ABM Treaty shows that the political problems of national missile defences probably can be overcome. In time the technical problems undoubtedly will diminish as well. Even if the political and technical problems never disappear, they seem increasingly manageable. What remains to be addressed are the regional riddles of theatre missile defences and the long-term challenge of terrorist missiles.

NOTES

1. Robert Jervis, *The Illogic of Nuclear Strategy* (Ithica, NY: Cornell University Press, 1989). Also see the contribution by Michael Quinlan in this volume.
2. With apologies to the late Herman Kahn, who coined the labels Type-I through Type-III deterrence, which he used to label different problems of deterrence between the United States and the Soviet Union, in *On Thermonuclear War* (Princeton, NJ: Princeton University Press, 1960).
3. Keith Payne, 'The Case for National Missile Defence', *Orbis*, Vol.44, No.2 (Spring 2000) pp.187–96. Payne also was the principal author of the highly influential report, *Rationale and Requirements for US Nuclear Forces and Arms Control* (Fairfax, Virginia: National Institute for Public Policy, Jan. 2001).
4. George Lewis, Lisbeth Gronlund and David Wright, 'National Missile Defence: An Indefensible System', *Foreign Policy*, No.117 (Winter 1999/2000), pp.120–37.
5. Michael O'Hanlon, 'Scholars need to bring Creative Thinking to the Debate over Missile Defence', *Chronicle of Higher Education*, 30 Nov. 2001, pp.B11–B13.
6. Gopal Ratham, 'Writing a missile shield rule book', *Defence News*, 30 August 2004, p.1.
7. *Report of the Commission to Assess the Ballistic Missile Threat to the United States: Executive Summary*, 15 July 1998.
8. Richard L. Garwin, 'The Rumsfeld Report: What we Did', *The Bulletin of the Atomic Scientists*, Vol.54, No.6 (Nov./Dec. 1998), pp.40–45.
9. Michael Dobbs, 'How Politics helped Define the Threat', *Washington Post*, 14 Jan. 2002, p.A1.
10. Although traditional security studies has resisted social constructivism – mostly because of its arcane language, I think – its stress on the role of beliefs in shaping political order is as relevant here as to any other aspect of international affairs. Alexander Wendt, *The Social Construction of International Politics* (Cambridge: Cambridge University Press 1999).
11. Remarks by the President on National Missile Defence, The White House, 13 Dec. 2001.
12. Dana Milbank, 'Criticism Softens on ABM Move', *Washington Post*, 22 May 2002, p.A28; John Vinocur, 'In private, US and Europe aren't Battling', *International Herald Tribune*, 17 July 2002, p.1.
13. 'Combating Terrorism: A Global Approach?', sponsored by Old Dominion University and Supreme Allied Commander, Atlantic, Norfolk, Virginia, 13–14 May 2002.
14. 'Foreign Minister Ivanov rules out Russia–US deal on ABM', *Segodnya*, NTV International, 30 May 2001 (FBIS translation).
15. Elaine Sciolino, 'Clinton and Putin unable to Agree on Missile Barrier', *New York Times*, 5 June 2000, p.A1.
16. Elaine Sciolino, 'Clinton finds Germans Critical of US Missile Defence Plan', *New York Times*, 2 June 2000, p.A10; Roger Cohen, 'Warm Welcome for "Putin the German"', *New York Times*, 15 June 2000, p.A12.
17. Erik Eckholm, 'China says US Missile Shield could force an Arms Buildup', *New York Times*, 11 May 2000, p.A1.
18. Patrick E. Tyler, 'Gingerly, NATO plans Broader Role for Moscow', *New York Times*, 7 Dec. 2001, p.A11; Judy Dempsey, 'Historic Accord gives Russia a Bigger Say in NATO', *Financial Times*, 15 May 2002, p.1.

19. Robert Cottrell, 'Closer Ties with the West attracts Muted Criticism', *Financial Times*, 15 April 2002, p.3; 'Putin's Unscrambled Eggs', *The Economist*, 9 March 2002, pp.54–5.
20. Christoph Bluth, 'Germany and Missile Defence: The Dilemmas Facing an Ally', *Jane's Intelligence Review* (Oct. 2001), pp.50–51; Harald Mueller, 'Germany Hopes it will Go Away', *Bulletin of the Atomic Scientists*, Vol.57, No.6 (Nov./Dec. 2001), pp.31–3.
21. For example, see Jessica T. Mathews, 'Estranged Partners', *Foreign Policy* (Nov./Dec. 2001).
22. A point made repeatedly in Hubert Vedrine, with Dominique Moisi, *France in an Age of Globalization*, translated by Philip H. Gordon (Washington, DC: Brookings Institution, 2001).
23. Although he never mentions missile defence, the general point is made by Ian Buruma, 'The Blood Lust of Identity', *New York Review of Books*, 11 April 2002, pp.12–14.
24. The shift in European priorities did not escape the editors of the *Washington Post*, which they juxtaposed in Dana Milbank, 'Criticism Softens on ABM Move', *Washington Post*, 22 May 2002, p.A28; and T.R. Reid, 'Resurfacing Animosity Awaits Bush in Europe', *Washiington Post*, 22 May 2002., p.A29.
25. Erik Eckholm, 'China says Next Move in Arms Talks is up to US', *New York Times*, 27 Feb. 2002, p.A5.
26. Aaron L.Friedberg, '11 September and the Future of Sino-American Relations', *Survival*, Vol.44, No.1 (Spring 2002) pp.33–50.
27. 'China's Response to Missile Defences: Confronting a Strategic Fait Accompli', *IISS Strategic Comments*, Vol.8, No.1 (Jan. 2002).
28. Although the 2002 US Nuclear Posture Review discussed nuclear options, raising alarm, this is not a departure from past American policy, which always countenanced possible first use. David E. Sanger, 'Thinking the Unthinkable Again', *New York Times*, 18 March 2002; and Richard D. Sokolsky and Eugene B. Rumer, 'Nuclear Alarmists', *Washington Post*, 15 March 2002, p.A23.
29. 'US installs first GMD anti-missile interceptor', *Jane's Missile and Rockets*, 1 Sep. 2004.
30. James Dao, 'Plan to stop Missile Threat could cost $238 Billion', *New York Times*, 1 Feb. 2002, p.A5.
31. See statements by two prominent Senators. Carl Levin, 'A Debate Deferred', *Arms Control Today* (Nov. 2001), pp.3–5; and Joseph R. Biden, Jr, 'Missile Defence Delusion', *Washington Post*, 19 Dec. 2001, p.A39.
32. Dennis M. Gormley, 'Enriching Expectations: 11 September's Lessons for Missile Defence', *Survival*, Vol.44, No.2 (Summer 2002) pp.19–35.
33. US Department of Defence, *Nuclear Posture Review* (Washington, DC: submitted to Congress 31 Dec. 2001, unclassified version released 8 Jan. 2002).
34. For example, see Vladimir Slipchenko, 'Point of View: Has the Circle Closed? Nuclear Deterrence has become Mired in Defects', *Armeyskiy Sbornik*, 1 April 2002 (FBIS translation).
35. Partrice-Henry Desaubliaux, 'Doctrine remains Deterrence', *Le Figaro*, 8 June 2001, p.7 (FBIS translation).
36. Jean Tandonnet, 'French Nuclear Deterrence in the Wake of September 11', *Defence Nationale* (May 2002), pp.19–27 (FBIS translation).
37. Robert Cooper, *The Post-Modern State and the World Order* (London: Demos, 1996).
38. Edward N. Luttwak, *Strategy: The Logic of War and Peace*, revised edition (Cambridge, Massachusetts: Harvard University Press, 2001).
39. Martin van Creveld, *The Transformation of War* (New York: Free Press, 1991), ch.7; William S. Lind *et al.*, 'Warfare in the 4th Generation', *Marine Corps Gazette*, Oct. 1989.
40. This point is explored in an exchange of letters between James M. Lindsay and Michael E. O'Hanlon and a response by Charles L. Glaser and Steve Fetter in *International Security*, Vol.26, No.4 (Spring 2002) pp.190–201.
41. Wyn Bowen, 'European Governments ponder Plans for GMD', *Jane's Intelligence Review* (Aug. 2001).
42. Thus Dean Wilkening wrote: 'non-state actors simply do not have the wherewithal to construct, purchase or operate 100,000 pound ICBMs'. Dean Wilkening, 'Counterterrorism is a Top Priority, so Why Rush to Kill the ABM Treaty?' *San Jose Mercury News*, 16 Dec. 2001.
43. Amnon Barzilay, 'Hot Debate over Future of Nautilu', *Ha'aretz*, 5 Dec. 2001.

PART III: DETERRENCE PRACTICE – THE FIVE ESTABLISHED NUCLEAR WEAPON STATES

United States Nuclear Strategy in the Twenty-first Century

JAMES A. RUSSELL AND JAMES J. WIRTZ

A revolutionary transformation is quietly occurring in US nuclear strategy and defence policy. It is quiet only because it is being overshadowed by the war on terrorism, by fundamental organizational changes in the US government that are flowing from the new requirements of homeland security, and by a chaotic international environment exemplified by the ongoing dispute between Israelis and Palestinians. It is revolutionary because it reflects a fundamental change in the threats, capabilities, philosophy and strategy that have preoccupied US nuclear planners since the 1950s. It also highlights significant changes in the way the US military is organizing to fight future wars. Like all revolutions, such fundamental change is bound to disturb both supporters and critics of the *status quo*. But at least from the perspective of realism, the transformation reflects a rational response to a changing threat environment, especially the end of the Cold War. The Bush administration has launched the first significant departure in US nuclear policy since the demise of the Soviet Union.[1]

The Bush administration's vision of the American nuclear future, articulated in its 2002 Nuclear Posture Review (NPR),[2] is part of a broader effort to restructure US defence policy. The NPR thus reflects the key concepts of dissuasion, deterrence, defence, and denial articulated in the Quadrennial Defense Review, which was released in the autumn of 2001. The NPR and QDR establish new priorities for US defence and foreign policy, turning the proverbial 'ship of state' onto a new course. The NPR incorporates a new framework for Russian–American strategic relations and a response to the ongoing proliferation of nuclear, chemical and biological weapons and long-range ballistic missiles. It also contains several paradoxes, not unlike earlier nuclear strategies. It reduces the overall number of deployed nuclear forces, while at the same time it places a renewed emphasis on US nuclear systems as weapons to be used in battle. It identifies the potential need for new types of nuclear weapons and delivery systems, while at the same time it suggests that precision-guided conventional weapons can accomplish many existing nuclear missions. It downplays the threat posed to the United

States by the largest nuclear arsenal in the world and instead highlights the threat posed by weak states or non-state actors armed with rudimentary nuclear, biological and chemical capabilities. It is a nuclear policy that makes a concerted effort to consign the defining feature of the Cold War – the Soviet–American strategic relationship of Mutual Assured Destruction (MAD) – to the history books.

To illustrate the Bush administration's new nuclear thinking, the article will first identify the factors that have led to the reassessment of US nuclear policy and strategy. It then describes the recent changes in US strategic thinking outlined by the Bush administration's Nuclear Posture Review. The article concludes with some thoughts on the NPR not as a cause, but as a response to a changing strategic landscape.

New Threats, New Opportunities

The Bush administration's nuclear policy reflects strategic, technological and political trends that have emerged and converged over the last decade. The collapse of the Soviet Union created the opportunity to foster a new strategic relationship between Russia and the United States. Administration officials believed that massive nuclear arsenals, which produced the situation of MAD, Cold War arms control agreements and a 'Cold-War mindset' were no longer relevant in Russian–American relations, especially as democracy and a market economy slowly emerged in Russia. Political disagreements no longer motivated the maintenance of large nuclear forces, and both Russia and the United States could benefit from savings generated by scaling back Cold-War nuclear arsenals. During the 2000 Presidential campaign, Bush supporters noted that even the existing arms control regime between Russia and the United States was counterproductive because it was intended to manage an adversarial situation and was preventing both sides from adjusting their force structures and doctrine in response to fiscal realities and new threats. In their minds, arms control was actually producing acrimony in an otherwise increasingly cooperative relationship.[3] For administration officials, the time had arrived to stop treating Russia as a potential adversary and to find a more cooperative way to manage strategic relations.

While many observers marvelled at the effectiveness of precision-guided air strikes during the 1991 Gulf War, advances in weapons technology did not stop there. The information revolution that occurred in commercial and social life in the 1990s continued to transform US military capabilities. Sometimes referred to as the Revolution in Military Affairs (RMA), the application of the information revolution to the realm of warfare is creating a precision-strike complex that integrates surveillance and reconnaissance sensors, information processing capabilities, tactical and operational communications, and long-range precision guided munitions. In real time, operational commanders can now use multiple data feeds from a variety of sensors (generically called the global command and control system, or GCCS) to create a coherent operational picture of the battle space that can be used to target everything from lone individuals to armoured divisions. This real-time capability to target precision-guided munitions did not exist ten years ago. Breaking a long-standing divide between conventional and nuclear forces, the Bush administration is interested in incorporating these new conventional capabilities into US strategic doctrines and force structures.

Over the last decade, official concern about the proliferation of chemical, biological and nuclear weapons and associated long-range delivery systems has grown. The Gulf War highlighted the new threat posed by long-range missiles and provided a hint of the changing threat environment that would be produced by the proliferation of chemical, biological and nuclear weapons. The 1995 National Intelligence Estimate 'Emerging Missile Threats to North America during the Next Fifteen Years', which depicted a relatively benign threat environment, was discredited by the 1998 Rumsfeld Commission Report and the August 1998 North Korean launch of a three-stage Taepo-Dong missile. The 1996 Aum Shinryko sarin attack in the Tokyo subway, the 1998 Indian and Pakistan nuclear tests, the end of the UNSCOM inspection regime in Iraq, the 9/11 terrorist attacks on the Pentagon and the World Trade Center, and the anthrax attacks in the northeastern United States have made the proliferation of weapons of mass destruction (WMD) a salient threat to the American public and US officials. In its report to Congress on 30 January 30 2002, the Central Intelligence Agency identified nine countries that are developing or seeking to acquire weapons of mass destruction.[4] Three of these countries, Iran, Iraq and North Korea, identified as an 'axis of evil' by President Bush in his 2002 State of the Union Address, were said to represent a particular threat to the United States. President Bush also has stated that he will not allow 'a nation such as Iraq to threaten our very future by developing weapons of mass destruction'.[5] The Nuclear Posture Review echoes this concern and increases the number of countries that represent a threat to the United States: 'North Korea, Iraq, Iran, Syria and Libya are among the countries that could be involved in immediate, potential, or unexpected contingencies'.[6] Various non-state actors and terrorist organizations, such as Al Qaeda, which are rumoured to be trying to acquire chemical, biological, nuclear and radiological weapons, also are depicted as posing a serious threat to the United States.

When combined, the trends that have emerged over the last decade have created a challenging set of circumstances for US elected officials and defence planners. On the one hand they have a strategic nuclear capability that has been optimized to deal with a threat that no longer exists and which is now viewed as a stumbling block to improved Russian–American relations. On the other hand, the failure of non-proliferation efforts during the 1990s now confronts US planners with a host of relatively small-scale threats (when compared to the Cold War challenge posed by the Soviet Union) that with little warning might become serious civil, political and military problems. Compared to at least the latter years of the Cold War, it now appears more likely that the US military might encounter opponents willing to use chemical, biological or nuclear weapons. At the same time, the RMA has provided planners with new ways to use conventional weapons to undertake missions once reserved for US nuclear forces.

The operational history of the US military since the early 1990s reflects these trends. Desert Storm, containment of Iraq, a commitment to transformation, war in the Balkans, counter-proliferation and now the war on terrorism, have slowly moved the Defense Department away from its traditional planning benchmark, the ability to fight two major theatre wars simultaneously. Instead, US forces have been continuously engaged somewhere over the last decade containing a crisis, responding to a disaster or actually engaged in open hostilities. The transition has been almost imperceptible, but now conflict is continuous and without borders. It is not true global war in the Cold-War sense of the term, but it is not without strategic objectives or risks. The challenge facing US planners is to develop policies that respond to this new strategic, technological and political landscape.

The End of Mutual Assured Destruction: The 2002 NPR

The Bush administration's NPR and the Quadrennial Defense Review indicate that Mutual Assured Destruction is no longer considered an acceptable basis for the strategic relationship between Russia and the United States. Assuring destruction of Russia under any circumstances is no longer viewed as the primary strategic concern that should preoccupy US nuclear planners. In his briefing to announce the unclassified summary of the Nuclear Posture Review, Assistant Secretary of Defense J.D. Crouch stated that the United States was now 'ending the relationship with Russia that is based on mutual assured destruction', adding that 'this seems to be a very inappropriate relationship given the kinds of cooperation, for example, that have been evinced in the last few months in the campaign against global terrorism'.[7] The actual NPR is even more unequivocal: 'As a result of this review, the United States will no longer plan, size or sustain its forces as though Russia presented merely a smaller version of the threat posed by the Soviet Union.' In other words, since Russia and its nuclear forces are viewed as a waning threat to the United States, deterring Russia will no longer dominate US nuclear doctrine and targeting.

Although administration officials never clearly articulated their plan to transform the Russian–American strategic relationship and it remains unclear whether any plan actually exists, changes in US policy are beginning to create a new strategic framework between the United States and Russia. Initiatives by administration officials to eliminate the last vestiges of this enduring rivalry are important in both a theoretical and practical sense. Unilateral US efforts to overcome lingering mistrust entail risk, which increases their credibility, and signals a commitment to eliminating the security dilemma that continues to plague Russian–American relations.[8] In other words, US officials recognized that nuclear doctrine and capabilities, not underlying political grievances or aggressive impulses, stand in the way of more cooperative Russian–American relations. They therefore undertook a series of unilateral initiatives – announcing a change in nuclear doctrine, negotiating reductions in strategic forces, introducing confidence-building measures – that they apparently hoped would reduce tension and foster better Russian–American relations. When viewed in this light, even withdrawing from the ABM Treaty becomes an extremely important and positive initiative by delivering a potentially lethal shock to the Cold War strategic framework that continues to govern Russian–American strategic relations. As Bush officials have repeatedly noted, the ABM Treaty was an outmoded document that stood in the way not only of US missile defence programs, but also in the way of a more cooperative strategic relationship with Russia. The United States–Russian arms control agreement signed by Presidents Bush and Putin in Moscow in May 2002 is also part of this new strategic framework. Even though the treaty limits the number of deployed nuclear warheads to a maximum of 2,200 by 2012, it is more of a political document than a mechanism for arms control and strategic stability. The treaty reflected changes in force structure already mandated by the NPR and may have been concluded to satisfy President Putin's political requirements for concrete evidence of his new partnership with Washington.

The ultimate challenge faced by administration officials in their effort to end the situation of MAD is that the nuclear balance between Russia and the United States is a strategic relationship, i.e., a relationship shaped by the actions and interactions of at least two parties. Avoidance of Armageddon during the Cold War, for instance, really required cooperation on the part of both superpowers since neither, by definition, had the capability to protect itself unilaterally from nuclear destruction.[9] Similarly, just because US policy-makers believe that concerns about nuclear weapons should no longer dominate Russian–American relations does not guarantee that Russian officials will go along with their American counterparts. Russians, after all, cling to their nuclear arsenal as the last vestige of their superpower status; dire warnings are heard in Moscow about Russia's potential vulnerability if the nuclear *status quo* changes, even as the Russian government struggles to find the money to maintain a shrinking nuclear force.

Bush officials' hopes of positively influencing Russian–American relations were in fact achieved by practical politics. By declaring peace, and taking concrete steps to back up their words, they undermined the strategic reasoning of all those who favour the military, institutional and diplomatic *status quo*. US policymakers are presenting their Russian counterparts with a difficult political challenge: How can hard-line Russians officials preserve a 'Cold-War' approach to Russian–American relations when US policymakers are clearly willing to reciprocate Russian concessions? The Putin government apparently has found it possible to live with a light US ABM system in return for a US agreement to further reduce the size of its nuclear arsenal to Russian levels, which are governed not by doctrine, but by a weak Russian economy. The administration's approach to dealing with Russia also challenges those who advocate traditional approaches to arms control and disarmament. When a disarmament advocate complained recently that the informal cooperation emerging in Russian–American relations lacked transparency because of the absence of formal agreements that could be vetted by the international arms control community, the audience broke out laughing.[10] It is possible that many existing arms control agreements will become increasingly obsolete as Russian–American strategic relations improve. Cooperative efforts among potential allies to foster peace, reduce nuclear forces and safeguard hazardous nuclear materials do not pose much of a threat to other nations; they do not need to be codified in formal treaties to reassure the international community. What is surprising is that the international community has failed to acknowledge the recent success of both Moscow and Washington in making further progress toward eliminating the hazardous legacy of the Cold War.

A New Triad

The NPR unveiled a new strategic triad, consisting of nuclear weapons and non-nuclear precision-strike capabilities, passive and active defences and a revitalized nuclear infrastructure. The Review's authors consider nuclear weapons to be only one element of an array of capabilities designed to address threats posed by the proliferation of chemical, biological and nuclear weapons and long-range ballistic missiles. Although the new strategic framework advanced by the Bush administration might be viewed as a logical outgrowth of policy since the end of the Cold War (i.e., further reductions in strategic forces and incremental movement toward a US–Russian relationship based on cooperation), the new triad concept represents a major departure in US strategic doctrine. Deterrence, defence and counter-force are now acknowledged components of US strategic (nuclear) doctrine. This doctrine will eventually be reflected in a new force structure, although the concepts and planning for this force structure do not yet exist.

The Bush administration's new strategic triad is intended to integrate defences (i.e., missile defence), nuclear weapons and 'non-nuclear strike forces'[11] into a seamless web of capabilities to dissuade potential competitors from mounting a military challenge to the United States,[12] to deter adversaries and to fight and win wars if deterrence fails. The NPR notes that the strike elements

> can provide greater flexibility in the design and conduct of military campaigns to defeat opponents decisively. Non-nuclear strike capabilities may be particularly useful to limit collateral damage and conflict escalation. The NPR emphasizes technology as a substitute for nuclear forces that are withdrawn from service. Global real-time command and control and reconnaissance capabilities will take on greater importance in the new strategic triad. Nuclear weapons could be employed against targets able to withstand non-nuclear attack, (for example, deep underground bunkers or bio-weapons facilities).[13]

The new triad will rely on 'adaptive planning' so that it can meet quickly emerging threats and contingencies. Advanced command, control and intelligence capabilities will integrate the legs of the triad, facilitating flexible operations. This emphasis on adaptive planning differs from the traditional approach taken to the development of the US nuclear war plan, the Single-Integrated Operations Plan (SIOP). The SIOP reflected a deliberate planning process that often took months or even years to complete and which generated a finite number of nuclear employment options for consideration by the President in his capacity as Commander in Chief.

Administration officials have suggested that the new triad would allow reductions in operational nuclear forces from the current START I levels of approximately 6,000 warheads each deployed by the United States and Russia. The Treaty of Moscow, signed on 24 May 2002, made this intention a reality as both Washington and Moscow agreed to reduce the number of their strategic operational warheads to between 1,700 and 2,200 by 2012.[14] In the US arsenal, the warhead reductions will come from the retirement of the MX Peacekeeper ICBM starting in 2002, the removal of four Trident submarines from strategic service and the elimination of the requirement that the B-1 bomber maintain a nuclear capability. Like the Clinton administration, the Bush administration will maintain a 'responsive' force (sometimes referred to as a reserve force) of warheads that could be brought back into service if necessary. Military planners probably have not finalized the size of the 'responsive' force, but in all likelihood it will number in the thousands of warheads.[15] Both the Bush and Clinton administrations maintained that it

FIGURE 1
JOINT STRATEGIC TARGET PLANNING STAFF EAGLE PATCH

This patch, worn by members of the JSTPS who worked at the Strategic Air Command (SAC), is now a symbol of a bygone era. JSTPS was the Joint Staff organization at SAC charged with generating the Single Integrated Operations Plan. Today their functions have been transferred to J5, US Strategic Command.

only makes sense to count warheads actually deployed or warheads that are available for battlefield use within a matter of days. In contrast, this response force (read 'hedge force') would only become available after an extended period of regeneration and redeployment – a process that could take months or even years.[16] The existence of this response force, however, has prompted concerns in some quarters. Critics charge that the reductions mandated by the Treaty are ephemeral because only counting operational warheads masks the true size of the strategic forces maintained by the United States. But these critics fail to recognize that the response force can serve as an important US bargaining chip in the effort to find a negotiated settlement to an increasingly important problem, eliminating the thousands of Russian tactical nuclear weapons that are not addressed by the Moscow Treaty.

The reduction in operational nuclear warhead level will be accompanied by the development of new capabilities. The centrepiece of these new capabilities will be missile defence. The Bush administration wants to spend $7.8 billion in fiscal year 2003 for a missile defence research and testing program that will eventually create a multi-layered defence against accidental missile launches and the relatively limited missile attacks that can be launched by America's likely adversaries. No longer constrained by the ABM Treaty after June 2002, the administration has launched a robust missile defence program that builds on the programs initiated by the Clinton administration nearly a decade ago. The current program includes boost-phase interceptors to attack enemy ballistic missiles while they are still over the opponent's territory. Because warhead debris would likely fall on the country launching the missile attack, these defences would serve to deter an adversary's use of nuclear, chemical or biological weapons. Administration officials want to allocate $598 million for the Airborne Laser (ABL), a speed of light 'directed energy' weapon, and $797 million for research on sea, air and space-based boost phase systems to defeat missiles while they are in the highly visible and vulnerable initial stage of flight. The administration also has bolstered the Clinton administration's mid-course ground-based interceptor program by proposing $534 million for an expanded test-bed for missile intercepts. $623 million for the Patriot PAC III will bolster terminal and point defence of critical facilities and forces. Patriot is primarily intended to be used by US ground forces to protect themselves from cruise missile and tactical ballistic missile attack. The administration has further earmarked $3.5 million for the Mobile Tactical High-Energy Laser that will give ground forces a directed energy weapon for use against enemy rockets, cruise missiles, artillery and mortar munitions.

The new triad concept highlights three profound changes in US strategic doctrine. First, it makes clear that deterring an all-out nuclear war between Russia and the United States is no longer the central feature of US war plans. US policymakers believe that a nuclear war between Russia and the United States is an extremely remote possibility and US nuclear policy and strategy now reflect this changing threat perception. Second, like the old triad concept, the new triad embodies an effort to increase the credibility of US strategic deterrent threats by increasing the range of options available to US officials. The old triad concept was intended to guarantee the availability of a massive response to nuclear attack, while the newly reconfigured triad is intended to guarantee that US policymakers will have an appropriate way to respond to different forms of aggression, thereby bolstering deterrence. Third, the new triad concept provides a way to sidestep bureaucratic resistance to changing what constitutes one of the most respected elements of the nuclear creed that shaped US nuclear doctrine: the sanctity of the old triad of forces and the focus on guaranteeing a massive nuclear response under any circumstances. The new strategic triad thus paves the way for further reductions in US strategic nuclear forces because it clears a path for the possible elimination of one of the legs of the old nuclear triad. The Bush administration's new triad concept thus constitutes an important facet of the quiet revolution taking place in US strategic nuclear doctrine.

Counter-proliferation, Conventional Counter-force and Nuclear War

Although there is little doubt that the Bush administration wants to eliminate nuclear deterrence as the basis of the Russian–American strategic relationship, it is clear that the NPR is not a blueprint for international disarmament. Reductions in operational warhead levels, deployment of missile defences, a shift to adaptive nuclear planning and new conventional precision-strike capabilities augur a new era in thinking about nuclear strategy and the relationship between nuclear weapons, deterrence and nuclear war. The NPR identifies new targeting priorities for nuclear weapons: hardened underground facilities housing command centres, underground facilities associated with chemical, biological or nuclear weapons, and mobile targets (such as missiles armed with WMD). The NPR states that there are nearly 1,400 underground sites worldwide that require targeting by the nuclear force because conventional weapons cannot destroy them. Thus there is a need to develop an earth penetrating capability to place these targets at risk. The NPR also calls for 'additional yield flexibility' for weapons in the stockpile and for 'warheads that reduce collateral damage'.[17] By identifying new targets and missions for nuclear weapons, it would appear that the United States would eventually have to design and build new weapons – a process that is made difficult if not impossible by the continued observance of the moratorium on nuclear weapons testing. To build new weapons, however, US weapons designers would have to conduct nuclear tests to certify that the weapons would actually work as advertised. Given that it is unlikely that the United States will abandon the testing moratorium if current circumstances continue, it is unclear how officials will overcome this fundamental inconsistency in the policies and capabilities advocated by the NPR.

One observer has noted that the NPR moves US strategy away from the idea of mutually assured destruction toward the concept of 'unilateral assured destruction, so that no dictator could seek safety for himself or his weapons of mass destruction in some deep bunker where no conventional weapon could destroy them'.[18] This description of the new nuclear strategy, however, is regrettable because it probably overemphasizes the degree to which officials are contemplating first use, let alone massive first use, of nuclear weapons. Much like criticism levelled against the Eisenhower administration's policy of massive retaliation, Bush officials were apparently concerned that the availability of only relatively large nuclear weapons reduced the credibility of the US nuclear deterrent because potential opponents might gamble that the United States would not respond with nuclear weapons to small-scale use of chemical or biological weapons.[19]

The NPR is intended to increase the range of options available to US officials to deal with adversaries armed with chemical, biological and nuclear weapons and long- range delivery systems. Clearly, precision-guided weapons are the preferred option when it comes to conducting pre-emptive attacks against an opponent's WMD infrastructure and delivery systems.[20] While it is politically difficult to justify the use of nuclear weapons in a preventative attack to prevent the use of nuclear weapons, the US nuclear arsenal provides escalation dominance. US nuclear superiority makes standing by and being forcibly disarmed in a conventional counter-force attack the only rational response available to the opponent. A range of US nuclear options thus makes it more likely that opponents with small WMD arsenals will lose rather than use their nuclear, chemical or biological weapons capabilities. Significant use of nuclear, chemical or biological weapons might generate a massive nuclear response from the United States, a perception that reduces incentives for initial escalation by US adversaries. Theatre and national missile defences backstop conventional counter-force attacks by destroying incoming warheads launched if counter-force and nuclear escalation dominance fails. There is a reason why the reader might find this sort of analysis hair raising: what has just been described is a form of nuclear war fighting. Moreover, this scenario is not hypothetical. It has been played out repeatedly in the effort to disarm Iraq, although US officials, international observers and scholars, with one notable exception, have failed to pay much attention to the emergence of preventive war in US counter-proliferation strategy.[21]

The message to state and non-state actors seeking to acquire or use WMD is unambiguous – the United States recognizes that it cannot prevent proliferation. Instead, it is preparing to target emerging nuclear, chemical and biological arsenals with conventional and, if necessary, nuclear forces. Pre-emptive attack has not been ruled out. President Bush told the country during his address to West Point cadets in June 2002 that the US security 'will require all Americans to be forward-looking and resolute, to be ready for pre-emptive action when necessary to defend our liberty and to defend our lives'.[22]

Does the NPR lower the nuclear threshold? The NPR explicitly mentions the idea of developing an earth-penetrating nuclear device to target underground facilities housing nuclear, chemical or biological weapons.[23] Secretary of State Colin Powell rejected this concern in testimony before the Senate Appropriations Subcommittee on Commerce, State and Justice and the Judiciary by stating: 'There is no way to read that document and come to the conclusion that the United States will be more likely or will more quickly go to the use of nuclear weapons'.[24] But critics find these sorts of statements disingenuous. During the Cold War, flexible, adaptive planning that integrated conventional and nuclear forces and operations was always criticized as lowering the nuclear threshold. And, when integration of conventional and nuclear operations was not criticized as a matter of deliberate policy, observers raised the possibility of inadvertent escalation. In other words, as the chaos and the fog of war grip the battlefield, nuclear forces inevitably will be used even if the order to use them is not given by national authorities.

Alternatively, the NPR's emphasis on conventional counter-force operations against a rogue's arsenal might lower the threshold at which an adversary will use WMD, especially if the adversary perceives its chemical, biological or nuclear weapons as a 'strategic' asset that guarantees national or regime survival. Such a scenario is not all that difficult to imagine in Iraq. Saddam Hussein views his WMD program as an instrument of regime and personal security, which is one reason why he has gone to such great lengths to avoid meeting his obligations to the international community. US nuclear escalation dominance might not stop Iraqi use of WMD in response to conventional counter-force attacks because Saddam might rationally believe that WMD could save his regime or guarantee his personal security. Disarmament by force thus becomes extraordinarily risky when dictators perceive it to be part of a larger attack directed against regime survival.

What critics fail to realize, however, is that the United States finds itself in a different situation when it comes to the use of nuclear weapons in likely contingencies. Unconstrained by the threat of retaliation in kind, it faces enormous incentives to pre-empt its opponents' use of chemical, biological or nuclear weapons. After all, the only realistic way of winning a nuclear war is to use nuclear weapons first (or at least prevent your opponent from using nuclear weapons). What incentives do US officials have to allow their opponents to be the first to use chemical, biological or nuclear weapons, especially if they have the means to disarm them before they have a chance to use their arsenals? One could argue that suffering a WMD attack would generate enormous political support for retaliation. One could also argue that no elected official is that cynical; leaders will take desperate action to avert disaster. Increasing the range of options available to the United States and its allies thus raises the nuclear threshold by creating ways to disarm opponents without using nuclear weapons.

Negative Security Assurances

An issue that has generated commentary is the relationship between the NPR and 'negative security assurances', i.e., the US policy of not using nuclear weapons against non-nuclear weapons states that are also signatories of the Non-proliferation Treaty (NPT). This policy was restated in a November 1997 Presidential Decision Directive:

> The United States reaffirms that it will not use nuclear weapons against non-nuclear-weapon States Parties to the [NPT] except in the case of an invasion or any other attack on the United States, its territories, its armed

forces or other troops, its allies, or on a State toward which it has a security commitment, carried out or sustained by such a non-nuclear-weapon State in association or alliance with a nuclear-weapon State.[25]

Critics allege that these so-called negative assurances have been called into question by some of the states identified as potential nuclear targets by the NPR. But the relationship between the NPR and negative security assurances is more complex than many critics suggest because it highlights the interaction between disarmament, deterrence and counter-proliferation policies.

The NPR names five states – Iran, Iraq, Syria, Libya and China – that could be involved in 'immediate' or 'potential' contingencies involving nuclear weapons. These countries, however, cannot be placed in the same category when it comes to the negative security assurances associated with the NPT. China is an acknowledged nuclear power that actually has a small force of intercontinental ballistic missiles capable of striking the United States. Negative security assurances offered by the United States were never intended to apply to China. Iraq and North Korea are signatories of the NPT, but both countries are not considered in 'good standing' when it comes to their obligations under the treaty. Iraq and North Korea are suspected of developing clandestine nuclear arsenals. US officials thus have little alternative but to treat Iraq and North Korea as *de facto* nuclear weapons states. Iran, Syria and Libya are believed to have significant chemical weapons arsenals.

Critics of the NPR state that the US use of nuclear weapons against non-nuclear countries would constitute a US violation of its pledge not to use nuclear weapons against states that lack a nuclear arsenal. The Bush administration has stated publicly that it intends to continue abiding by its policy of negative security assurances, but, like previous administrations, it has suggested that ambiguity exists in situations where the United States or its military forces have been subjected to an attack by weapons of mass destruction (WMD). In other words, significant use of chemical, biological or radiological weapons against the United States or its forces undermines the policy of offering negative security assurances. Because the United States abides by its treaty commitments to forego developing or employing chemical or biological weapons, it cannot respond in kind in the aftermath of chemical or biological attacks that inflict thousands or even millions of casualties. If the United States is going to respond to a mass casualty attack using weapons of mass destruction, it only has nuclear weapons in its arsenal to use in a retaliatory attack.

What critics of the NPR fail to understand is that the inability of disarmament institutions and agreements to stop the proliferation of significant chemical, biological and nuclear capabilities – not the NPR itself – lies at the heart of the debate about negative security assurances. The negative security assurances offered by the United States were made in the context of the NPT to foster non-proliferation efforts and to reward states that agreed not to acquire nuclear weapons. These negative security assurances were not intended to undermine similar efforts to block the spread of chemical and biological weapons (i.e., the Chemical Weapons Convention and the Biological Weapons Convention). If one follows the logic of critics of the NPR, states that employ chemical or biological weapons need not fear retaliation in kind (because these weapons are banned by international agreement) or nuclear retaliation because of negative security assurances associated with the NPT. States that violate international agreements would thus be given a 'free ride' when it comes to threatening to use or actually using chemical or biological weapons. Giving free rides to states that violate international non-proliferation norms and agreements is not conducive to bolstering global efforts at disarmament. Additionally, the principle of reprisal could justify a US nuclear response to the use of nuclear, chemical or biological weapons. Under reprisal theory, the United States would be allowed to respond to illegal and illicit acts in any way deemed appropriate to stop such acts, even if the US response also involved actions that under normal circumstances might be considered to be illegal acts. Certainly the massive use of chemical or biological weapons against the United States or its allies would be catastrophic, prompting US officials to take extraordinary steps to protect US interests. Once the illicit actions have ceased and other nations once again abide by their legal, political and moral duties, then the practices and pledges associated with normality also resume.

The whole issue of negative assurances has arguably been subsumed by the new threat environment, which in turn underlies a major premise of the NPR: that nuclear weapons could be used in a wider number of circumstances on different kinds of targets than had previously been the case. States that have signed the NPT are offered no potential 'relief' from being targeted due to negative assurances, and the NPR in fact identifies a number of so-called NPT states (Iran, Iraq, Syria, Libya and China) as targeting priorities due to their own actions. One could also argue that the negative assurance issue has been subsumed by the new targeting requirements to hit underground facilities and mobile relocatable targets. With the movement of WMD facilities and storage bunkers underground to avoid being targeted by conventional means, a new nuclear targeting requirement has been created that the United States cannot ignore if it is to maintain a credible deterrent. Conventional munitions cannot destroy hardened underground facilities, hence the efforts identified by the NPR to modify the B-61 nuclear bomb to give it an earth-penetrating capability.

Concerns that the United States will violate its NPT negative security assurances are being blown out of proportion. Critics seem to extend these assurances to states that have overt or clandestine nuclear arsenals and to states that violate international norms and treaties against developing, stockpiling or using biological and chemical weapons. Clearly the Bush administration has voiced no intention to be the first to use nuclear weapons against states that lack weapons of mass destruction. The administration's preference is not to use nuclear weapons – hence the stated intention in the NPR to use conventional weapons in a 'strategic' context. The NPR debate, however, does focus attention on a disturbing international trend. Even as the United States and Russia reduce their strategic nuclear arsenals, other state and non-state actors continue in their quest to bolster their nuclear, chemical and biological weapons capabilities. Whenever policies that are intended to foster disarmament – such as the negative security assurances associated with the NPT – confront flagrant efforts to obtain weapons of mass destruction, the connection between policy and reality will be strained. The inability of disarmament policies to cope with these circumstances has more to do with bad situations, not the bad intentions of the policymakers involved.

Conclusion

Some readers might object to the idea that the NPR represents something fundamentally 'new' in US nuclear strategy because the NPR draws on ideas and policies that have emerged in US strategic thinking over the last fifty years. They have a reasonable point: the NPR did not emerge from a strategic or historical vacuum. Since the late 1960s, for example, planners have suggested that the United States should seek flexible response options to deter attacks against members of the North Atlantic Treaty Organization so that nuclear weapons use would not automatically lead to a massive nuclear exchange with the Soviet Union. As the Cold War continued, the SIOP also offered more nuclear options short of an all-out attack. Many observers also have been uncomfortable with MAD and the fact that the threat to kill millions of people was used as an instrument of strategic stability. Others have championed the idea that active and passive defences should play a larger role in nuclear strategy and that the ABM Treaty should be scrapped. A Defense Department report published in 1988, 'Discriminate Deterrence: Report of the Commission on Integrated Long Term Strategy', for instance, identified emerging threats that needed to be addressed by more closely integrating offensive and defensive capabilities into US nuclear and conventional strategy.[26] Much like the NPR, the report urged the Defense Department to start looking at broadening the targets that could be hit by conventional means and more closely integrating conventional and nuclear forces as part of the nation's 'strategic' deterrent. Thus, in terms of offence–defence integration, turning away from MAD and better integrating nuclear and conventional forces and strategy, the Bush administration is implementing ideas that are not without historical or policy precedent.

The NPR, however, does represent a fundamental departure in US thinking about deterrence. First, it abandons MAD as the basis of the Russian–American strategic relationship and it eliminates Russia as the benchmark for sizing US nuclear forces. Second, it seeks to substitute conventional forces for nuclear capabilities to serve as a strategic deterrent; in the past the goal of strategy was to find ways to couple conventional and nuclear force structures so that they could function in a mutually supportive way to bolster conventional and nuclear deterrence. Third, the formal integration of offence and defence to bolster deterrence by denial is a departure from the past, even if the mechanisms and organizations to integrate these forces are still on the drawing board.

Despite what critics charge, the real paradox inherent in the NPR is that even though it appears to make nuclear use more likely, it actually reflects the tradition of nuclear non-use that has emerged since the end of the Second World War. Clearly some factor other than cost-efficiency or military utility has shaped US policy when it comes to weak states that brandish nuclear, chemical or biological weapons. US officials could have responded to the proliferation of nuclear, chemical and biological arsenals and long-range delivery systems with a simple threat. They could have stated that any use of WMD, any conventional strike or any unconventional attack would be met with a massive use of nuclear weapons.[27] Instead of relying on this nuclear threat, they are searching for options to deter and defeat WMD armed adversaries with significantly less force than an all-out nuclear attack.

Disarmament advocates will decry the NPR as a disaster because in their eyes it undermines efforts to delegitimize the possession and use of nuclear weapons. But they fail to acknowledge the fact that the document declares a historic end to the Russian (Soviet)–American strategic relationship based on the threat of nuclear annihilation. They also do not seem to understand that despite much effort, good intentions and hope, the failure of the non-proliferation regime in the 1990s was the necessary condition for the Bush administration's NPR. Sadly, the United States must prepare to deal with several adversaries that are equipping themselves with weapons of mass destruction.

The potential for overwhelming retaliation in kind no longer restrains US defence planners as they contemplate the potential use of nuclear weapons to disarm likely adversaries. But observers also need to keep in mind that outside of a few pockets of support, US military officers have never been fans of nuclear weapons. They generally have been considered to be little more than a maintenance, security and administrative nightmare. And because they tend to eliminate technical, numerical, organizational and professional disparities between forces, US military planners probably see little military advantage in being first to use nuclear weapons in a conflict. The NPR reflects this bias against nuclear first use and nuclear weapons generally, while suggesting that American planners have been asked to devise ways to deter, fight and win nuclear, chemical and biological war.

One immediate result of the NPR appears inescapable. A negotiated or unilateral reduction in nuclear warheads to less than one-third of today's levels will force a profound change in the way US officials and planners think about the role of nuclear weapons in defence strategy. With a Cold War arsenal numbering approximately ten thousand warheads, planners were afforded the luxury of nearly endless redundancy in systems and the ability to place multiple weapons on priority targets. But the NPR's dramatic reduction in numbers will first force planners to make harder choices in targeting decisions – possibly even causing a return to counter-value targeting. One can only hope that these reductions will evolve into a healthy exercise that produces a rational reassessment and integration of strategy, doctrine and force structure.

NOTES

This chapter was originally drafted in 2002. This chapter represents the views of the authors, not the views of the Department of the Navy, Office of the Secretary of Defense or the US Government. The authors would like to thank Elizabeth Skinner for her editorial contributions.

1. The last significant departure in US nuclear policy, strategy and doctrine occurred on 27 September 1991 when President George H.W. Bush announced a series of unilateral initiatives: (1) eliminating tactical nuclear weapons deployed with US military units; (2) ending strip alert for the US strategic bomber force; (3) accelerating force reduction called for by START I; and (4) canceling several strategic systems (e.g., rail-mobile MX, Midgetman and the short-range-attack missile II). These initiatives virtually ended the US nuclear force modernization program and were a significant first step in a decade of force reductions. See Ronald E. Powaski, *Return to Armageddon* (New York: Oxford University Press, 2000), pp.130–33.
2. Excerpts from the classified version of the report were first reported in the *New York Times* and the *Los Angeles Times*. Most of the NPR text has been posted on the globalsecurity.org website at ⟨http://globalsecurity.org/wmd/library/policy/dod/npr.htm⟩. This quotation is taken from that text cited as the NPR's Executive Summary on p.1, which was released by the Department of Defense. Other quotations come from the global security website, although the authors have no way to confirm whether this is the actual report.
3. Robert Joseph, 'The Changing Political–Military Environment', in James J. Wirtz and Jeffrey A. Larsen (eds), *Rockets' Red Glare: Missile Defenses and the Future of World Politics* (Boulder, CO: Westview, 2001), pp.55–78; and Bradley Graham, *Hit to Kill* (New York: Public Affairs, 2001).
4. Unclassified Report to Congress on the Acquisition of Technology Relating to Weapons of Mass Destruction and Advanced Conventional Munitions (1 Jan.–30 June 2000, Central Intelligence Agency.
5. News transcript from the White House; President Bush press conference transcript from 13 March 2002.

6. Nuclear Posture Review, p.16. By contrast, the NPR does not depict Russia as a country of immediate or even potential concern.
7. News transcript from the United States Department of Defense, J.D. Crouch, Assistant Secretary of Defense, International Security Policy, Wednesday, 9 Jan. 2002, p.3.
8. For a discussion of how risk communicates commitment see Robert Jervis, *The Logic of Images in International Relations* (New York: Columbia University Press, 1989); and Deborah Larson, 'Crisis Prevention and the Austrian State Treaty', *International Organization*, Vol.41, No.1 (Winter 1987), pp.27–60.
9. Richard Harknett, 'State Preferences, Systemic Constraints, and the Absolute Weapon', in T.V. Paul, Richard Harknett and James J. Wirtz (eds), *The Absolute Weapon Revisited: Nuclear Arms and the Emerging International Order* (Ann Arbor, MI: The University of Michigan Press, 1998), pp.47–72.
10. James Wirtz notes taken at the 12th Annual International Arms Control Conference, Sandia National Laboratories, Albuquerque, New Mexico, 18–20 April 2002.
11. Department of Defense news transcript, 9 Jan. 2002, p.6.
12. The concept of dissuasion is a new term in US doctrine. It apparently suggests that US military forces will be so technologically and operationally superior, that potential competitors will abandon efforts to challenge the United States. We would observe that the efforts at dissuasion might simply channel the military strategies and capabilities of potential competitors away from US strengths to attack US vulnerabilities, i.e., to adopt asymmetric strategies.
13. Nuclear Posture Review, pp.12–13.
14. Department of Defense news transcript, 9 Jan. 2002, p.8.
15. The Nuclear Posture Review states (p.32) that there are 8,000 warheads in the active nuclear stockpile. Presumably, these warheads form the backbone of the responsive force. The Natural Resources Defense Council estimates the hedge force may total as many as 15,000 warheads. See NRDC Backgrounder, 'Faking Nuclear Restraint: The Bush Administration's Secret Plan for Strengthening US Nuclear Forces', 13 Feb. 2002.
16. Statement of the Honorable Douglas J. Feith, Undersecretary of Defense for Policy, Senate Armed Services Hearing on the Nuclear Posture Review, 14 Feb. 2002, p.4.
17. Nuclear Posture Review, pp.46, 34–5.
18. John H. Cushman, Jr, 'Rattling New Sabers,' *New York Times*, 10 March 2002.
19. Lawrence Freedman, *The Evolution of Nuclear Strategy* (New York: St Martin's Press, 1989), pp.76–169.
20. The NPR, however, explicitly mentions the idea of developing an earth-penetrating nuclear device to target underground facilities housing WMD. This idea probably is a reflection of simple operational necessity rather than strategic choice. Some bunkers are so well constructed and deeply buried, they require enormous explosive energy to be efficiently coupled to the ground to destroy them; i.e., a relatively large earth-penetrating nuclear warhead is needed to guarantee their destruction.
21. James J. Wirtz, 'Counterproliferation, Conventional Counterforce and Nuclear War', *Journal of Strategic Studies*, Vol.23, No.1 (March 2000), pp.5–24
22. For President Bush's West Point speech see ⟨http://www.whitehouse.gov/news/releases/2002/06/20020601-3.html⟩.
23. Nuclear Posture Review, pp.12–13.
24. Phillip Bleek, 'Nuclear Posture Review Leaks; Outlines Targets, Contingencies,' *Arms Control Today*, Vol.32, No.3 (April 2002), p.1.
25. Powaski, *Return to Armageddon*, pp.207–8.
26. *Discriminate Deterrence: Report of The Commission on Integrated Long-Term Strategy*, co-chairmen Fred C. Ikle and Albert Wohlstetter, Washington, DC: US Government Printing Office, Jan. 1988.
27. Russian officials have apparently adopted this sort of nuclear doctrine.

A Few Speculations on Russia's Deterrence Policy

ALEXANDER A. PIKAYEV

Even a decade after the Soviet collapse and despite the unprecedented economic decline that took place in the 1990s, the Russian Federation still remains one of the two global nuclear superpowers, possessing deployed nuclear forces at levels comparable to or, probably, even exceeding those of the United States. There is detailed information on Russian strategic nuclear capabilities because, under the US–Russian START I Treaty, Moscow and Washington are obliged to exchange data on their strategic nuclear systems and their deployment. As of 2004, Russia deployed approximately 5,500 strategic nuclear warheads mounted on both land- and sea-based ballistic missiles, as well as on heavy bombers. At the same time, the Russians have never officially disclosed the number of their tactical nuclear weapons. The estimates vary considerably, but it is believed that perhaps a number in the low thousands are still deployed on the ground with several more thousands kept in central storage sites ready for return to their delivery vehicles.

Unfortunately, very little is known about modern Russia's nuclear strategy, nor of Moscow's vision about nuclear deterrence. In recent years, only two official documents have been published in which the role of nuclear weapons in Russia's military thinking has been mentioned. They were: the National Security Concept of the Russian Federation, approved by an Order of President Putin No.64 from 10 January 2000; and the Military Doctrine of the Russian Federation, approved by the President's Order of 21 April 2000. The provisions of both documents devoted to nuclear weapons fall far short of a detailed explanation of Russia's nuclear policy. Nevertheless, together with the 1993 Draft Military Doctrine they represent the only available official sources on the issue.

A question remains, however, over the extent to which those documents reflect the real up-to-date attitude towards nuclear issues. In post-Soviet Russia, written doctrinal documents have often become obsolete even before they have been approved and published. The same thing could apply to the 2000 Concept and Doctrine as they were prepared in the aftermath of the 1999 War in Kosovo, the bitterest point in relations between Russia and the West since the end of the Cold War. Since they were issued, one has witnessed rapid recovery of the Russia–Western, and particularly, the US–Russian interaction. It has become especially clear after the 11 September 2001 attacks against the United States. Therefore, both documents are very likely to have been based on political analyses quite different from those that might be made nowadays. Consequently, Russia's nuclear thinking since 2000 could have changed accordingly. As a reflection of that, in 2004 Russia's Security Council announced its intention to develop a new National Security Concept.

Another ambiguity is represented by uncertainties regarding the future development of Russia's nuclear and conventional forces. Since the Soviet collapse, Moscow has been obliged regularly to revise its official force projections, partially because of the fact that the economic situation has become worse than expected, and partially due to a rapidly changing international environment. Particularly, in the 1990s developments in Russia's strategic forces were closely linked to the conditions of the US–Russian START II Treaty, signed in January 1993 but ratified by the Russian Federal Assembly – the Parliament – only in 2000. Another prerequisite was that another important US–Russian agreement – the 1972 Anti-Ballistic Missile (ABM) Treaty would remain in force. However, in late 2001 and in 2002 under the new US–Russian strategic framework both agreements have collapsed, which has opened the door for a new round of discussions on the future direction of the modernization of strategic nuclear forces. Thus, the nuclear thinking reflected in both 2000 documents would not necessarily survive until end of this decade, if nuclear development plans have to be significantly reconsidered.

Due to a lack of publicly available data, and because of existing objective uncertainties one cannot provide a clear and complete picture of Russian deterrence policy. The only possibility is to speculate on the basis of known documents and data and to try to put together the fragmented pieces of what is publicly available.

The Evolution of the Role of Nuclear Weapons in Russian Military Thinking

During the last decades of the Cold War the Soviet Union enjoyed considerable conventional predominance over all potential adversaries on the Eurasian landmass. The Politburo could confidently calculate that its military could reach the Rhine within 48 hours, and the English Channel within 72 hours of a large-scale offensive operation. Therefore, there was no reason to consider strategic nuclear weapons as a war-fighting tool. Instead, it was believed that the strategic arsenals could play the role of an intra-war deterrent against the possible use of the US strategic forces (and, probably, those of Britain and France). The role of tactical nuclear capabilities was not that clear. Some Russian military authors believed that they could possess a purely military war-fighting role. For instance, they could be used in order to break up antitank defence, or for destroying concentrated adversary forces and equipment. However, those thoughts on using tactical nuclear arms were not likely to be shared by the top political and, to a lesser extent, the military leadership. Being confident in its conventional predominance, the Soviet Union could safely declare a policy of no-first-use of nuclear weapons, since it might reasonably expect to win a major war in Europe without launching any nuclear warhead.

The transformation of the geopolitical landscape in Europe in the late 1980s and early 1990s has led to a situation where Moscow's conventional might has been dramatically eroded. Within five years – between the GDR collapse in 1989 and the completion of the withdrawal of Russian troops from Germany and the Baltic States, the depth of defence was decreased by a factor of five – from 2,000 to 400 kilometres. Before 1994 Russian troops were stationed at the River Elbe in the middle of Germany, now they are deployed just 400 kilometres to the west of Moscow at the border with the Baltic States. In 1991 the manpower of the Soviet armed forces was approximately five million. By 2004, the Russian forces had been downsized to 1.2 million, and further reduction is expected. In terms of major military equipment, the 1980s Warsaw Pact predominance over NATO by a factor of two-to-three has been changed into the opposite: three-to-four times NATO predominance over Russia in the European zone. Conventional deployments in the Far East have possibly been degraded to an even greater extent.

It is not surprising that under conditions of such a rapid degradation of Russian conventional forces the military increasingly came to rely on its still mighty nuclear capabilities. This meant that the nuclear weapons could be needed not only in response to nuclear attack, but also in the case of conventional aggression. Consequently, the Soviet pledge of nuclear no-first-use could not be complied with anymore. The political leadership had to accept the first-use option in late 1993, when it became dependent upon the military after the latter helped the Yeltsin administration to topple a pro-Communist *coup d'etat* in October 1993. For the first time, Moscow effectively officially denounced the no-first-use pledge in a Draft Military Doctrine published in November 1993.

Nuclearization of Russian military thinking has become obvious since the end of the first war in Chechnya (1994–96). Driven by concerns about NATO eastward enlargement, in 1997 the leadership nominated Igor Sergeyev as Defence Minister. Before that, he had commanded the Strategic Rocket Forces (SRF), managing a cornerstone of Russia's strategic triad. Under him, more than half of defence procurement was spent on nuclear-related needs. During his term as Defence Minister, the new *Topol M* (SS-27) intercontinental ballistic missile (ICBM), and the *Iskander* dual use tactical land-based ballistic missile were commissioned.

The next round of nuclearization started in 1999, during NATO's War in Kosovo. On 30 April at the meeting of the Russian Security Council, President Yeltsin reportedly asked why the Russian position on Yugoslavia was so openly ignored by the West despite the fact that Moscow still possessed huge nuclear stockpiles? That meeting has triggered thinking on how nuclear weapons could be used for gaining political goals in times when conventional resources have become inadequate. Some generals started delivering the opinion that early first use of nuclear weapons was possible: in the early stages of a conflict, or even in time of crisis. In practical terms, the Russian military started involving nuclear forces more actively in peacetime military operations. During the *West-99* military manoeuvres in Kaliningrad, a scenario of using tactical nuclear weapons to halt non-nuclear aggression was elaborated. In 1999–2001 Russian strategic bomber forces, which had been generally grounded for almost a decade, launched a relatively ambitious patrolling mode, resuming their Cold War type training flights as far as Iceland and even to Cuba. Beyond a purely military rationale, the task of that increased activity was clearly of a political nature – to incorporate the last remaining superpower asset into attempts to gain peacetime political dividends.

However, since 2000 the nuclearization trend has been halted and even reversed. Partially, this can be explained by interagency competition inside the Russian armed forces. The conventional armed services were disappointed by what they perceived as an imbalanced procurement policy in favour of nuclear-related forces. But the primary reason was a general shift in threat perceptions resulting from the second Chechen war and the change of administration in the Kremlin. The second Chechen war, which started in August 1999, demonstrated a lack of basic conventional equipment needed for counter-guerrilla operations: all weather helicopters; non-wire communications systems, etc. In broader terms, it demonstrated that, despite all the disagreements with the West, the threat of a large-scale war in the Western strategic azimuth remains largely theoretical whereas in the South the threat of war is a real and present danger. Nuclear weapons cannot be used for winning those low-intensity conflicts along the Southern periphery of Russian borders. At the same time, they divert scarce resources from the procurement of the weaponry needed for conducting such warfare.

As a result, in 2000 a dramatic decision was made on de-nuclearizing Russia's military policy. Accents in procurement were shifted in favour of conventional forces. In 2001, for the first time since the Soviet collapse, not a single new strategic ballistic missile was operationally deployed.

Pro-nuclear Marshal Sergeyev was replaced in his position as Minister of Defence, and the Strategic Rocket Forces, the only armed service institutionally interested in enhancing the role of nuclear weapons, have lost their status as a separate armed service and been downgraded into a lower level military bureaucracy (*rod voysk*) subordinated to the General Staff.

Increased Priorities Versus Falling Numbers

While following the debates around nuclearizing Russian military thinking from 1992 to 2000, one should take into account that those trends took place in the environment of a considerable de-nuclearization of Moscow's security policy in general, where military priorities played a much more peripheral role than in Soviet times. The 2000 National Security Concept placed domestic challenges to national security above international challenges. Among the latter, military threats were mentioned below political challenges and terrorism; nothing was said about a risk of nuclear attack against Russia. The Concept's Section IV, which was devoted to the tasks of maintaining national security, gave first place to economic goals and second place to foreign policy tasks. Then it mentioned the democratic political system, the solution of multiple social problems, and ecology. Only after that long list of national security tasks came military security.

Nuclear matters were mentioned in the National Security Concept only three times; three paragraphs were dedicated to them in a 20-page long text. Interestingly, the task of safe dismantlement of weapons of mass destruction and related equipment (for instance: nuclear powered submarines and surface ships; rocket fuel) was also placed above mentioning nuclear weapons in a traditional military context.

This marginalization of the role of nuclear weapons in the National Security Concept reflected real developments in Russia since the Soviet collapse. While during the Cold War nuclear matters occupied a central role in Russian foreign and security policy, including the Kremlin's relations with the United States, since the Soviet collapse they have been replaced by relations with international financial organizations, the tasks of promoting exports and accessing various international institutions, such as G-8, various export control clubs, and the World Trade Organization. More recently, international terrorism has firmly occupied top positions in the Kremlin's list of foreign and security priorities. Even with much reduced military activity abroad, the Russians tended to use peacekeeping as a primary military tool for preserving their interests in the former Soviet space and in the Balkans.

The 1997 to 2000 imbalances in defence procurement policy in favour of nuclear-related forces took place in an environment when procurement overall has dramatically decreased from 1980s levels. In 1992 alone, the federal military order was decreased by a factor of ten compared to the previous year. It is likely that the trend continued for a few years thereafter. Although there are no directly available figures to illustrate the procurement decline, it might be done by showing decreases in overall defence spending. It is believed that in the Soviet times Moscow spent annually around US $100bn for its military. For 2005, the defence budget was requested at slightly less than Roubles 53bn, or approximately US $18bn at the market currency exchange rate.

These dramatic decreases have significantly affected nuclear procurement as well. Since 1992 Russia has not commissioned a new strategic nuclear submarine (SSBN). Construction of *Yury Dolgoruky*, a new Borei-class SSBN started in November 1996. She was to have been commissioned in 2002, but the completion has been delayed indefinitely due to the absence of sea-launch ballistic missiles (SLBM) to arm the new boat. Russia failed to develop a new SLBM. The *Bark* SLBM project was halted in 1998 due to failure of the flight test programme. Instead, development of the *Bulava* SLBM was ordered in the same year. Reportedly, it entered the flight test stage in 2004, but its future remains unclear. Production of heavy bombers has also been halted, with only those Tu-160 Blackjack aircraft, construction of which had been started in Soviet times, being slowly completed since 1992. In the field of land-based strategic ballistic missiles, procurement has never exceeded ten missiles annually, which represents a tenfold decline from the Soviet peak rate. For 2005, the Ministry of Defence plans to purchase four ICBMs.

Financial shortages affected not only development and procurement, but also maintenance of existing forces. SSBNs were decommissioned ahead of the schedule required by the START I Treaty. Because of inadequate maintenance, even relatively new SSBN types will have to be decommissioned within the next five years. According to the Russian application for US Cooperative Threat Reduction (CTR) assistance aimed at facilitating Russia's nuclear disarmament, five out of six existing Typhoon-class submarines and one of seven Delta IV-class SSBNs should be destroyed by 2007. It is very likely that by the end of this decade, unless new boats are commissioned, the Russian Navy could operate no more than seven strategic submarines instead of the 62 it commanded in 1990.

According to official plans made publicly available in December 1998, by 2010 the Russian authorities expected that only 70 SS-25 mobile single warhead ICBMs would remain operational from 1,064 ICBMs deployed in 1990. To them will be added an unknown number of new SS-27 land-based strategic missiles, three dozen of which have been commissioned since 1998. If the present ICBM procurement rate were to be maintained for the rest of this decade, by 2010 the SRF would operate no more than 150 ICBMs. A similar decline would affect heavy bombers. According to some estimates, by 2010 the Air Forces could command on no more than 20 strategic aircraft compared to 162 in 1990.

A high rate of decommissioning and much lower new production of nuclear warheads accompanied the downward trends in strategic nuclear delivery vehicles. According to the US estimates, in the 1990s the Russians dismantled between 1,000 and 3,000 warheads (both strategic and tactical) annually. Regarding new warhead production, since Soviet times it has decreased by a factor of twenty. Drastically reduced warhead production together with a massive withdrawal of tactical nuclear weapons from military units to central storage sites or for dismantlement most certainly is causing continuing downward trends in tactical nuclear arsenals as well.

Therefore, the nuclearization of Russian military thinking was only relative and developed against a background of the marginalization of the military component in national security priorities, and a dramatic decline in investment in developing, procuring and maintaining nuclear weaponry. As a result, by 2010 the Russians might possess approximately 1,000 – or even less – deployed strategic nuclear warheads. This would be five times less than they deployed in 2004, or 2.2 times below the upper ceiling of the United States/Russian Moscow Strategic Offensive Reductions Treaty, concluded in May 2002. Whether these numbers would be sufficient for fulfilling the ambitious deterrence and war fighting tasks postulated for nuclear weapons by the 2000 Military Doctrine remains a question to be addressed below.

The Role of Nuclear Weapons in the 2000 Military Doctrine

The 2000 Military Doctrine gives a high place to the role of nuclear deterrence in reducing any direct military threat to the Russian Federation. In Part I, Section 4 the document stated:

> Under present conditions the threat of direct military aggression in its traditional forms against the Russian Federation and its allies has been reduced due to positive changes in the international environment, pursuit of an active, peace-loving, international course on the international stage by our country, maintaining Russian military capabilities, above all, the nuclear deterrent, at a sufficient level.

According to the phrasing of this text, the role of the military capabilities was placed behind the general international environment and Russian foreign policy. However, nuclear deterrence was mentioned as a primary element in maintaining military capabilities at a sufficient level. It could be evaluated as a vision that nuclear deterrence represents the most important factor among all other military – but not political – means of reducing the risk of direct military intervention against Russia.

Similar provision was incorporated into Part I, Section 7 of the Doctrine, devoted to maintaining military security. It says, 'The Russian Federation keeps its status of nuclear power for deterring (preventing) aggression against itself and (or) its allies'. It could be seen as a vision that nuclear capabilities are needed to cope with an aggression of any kind, including conventional. Furthermore, both Sections 4 and 7 show that Russia's nuclear deterrent is to be used to provide *extended deterrence* – protecting not only Russia itself, but its allies as well. The word *preventing* aggression permits very wide speculation about the possibility of preventive use of nuclear weapons. Of course, Section 7 permits the first use of nuclear weapons, but the clause on preventing aggression might refer not only to using nuclear arms during war, but in a crisis as well. For instance, one could try to prevent aggression by launching a surprise nuclear attack against military concentrations of a potential adversary even before hostilities start – in time of crisis.

Another interesting element of Section 7 is the implicit recognition that, for the foreseeable future, Russia will have to maintain a nuclear deterrent and is not ready to abolish it completely. In the same Section, it is stated that Russia 'is ready for further reductions of its nuclear weapons on a bilateral base together with the United States, and on a multilateral base together with other nuclear countries, down to *minimum levels*, which meet the requirements of strategic stability' [emphasis added]. In fact, for the foreseeable future, Moscow, like the other nuclear capitals, is not ready for complete nuclear disarmament, nor for deep unilateral nuclear cuts. However, cooperative nuclear reductions – both bilateral and multilateral – are considered as desirable.

Section 8 of Part I of the 2000 Doctrine occupies a key position in formulating the role of nuclear weapons. It opens with an intriguing statement:

> The military security of the Russian Federation is provided by a sum of all the forces, means and resources it possesses. Under modern conditions, the Russian Federation relies on a need to possess nuclear capabilities enabling it a guaranteed possibility to inflict damage of predetermined [or pre-calculated][1] scale to any aggressor (a state or a coalition of states) under any circumstances.

The provision could be interpreted as Russia's nuclear deterrent should be survivable and flexible enough to inflict not only massive retaliation, but also pre-calculated damage. This would mean that the ideas of *limited strikes and flexible response* are something which represent integral parts of Russian nuclear thinking. Mentioning 'under any circumstances' means that the Russian nuclear deterrent could be used under all conditions – in a first nuclear strike, launch-on-warning (after the adversary's nuclear forces were launched, but still before they reached their targets in Russia), and launch-under-attack (after the enemy's warheads have hit their targets). The last scenario requires a significant level of survivability of nuclear forces and maintenance of reliable command and control over them in wartime. Indeed, launch-under-attack imposes very high requirements on survivability of forces and command authorities – they should be able to survive, calculate, make damage assessment, communicate, send orders, and be able to launch all or a part of surviving forces under conditions of heavy destruction and losses inflicted by an adversary's first nuclear attack.

Conceptually, the phrase 'under any circumstances' could also involve nuclear attack in a crisis. This corresponds to the mention of the role of nuclear weapons as a tool for 'preventing' aggression.

Section 8 also contains criteria for using nuclear weapons – under what conditions and against whom they could be launched. It states:

> The Russian Federation reserves the right to use nuclear weapons in response to the use of nuclear arms and other weapons of mass destruction against itself and (or) its allies, as well as in response to large-scale aggression with the use of conventional weapons under situations critical for the national security of the Russian Federation.

This provision confirms that the Russian nuclear deterrent has to fulfil an extended deterrence mission to protect not only Russia *per se*, but its allies as well. Furthermore, like the United States, Russia could use nuclear weapons not only if somebody launches a nuclear attack against itself or its ally, but also in response to the use of other weapons of mass destruction, such as chemical, biological or maybe radiological arms. However, Russia's nuclear launch under those circumstances would not be automatic, since Moscow only 'reserves the right' to nuclear response.

Probably, the most important aspect of this paragraph is a separation between responding to attack with weapons of mass destruction, and Russia's use of nuclear weapons in the context of 'a large-scale conventional aggression'. The document, in fact, hints that the probability of nuclear response in that case is lower than in response to WMD attack. Beyond the wording 'reserves the right', the provision establishes additional criteria for a nuclear response – nuclear weapons could be used 'under situations critical for national security'. The presence of the additional criterion might demonstrate that the use of WMD would be more likely than conventional aggression to trigger a nuclear response from Russia.

The criterion adds more ambiguity to the scenario of a large-scale conventional attack. WMD attack is a clear action, which could trigger Russian nuclear retaliation. Large-scale conventional aggression would trigger nuclear responses only if somebody in the Kremlin decided that a situation had emerged *critical to national security*. The Russian military explained that criterion as meaning that the nuclear response would be a weapon of last resort, when all other means to halt aggression have failed. This means that nuclear weapons would be used only when the risk of Russian defeat was unacceptably high. However, no clarifications of that kind were included in the document. At least, one could expect wording more explicit than *national security*, maybe *critical to national survival*. Since that did not happen, one might suspect that the vague term *critical to national security* had been chosen deliberately in order to hint about other scenarios of nuclear response. Strictly speaking *critical to national security* may apply not only to the last stage of conventional war, but to early stages of the conflict, or even to a time of crisis. As was mentioned above, large-scale military concentration near the border in numbers perceived sufficient to inflict military defeat could, in principle, be considered as a situation *critical to national security*, and thus permitting use of nuclear weapons in order to disrupt the concentration in a preventive attack. This assumption is compatible with the provisions of Sections 4 and 7, which could be read as permitting preventive *early first use*.

The follow-on text provides the criteria for states and circumstances against which Russian nuclear weapons could be used. It states:

> The Russian Federation will not use nuclear weapons against State Parties of the Nuclear Non-Proliferation Treaty, not possessing nuclear weapons, except in case of attack on the Russian Federation, Armed Forces of the Russian Federation or other troops, its allies or a state towards which it possesses security obligations, made by or supported by a country, not possessing nuclear weapons, together or possessing alliance obligations with a nuclear weapons state.

To an extent, this paragraph confirms suspicions that Russia's nuclear weapons are not considered as a weapon of last resort, and their *early first use* is another implicit option. It especially mentions that an attack on Russian Armed Forces and other troops could trigger nuclear retaliation. This might be interpreted only in a way that such retaliation could be prompted by an attack on Russian forces deployed abroad – an action clearly less dangerous than the threat of complete Russian military defeat.

This provision puts the majority of the CIS neighbours under the risk of Russian nuclear retaliation – if they attack the Russians. Only Iran, North Korea (as long as they would not possess nuclear weapons) and, perhaps, Mongolia, could reliably consider themselves as exempt from the notion. They are NPT State Parties and their attack on Russian troops together or in alliance with a nuclear power is inconceivable under the recent geopolitical paradigm. The expression *alliance obligations* is also vague. Indeed, attack on Russian forces made by any NATO member, for instance, Turkey, clearly falls under the provision of Section 8: NATO has three nuclear member states. But whether it is true for Afghanistan and Uzbekistan, which do not possess formal alliance relations with any nuclear power, but host nuclear powers' troops on their territories? Or what is the situation of Georgia, which hosts US military advisors?

There is a contradiction between the two above-mentioned paragraphs of Section 8. The former stated that the Russians *reserve the right* to use nuclear weapons in the case of a WMD attack against Russia. The latter provision states that nuclear weapons would not be used against non-nuclear NPT State Parties, even if they attack Russia or its allies and forces abroad, but not together or in alliance with other nuclear powers. Does it mean that such countries could be exempt from Russian nuclear retaliation, even if their attack involves use of chemical, biological and radiological weapons?

Part II of the Military Doctrine is entitled 'Military and Strategic Pillars' and is devoted to description of the characteristics of modern wars and conflicts. Section 3 of Part II describes common characteristics of modern warfare. Particularly, it says that the risk of escalation of hostilities during war is highly probable, involving 'expanding the range of equipment used, including weapons of mass destruction'. Section 9 of Part II describes a large-scale war, which involves a large amount of countries from various regions. The war could be a result of escalation of armed conflict, local and regional wars. A conventional large-scale war 'has a high probability of escalating into a nuclear one with catastrophic consequences for civilization, activity and existence of mankind'. Section 11 states that large-scale war requires 'maintaining reliable state and military command', and it might be protracted with major military tasks reached in its follow-on and final stages. According to Section 14, in large-scale and regional wars, the Russian Armed Forces must 'inflict a defeat on an aggressor, forcing it to halt hostilities under conditions complying with the interests of the Russian Federation'. Furthermore, Section 16 states that the Armed Forces must be ready to

> carry out operations (both offensive and defensive) under any form of eruption of hostilities and to conduct wars and armed conflicts under conditions of massive use by an adversary of modern and future combat means of destruction, including weapons of mass destruction of all types.

All the above-mentioned citations demonstrate that Russian military thinking includes a vision of conducting large-scale *protracted* war, which might involve a massive use of nuclear weapons. This corresponds to several provisions incorporated into Part I of the document. The Armed Forces must be ready to conduct warfare in the environment of nuclear weapons use for a long period of time. The command-and-control system should be highly survivable and function reliably during protracted nuclear warfare. Part II mentions that nuclear weapons could be used in large-scale and regional wars only, but does not mention their use while describing local wars and armed conflicts. At the same time, that possibility is not excluded completely, since Section 3 said that all types of modern warfare could very likely escalate to a nuclear one. This might mean that the Doctrine implicitly permits nuclear early first use even under conditions of low intensity 'armed conflict' and local war.

In sum, the 2000 Military Doctrine sees the possibility of using nuclear weapons under all types of warfare, especially in regional and large-scale wars. A nuclear war could be protracted and during it nuclear weapons could be used more than once. With minor exemptions, the first use of nuclear arsenals has been permitted. It could be done not only as a last ditch effort aimed at preventing military defeat, but also in a preventive way during the early stages of warfare, even in a crisis, before hostilities have erupted. The nuclear weapons should defend not only the Russian Federation *per se*, but its allies and forces deployed abroad as well. All this imposes a very low nuclear threshold, and a nuclear response might be triggered by an attack against a Russian military base abroad by a country possessing poorly defined allied obligations with a nuclear power.

Prospects for De-Nuclearizing Russia's Military Thinking

Nuclearized military thinking, which is reflected by the 2000 Military Doctrine, could hardly correspond with the changing emphasis on defence procurement policy and threat perceptions made by the Putin administration in 2000/01. The Doctrine's provisions on large-scale warfare and protracted nuclear war, gradual nuclear response, use of nuclear weapons against allies of nuclear powers clearly points, albeit indirectly, to the fact that one of its primary scenarios involves massive nuclear exchange with a mighty nuclear power and its systems of alliances – no one else except the United States and NATO fits into that category. This should not mislead, because the Doctrine has been developed in the post-Kosovo environment – i.e. shortly after the bitterest crisis in relations between Russia and the West after the end of the Cold War.

As was mentioned above, the Putin administration has significantly changed its foreign policy and security priorities, making them more pro-Western and more realistic. This highlighted major deficiencies of the Doctrine's nuclear vision. A need to conduct protracted nuclear warfare and to maintain efficient command-and-control systems during that war was not considered to be realistic even in the time of the Cold War, and sounds even less so when Russia's command and control faces problems in its peacetime activities. Maintaining nuclear forces of the size necessary for protracted nuclear warfare also seems unrealistic given the expected drastic downsizing of Russia's nuclear arsenals and the huge economic asymmetries with the United States.

It is not surprising that in 2002 Russian officials started to make statements which sounded like a revision of the approaches on which the 2000 Doctrine was based. Indeed, Russia's role as 'multi-regional' power imposes much lower requirements on its nuclear capabilities than the Soviet Union needed. Russia does not need extended deterrence against the West. No one post-Soviet state (except, maybe Belarus) asks Moscow for that kind of umbrella. At the same time, for political reasons, Russia itself is not ready to provide nuclear guarantees for those countries which might be interested in them, hypothetically, Iraq, North Korea or even Cuba. Therefore, *vis-à-vis* the West, Russian nuclear arsenals should provide deterrence only for Russia itself, and the role of such deterrence has been decreasing since 1999, given the improving political environment in the relationship and the shifting of US security priorities away from Europe. Deterring attack against the national territory requires less ambitious forces than the task of providing a nuclear umbrella for allies, especially against a mightier coalition. Given Western sensitivities to the consequences of a potential use of nuclear weapons, perhaps, maintaining smaller asymmetric forces could be enough to provide reliable deterrence. This permitted Russian military thinkers to accept the idea that they not only *cannot* maintain strategic nuclear parity with the United States, due to economic constraints, but they probably *do not need* it at all.

In the early 1990s several Central Asian nations sought Russian security guarantees against China, and a very different sort of assurances – against Islamic fundamentalism. In fact these guarantees (plus assurances *vis-à-vis* Uzbek regional ambitions) still determine the value of a Collective Security Treaty in the eyes of Kazakhstan, Kyrgyzstan and Tajikistan. It is not surprising that the three nations want to keep these nuclear guarantees even in the case of the establishment of the Central Asian nuclear weapons free zone. Given significant asymmetries in sizes of nuclear capabilities between Russia and China in Moscow's favour, extended nuclear deterrence in the region still works and will work for the foreseeable future.[2] Beyond that, the establishment of the Shanghai Cooperation Organization (SCO) in 2001 has made Beijing a regional partner in dealing with the Islamic challenge. Thus deterring it became a much less pressing task.

The defeat of the Taleban and the continuing US military presence in Uzbekistan, Kyrgyzstan and Tajikistan has become an additional factor alleviating security pressure in Central Asia. For a while, at least, Afghanistan has ceased serving as a rear base for Islamic combatants in the region. Simultaneously, the US presence, especially payments for using bases, has increased the self-confidence of Central Asian leaders. The US deployments also (so far) provide higher confidence *vis-à-vis* China, thus further decreasing the perception both in Moscow and the Central Asian capitals of a pressing need to deter the Chinese by means of a Russian nuclear umbrella.

The picture in the other key area, the Caucasus, is mixed. There Russia possesses only one ally, Armenia, which it provides with security guarantees against Turkey and probably Iran. Russian military and border troop bases in Armenia, although recently reinforced, host troops in clearly insufficient numbers to deter a hypothetical large-scale offence. Prospects for their reinforcement in wartime also remain doubtful given the uncertain access to Armenian bases through Georgian territory. Therefore there might be a motivation to involve nuclear weapons in order to enhance the security umbrella for Armenia, despite the fact that there is no conceivable risk of nuclear attack against that country.

In broader terms, the recent downsizing of Russia's military contains a risk of nuclearization of scenarios of local warfare. The 1.2 million personnel of the Russian Armed Forces are facing potential contingencies around the 60,000 kilometres of Russian borders. At some points, Russia employed up to 50,000 troops in Chechnya. Given a need for rotation of troops involved in warfare, the expected size of the ground forces would be insufficient for conducting more than one low-intensity counter-guerrilla conflict. This could stimulate the incorporation of nuclear weapons into warfare scenarios involving medium-size non-nuclear powers located in regions of concern. If that happens, the role of tactical nuclear weapons could increase, since militarily they could be used more easily in such local warfare options.

In sum, one could expect a shift in Russia's nuclear thinking away from traditional scenarios of central United States–Russian protracted nuclear war, with its requirements for maintaining strategic nuclear parity and the ability to employ flexible intra-war responses. This would mean considerable expense, unbearable for the Russian economy. Those requirements might be also unnecessary since inferior forces might be sufficient to deter attack against Russian national territory *per se*. At the same time, there is a possibility of nuclearizing local warfare scenarios, with a higher role for tactical nuclear weapons. In some cases, those regional nuclear missions would involve a very low nuclear threshold.

NOTES

This chapter was originally drafted in 2002.

1. Added by author as another possible translation of the word *zadanny*.
2. So far, China lacks deterrence capabilities *vis-à-vis* Russia: its nuclear forces are unable to inflict assured destruction on Russia's European part, where the major urban centres and economic assets are concentrated.

Redefining Strategic Stability in a Changing World: A Chinese View

ZHONG JING AND PAN ZHENQIANG

The concept of strategic stability can be defined as an enduring situation, in which various strategic forces in the world are able to establish and sustain a strategic framework for basic relations between and among them, and an adequate sense of security. Reflecting generally a balance of force, and moreover a balance of core interests among major powers, strategic stability is usually based on certain military and security arrangements through legally binding mechanisms or other institutions.

Ideally, strategic stability must also take into consideration the legitimate requests of all the other countries for insuring their own sovereignty and security. It is, therefore, a process of joint participation and mutual interaction by all the members of the international community.

Strategic stability thus is closely related to the existing world structure, international mechanisms and norms of behaviour in international relations. In a situation of strategic stability, there is little incentive for any major power to change unilaterally these existing arrangements by force.

Strategic Stability in the Cold War Years

Two phenomena dominated efforts to seek strategic stability throughout the Cold War years.

The first phenomenon is the emergence of a bipolar structure, in which the two superpowers, the United States and the Soviet Union, competed for world domination. The end of the Second World War soon witnessed the emergence of two confronting camps, each dominated by one superpower. This antagonism covered virtually all fields, underpinning the basic trends of the world situation. Under the circumstances, strategic stability built in those years was bound to reflect a balance between the two major powers on the basis of rigid confrontation. The zero-sum nature of state-to-state relations persisted even when détente began to materialise towards the end of the Cold War.

The second phenomenon is the emergence of nuclear weapons with unprecedented destructive power, which led relations between the United States and the Soviet Union at the outset of the Cold War to evolve chiefly around the struggle for nuclear supremacy. In the late 1940s and early 1950s, when the United States had a monopoly on nuclear bombs, Washington was preoccupied with establishing strategic stability on the basis of the perpetuation of that monopoly. The United States effort failed rather quickly as the Soviet Union soon acquired its own nuclear capability. Competition continued in the ensuing years, resulting in the accumulation of huge nuclear arsenals by each of the two superpowers. By the beginning of the 1970s, each had the capability of eliminating the other side several times.[1] The risk of nuclear war dramatically increased. Meanwhile, nuclear competition between these two major powers had also given rise to increasing risks of nuclear proliferation and to a worldwide effort to halt the nuclear arms race and to achieve nuclear nonproliferation. The nuclear issue became the top priority in international relations.

As a result of these two phenomena, the strategic stability achieved in the Cold War years inevitably bore some distinct characteristics.

First, the nuclear balance between the United States and the former Soviet Union became the central theme for strategic stability. In 1972, the two countries signed the Anti-Ballistic Missile Treaty and the SALT I agreement, which basically banned the development of strategic defensive forces while exercising some limit on the development of this strategic offensive forces. The arrangement was based on the rationale of so called Mutual Assured Destruction (MAD), that is, the assurance, because of the deliberate prohibition of strategic defense, that each side had the capability to wipe out the other. This MAD situation was believed to be effective in preventing nuclear war, as neither side dared to launch a preventive nuclear strike lest the attack should lead to retaliation and bring about virtual self-destruction. MAD thus was not only a fact of life, but also a theory, which constituted the conceptual basis for the strategy of deterrence that both superpowers were believed to embrace. According to the deterrence strategy, the focus was on the prevention rather than the actual fighting of a nuclear war. Thus, a nuclear balance was achieved between the two superpowers in terms of identical nuclear doctrine as well as nuclear force structure. And it was based on this nuclear balance that strategic stability was finally established. It was, indeed, a balance of terror, codified by the ABM Treaty and other related nuclear agreements; it nevertheless served as one of the important pillars for world strategic stability.

But strategic stability went beyond the manipulation by the two superpowers even in the Cold War years. With the development of the world campaign for peace, nuclear disarmament and nonproliferation, tension between the nuclear weapons states (NWS) and non-nuclear weapons states (NNWS) increased. On the other hand, the international community also saw increasing common interests in averting the danger of nuclear war. This situation led to the conclusion of a number of important multilateral treaties like the Partial Test Ban Treaty (PTBT) in 1963 and the Nonproliferation Treaty (NPT) in 1968. The NPT, in particular, stipulated different obligations for the NWS and NNWS respectively. The NWS pledged to carry out nuclear disarmament and eventual complete prohibition and thorough destruction of all their nuclear weapons, and to assist the NNWS in the development of peaceful use of nuclear energy. In exchange, the NNWS renounced the acquisition of nuclear weapons. The balance of different obligations between these two categories of countries became another important pillar for the sustainability of strategic stability in the Cold War years.

Strategic stability in the Cold War years was further consolidated as it was institutionalized based on the gradual establishment of a series of arms control and disarmament mechanisms and regional security arrangements both at bilateral and multilateral levels. They included, for example, the United States–Soviet Union bilateral negotiations, the Mutual Balanced Force Reductions talks in Central Europe (MBFR), the multilateral arms control and disarmament negotiations in the Conference on Disarmament in Geneva, peacekeeping activities under the auspices of the United Nations, and many others. All these were successful in producing a number of legal documents. Combined, they reflected the convergence of interests of the majority of members of the world, as well as their political willingness to accept certain constraints on their actions in the international arena. Because of the above-mentioned characteristics, the implications of strategic stability in the Cold War years were mixed.

On the positive side, strategic stability contributed in a significant way to the maintenance of peace in general and the curbing of nuclear war in particular. Large-scale conventional war between the two major powers or between NATO and the Warsaw Pact did not take place due to the fear of such a war being escalated into a nuclear exchange. Like two scorpions in a bottle, the two superpowers were virtually locked in an impasse (called strategic stability); neither side thought a major war would be in its best interests.

Strategic stability in the Cold War years also helped develop a useful code of conduct, particularly for the major powers in their involvement (or non-involvement) in regional conflicts as well as in regional arrangements for peacekeeping or peacemaking. Despite numerous regional conflicts and local wars, these instabilities and turmoil did not in general significantly jeopardize global strategic stability.

Last but not least, the role that legal arms control and disarmament mechanisms, established in the Cold War years, played in maintaining strategic stability and mobilizing the international effort for further arms control and non-proliferation progress should not be underestimated. As the Chinese foreign minister has put it,

> thanks to joint efforts over the years, the international community has established a set of relatively complete legal systems for arms control and disarmament. As an important component of the global collective security framework with the United Nations at its centre, this system has increased the predictability of international relations and played an important role in safeguarding international peace, security and stability.[2]

In the nuclear field, it was helpful in further regulating the rules of the nuclear game, and ensuring that the on-going nuclear arms race between the two superpowers remained on a controlled track. After the Cold War was over, this existing legal system continued to promote the arms control and disarmament process. During the whole of the 1990s, the international effort for arms control succeeded in producing further important conventions or treaties like the Chemical Weapons Convention (CWC), the Comprehensive Test Ban Treaty (CTBT) and the agreement of indefinite extension of the NPT, among others. All these achievements will continue to be important elements in establishing new strategic stability in the twenty-first century.

On the negative side, strategic stability in the Cold War years always bore some inherently irrational elements. It primarily catered to the convenience of the world competition of the two superpowers. Their chief concern was the insurance of 'a stable conflict' between themselves rather than a halt to it.[3] With inevitably deep-rooted suspicion and fear, lest the other side move ahead in the competition for military superiority, deterrence became the source of a continuing arms race between the two superpowers. In fact, in the strategic framework they had agreed to establish, the arms race (the nuclear arms race in particular) never ceased; preparation for fighting a nuclear war never relaxed. This situation led to the continuing expansion of the two major powers' nuclear over-kill capabilities beyond any reasonable calculations.[4] Strategic stability was precarious. The world still lives under the shadow of the spread of nuclear weapons and the danger of a nuclear war.

The irrationality also found expression in the discriminatory nature of the differing obligations under the NPT. Furthermore, while the overwhelming majority of NNWS largely (except for a few exceptions like Israel, India and Pakistan) observed their commitment not to acquire nuclear capabilities, the NWS had yet to honour their obligations. The failure on the part of NWS raised a serious moral obstacle to the strengthening of the nonproliferation regime; it also increased the confidence gap between NNWS and NWS.

In a larger security context, strategic stability in the Cold War years seemed to focus single-mindedly on the military balance between the

United States and the Soviet Union. Many regional conflicts and disputes were either set aside or frozen along the ups and downs in the relations between the two superpowers. These issues were, however, by no means solved. They contained potential instabilities that would invariably affect future stability once the old strategic stability became eroded. The developments in the post-Cold War era have amply demonstrated the weakness of the Cold War strategic stability. Every year during the 1990s there were over 30 local wars or violent conflicts throughout the world, which became the prime source for the turbulence and instability of the world today.[5]

A Changing Security Environment in the Post-Cold War Era

The end of the Cold War fundamentally changed the world strategic environment; the world is entering a transitional period. Many security arrangements that contributed to strategic stability in the Cold War years seemed increasingly irrelevant to meeting the new challenges; others, however, have persisted, or need to be retained to ensure peaceful and stable transition in the changing world. Greater complexity, uncertainty and unpredictability have become hallmarks of the world strategic situation in the new century.

A number of important changes will most affect the strategic stability built in the Cold War years: the Soviet Union has disintegrated; the bipolar system has collapsed; the world finds a single remaining superpower with increasing power and ambition, although multipolarity is also evidently a clear trend in the development of the international situation. This change has been leading all countries, major powers in particular, to the readjustment of their power alignments, threat perceptions, strategic objectives and security strategies. Inter-state relations are no longer defined simply on a foe-or-friend basis.

On-going economic globalization has been profoundly changing the economic and trade relations of various nations in the world. Interdependence and mutual constraints are greatly enhanced as a result. Meanwhile, globalization has also given rise to an enlarged gap between rich and poor, and North and South, owing to the inequality in economic competition.[6] Economic security has become increasingly conspicuous in the security outlook of all nations.[7]

Rapid development of high technology has become a double-edged sword in developing new capabilities, shaping new ways of life and thinking, and generating new threats to nations. Non-traditional security threats are emerging as an increasing security challenge to the whole world at such a fast speed and great magnitude that no nation can single-handedly handle the issue.[8] As the 11 September events illustrated, as a state builds on greater strength, its society and individuals could become more and more vulnerable.

The end of the Cold War makes obsolete the ideological criterion of defining friend and foe by judging whether they are communist or capitalist. But unbalanced development also provides great incentives for the rise of religious fundamentalism. Closely linked with nationalist or separatist elements in economically backward areas, the fundamentalism feels no restraint in asserting its own values and imposing its will on others by all the means it can lay its hands on. It does not care what the cost might be for launching such attacks. Indeed, as the 11 September events again demonstrate, the fundamentalist force has become the most dangerous international terrorist group, and poses a new challenge to the security of the world of a magnitude unimaginable in the past.

On the other hand, it should also be noticed that as the Cold War ended in an abrupt and peaceful manner, some elements which were indispensable for strategic stability in the past could not disappear overnight, and would persist into the future.

In the nuclear sense, the world remains very much a bipolar structure, based on the MAD impasse of the two nuclear superpowers. Despite the disappearance of the Soviet Union, and the dramatic weakening of its successor, Russia, Moscow has still inherited a huge nuclear arsenal, enough to wipe out America more than once. This fact of life will perhaps continue to live with us at least for the next several decades.

Also, for all the effort to harmonize relations between major powers as partnership, deep-rooted suspicion and distrust persist. Military alliances continue to exist and are even strengthened. Nations are still divided based on perceived different values, and different geopolitical and economic interests.

The security concept generated from military confrontation in the Cold War still lingers in many countries. This Cold War mentality, coloured with rigid ideological prejudice, tends to continue to look at the world as a 'jungle full of poisonous snakes', and is only too happy to resort to a confrontational approach to security issues.

Two Contrasting Approaches to Future Strategic Stability

Faced with a complex reality, it is obvious that all countries, major powers in particular, are striving to take measures to adapt to the new situation and enhance their security. During the process it is obvious, too, that all members of the international community share common concerns that efforts made by various countries to augment their own security should not jeopardize the prospect of strategic stability in the future. Judging from recent developments, two contrasting approaches towards the issue are now before us.

One approach is well represented by the policies of the Bush administration. President Bush and his team have pledged to build a ballistic missile defence (BMD) system at the expense of the ABM Treaty. They hope to bypass formal arms control constraints and instead to continue to keep a large nuclear arsenal despite so-called deep unilateral cuts in nuclear weapons. They are determined to reject the CTBT; plan to develop new capabilities in space; and to formulate a new capability-based strategy that is said to cope with all possible future military threats to the United States. According to the Bush administration, all these measures are intended to eliminate immoral MAD constraints, and provide the United States with more flexible options and maximum freedom of action. The international community at large, however, is greatly disturbed by this obviously unilateral, confrontational approach that builds its own security on the insecurity of others. Many critics have argued that Washington seems too intent on the utility of military superiority, as if it still lives in the Cold War world. Others offer the criticism that the United States is actually seeking absolute security, an objective which, like running after its own shadow, would never be reached for all the advantages that a superpower enjoys. On the contrary, the repercussions of the US approach to the peace and stability of the world could be disastrous. Take the international effort for arms control and disarmament, for example. One has good reasons to wonder, if Washington's approach prevails, whether all the achievements accumulated in the field over half a century will be blown away and leave the world without any consensual rules of the game. To see the differences and overlapping points between Bush's approach and the Cold War approach, see Figure 1.

Having examined Figure 1, it is fair to say that what the Bush administration is intending to do is to discard what should be retained, and to retain what should be discarded. No one questions the legitimacy of a state seeking a new strategic framework to adapt to the new situation and enhance its own security. But if one builds one's own security on the insecurity of others, and aims to ensure oneself the maximum freedom of action in the international arena without caring about the implications to others, the result will be greater instability, followed by a chain of actions and reactions. No one will feel safe, not even the United States.

Washington's actions make it urgent to draw the world's attention to the other approach to future strategic stability that the majority of the international community embraces. This approach is built on a new security concept,[9] which is characterized by:

- *Co-operation and not confrontation.* Despite many tensions and disputes in the present world, common or parallel interests still outweigh differences and conflicts among various countries. Moreover, solutions

FIGURE 1
COMPARISON BETWEEN THE COLD WAR AND BUSH ADMINISTRATION
APPROACHES TO STRATEGIC STABILITY

	Bush Administration Approach	Cold War Approach

Where they overlap	• Confrontational approach
	  • Focusing on military superiority
	  • Rigid ideological biases
	  • Stressing the role of nuclear weapons	

Where they differ	• Curbing nuclear war by acquiring both offensive and defensive capabilities	• Curbing nuclear war by striking a balance based on preserving mutual vulnerability between the two superpowers
	• Counter proliferation chiefly by using force, even unilaterally	• Nonproliferation chiefly through arms control and international cooperation
	• Strong aversion to arms control and disarmament, including legally binding treaties	• Using arms control regimes as important instruments for strategic stability
	• Building military capability in space	• Preventing an arms race in space
	• Refusing to accept constraints in order to maintain maximum freedom of action	• Both parties willing to accept certain constraints in their military actions

to many new security threats demand greater international co-operation or collaboration. The current anti-terrorist war has amply proved once again that no country can single-handedly handle them. Likewise, the future peace and stability of the world can only be achieved through broad international co-operation on the basis of equality and mutual respect.

- *The necessity of keeping nuclear stability.* No one has particular partiality for the value of MAD. It should disappear at the earliest possible date. But to be realistic, the American recipe of developing the BMD system may most probably not be useful, given Russia's determination to keep its powerful nuclear deterrent. In the short or medium term, therefore, to preserve the ABM treaty and allow the MAD situation to continue may be the second-best solution in the best interests of the international community, including the interests of the United States. In the long run, the only meaningful approach to getting rid of MAD is nuclear disarmament. That is, the United States and Russia should take the lead in genuine, irreversible and verifiable deep cuts in their nuclear arsenals so as to create favourable conditions for all nuclear weapon states to reduce nuclear weapons together until the realization of their complete prohibition and thorough destruction.

- *Stability in a larger context.* The new situation in the post-Cold War era evidently calls for a new stability beyond a mere military balance between major powers. Looking into the future, issues that will most threaten the security of the world may most probably be those issues of a political, economic and even cultural nature. In particular, the increasing discrepancy between rich and poor and North and South owing to uneven economic development has already become the prime cause of both global and regional disturbances and conflicts. Solution of the issue may well be the key to future strategic stability in the world. Of course, all of these problems cannot be expected to be solved solely by military means.
- *Joint participation.* The trend of multipolarity also demands increased interaction between and among all members of the international community in order to establish strategic stability, in which everyone has an adequate sense of security. This is particularly essential in the solution of regional conflicts to avoid manipulation by one major power or power group. In this regard, the role of the United Nations will perhaps continue to be irreplaceable. For the differences and overlapping points between the multilateral and co-operative approach and the Cold War approach, see Figure 2.

Practical Issues to be Solved

Opponents argue that the multilateral and co-operative approach to future strategic stability is perhaps too idealistic to realize. True, no one expects this will happen tomorrow. But as multipolar trends and globalization develop in depth, and the globe becomes smaller and smaller, with nations increasingly sharing interests and facing common threats, the world will have no alternative to a multilateral and co-operative approach to sustaining strategic stability in the future. The key lies in the change of the security concept, and the acceptance of the future world as a convergent one, in which everyone has an equal share of security and responsibility. Otherwise, our fear will become a self-fulfilling prophecy. In order to contribute to the effort for future strategic stability, three issues need particularly to be handled in the security and military field in the current situation:

FIGURE 2
COMPARISON BETWEEN MULTILATERAL CO-OPERATIVE APPROACH AND THE COLD WAR APPROACH TO STRATEGIC STABILITY

	The Multilateral Co-operative Approach	The Cold War Approach
Where they differ	• Co-operative approach • Stressing strategic stability beyond military balance • Stressing common interests based on increasing interdependence and facing common threats • Stressing reducing dependence on nuclear weapons through nuclear disarmament	• Confrontational approach • Focusing on military superiority • Rigid ideological biases • Stressing the role of nuclear weapons, but curbing the nuclear war by preserving the balance between the two superpowers
Where they overlap	• Preservation of ABM treaty • Opposition to BMD • Prevention of an arms race in space • Non-proliferation through arms control efforts and international co-operation • Using arms control regimes as instrumental to strategic stability • All parts willing to accept certain constraints in their military actions	

- *Further improvement of major power relations.* At present, all the major powers enjoy working relations among themselves. But to further enhance confidence in each other, all these powers should each make their strategic objectives more transparent; respect the core interests of other countries; and solve their differences through consultation and mutual compromise. All these are of vital importance to a propitious strategic framework, in which peace and stability are embedded.
- *Restoring confidence in nuclear stability among nuclear weapon states.* That confidence is now being seriously eroded by the United States' resolve to withdraw from the ABM Treaty, and to accelerate the

development and deployment of a seemingly open-ended missile defense system. In the near future, the implications of the American actions are more political and psychological rather than military since no one is sure of the size, nature and the timeframe of the intended system. But once Pandora's box is opened, the situation can become very unpredictable and negatively affect the threat perceptions of the other nuclear weapons states. To restore confidence in future nuclear stability, some amending measures on the part of the United States seem necessary. The United States has now a special obligation to demonstrate to the other nuclear weapons states by deeds rather than by words that the system is truly defensive, and is not intended to change the existing world nuclear structure by its deployment. It will be also helpful if Washington expresses its willingness to join international efforts for progress in arms control and disarmament.

- *Sustaining the world coalition against terrorism.* The United-States-led world campaign of counter-terrorism in Afghanistan has already become a showcase of the value of international co-operation for the common good of the international community. While operations in the country proved very successful thanks to the solidarity of almost all the countries behind Washington, the coalition could be fragile if mishandled. In this connection, all the major powers have a special responsibility to refrain from gaining unilateral advantage under the pretext of counter-terrorist actions. That will almost surely lead to the break-up of the coalition, creating a very negative impact on world strategic stability in the future.

China's Position on Strategic Stability

As the largest developing country in the world, China consistently values the importance of keeping a peaceful and stable international environment so that it is able to concentrate on domestic development. Global strategic stability is therefore one of the most significant conditions for that environment. Naturally China has always been positive in supporting strategic stability through international co-operation. Equally important, as a regional power limited in terms of strength and influence, China has never been in a position to play a prime role in the development of the international situation. China's position has always been defensive and reactive to what is happening rather than one of initiating provocative challenges to others. This constraint explains the seeming contrast of Beijing's strong concerns for preserving strategic stability with its limited action role.

That does not say that China is not an important country for establishing and preserving world strategic stability. During the Cold War years, although

Beijing was a junior player in the nuclear game, its self-restraint in nuclear policy still contributed towards preserving the nuclear balance between the United States and the Soviet Union. The increasingly active involvement of China in arms control negotiations and strengthening nonproliferation was also conducive to the solidarity of the international effort for peace and disarmament, thereby exercising great constraint on the two superpowers in their actions.

In the post-Cold War era, one can expect that China will play an increasingly important role in promoting strategic stability with its rapid economic development and further integration into the international community. But China's attitude towards the changing world is both active and pragmatic. Acknowledging the fast-changing nature of the world situation, Beijing calls for the re-establishment of strategic stability through increasing co-operation based on a new security concept. China is therefore a strong supporter of the multilateral and co-operative approach to reestablishing strategic stability. At the same time, China holds that while one needs to change the Cold War mentality in the process, one perhaps also needs to retain those arrangements from the Cold War years that will still play significant roles in maintaining peace and stability in the future. The ABM Treaty is a case in point. The strong opposition by China to the abrogation of the treaty is not only because China has benefited from it since the nuclear balance between the two nuclear superpowers gave much room for the effectiveness of Beijing's small nuclear force. It is also because the treaty provides a basis for nuclear stability in the world. Preserving the ABM Treaty today is necessary to create the conditions needed to get rid of it in the future.

This does not suggest that China favours the MAD situation permanently. As a matter of fact, China has never endorsed the concept of deterrence – the conceptual basis for the MAD situation. In China's view, deterrence implies a certain legitimacy of nuclear weapons, thereby running contrary to the objective of nuclear disarmament that China has consistently sought. Deterrence also generates fears of being overtaken by other side(s), and the breaking of the balance. It is the source of the endless nuclear arms race. China, therefore, seeks to change the irrational situation exactly through first casting away the concept of deterrence and the utility of nuclear weapons.

How to do it? In China's view, it is certainly the responsibility of all the nuclear weapons states. Given the existence of the huge nuclear arsenals in the world, China calls for, as a first step, reducing the role of nuclear weapons solely to retaliation for a nuclear attack (that is, each nuclear weapons state should undertake not to be the first to use nuclear weapons). On the basis of this commitment, each of these nuclear weapons states should then honestly undertake its obligation of nuclear disarmament until the complete prohibition and thorough destruction of all nuclear weapons is achieved. When there are no nuclear weapons, there will be no MAD, nor the necessity for the ABM Treaty.

NOTES

The views in the paper are entirely the authors' own and do not necessarily represent those of the National Defense University or any other organization.

1. According to the estimate of the Institute for Strategic Studies in London, the United States deployed 294 ICBMs, 155 SLBMs, and 600 strategic bombers; the Soviet Union deployed 75 ICBMs, 75 SLBMs and 190 strategic bombers. See Wang Zhongchun and Wen Zhonghua, *The Undissipated Nuclear Clouds* [in Chinese] (Beijing: NDU, 2000), p.75.
2. Tang Jiaxua, at the opening ceremony of the International Conference on a Disarmament Agenda for the 21st Century, sponsored by the United Nations and the People's Republic of China, Beijing, 2 April 2002.
3. Camille Grand, *Ballistic Missile Threats, Missile Defenses, Deterrence, and Strategic Stability*, Occasional Paper No.5, (Monterey, CA and Southampton: Monterey Institute of International Studies and Mountbatten Centre for International Studies, March 2001), p.6.
4. According to one estimate, the United States had deployed 9,376 operational nuclear warheads and 5,000 non-operational nuclear warheads; Russia deployed 9,196 operational nuclear warheads and 13,500 non-operational nuclear warheads by January 2001. See Hans M. Kristensen, 'The Unruly Hedge: Cold War Thinking at the Crawford Summit,' *Arms Control Today* (Dec. 2001), pp.8–12.
5. For detailed description of these armed conflicts, see *SIPRI Yearbooks* in the 1990s.
6. See Charles E. Morrison, 'Globalization, Vulnerability and Adjustment', *PacNet Newsletter*, No.32 (11 August 2000). Morrison pointed out that 'it is widely argued that globalization increases economic disparities between those better able to take advantage of globalizing forces and those unprepared for it. The relative income gaps between and within countries are widening. The income ratio of the richest fifth of the world's population and its poorest fifth have increased from 30 to 1 in 1960, to 60 to 1 in 1990, and 74 to 1 by 1997.'
7. See Zhu Yangming *Asia-Pacific Security Strategy* (Beijing: The Military Science Publishing House, 2000), pp.181–2.
8. See Paul Stares *'New' Or 'Non-Traditional' Challenges*, paper presented at a conference on The United Nations and Global Governance in the New Millennium, Tokyo, 19–21 January 2000, available at ⟨http://www.unu.edu/millennium/stares.pdf⟩. Stares said that 'the range of conceivable security concerns broaden dramatically–some would argue limitlessly–to include a host of economic, social, political, environmental, and epidemiological problems. Whether they emanate from outside or inside the boundaries of the state is immaterial to their consideration as security threats. Likewise, whether they are the product of the deliberate or inadvertent acts is irrelevant. The harmful impact on the individual or the surrounding ecosystem is what matters. What makes problem "new" or "non-traditional" threats, therefore, is not that they are truly phenomena or products but rather that they are now treated as security concerns.'
9. For more information on China's security concept, see the Ministry of Foreign Affairs, *New Concept of Security Advocated by China*, ⟨http://www.fmprc.gov.cn/eng/5053.html⟩, April 2002.

France, the United Kingdom and Deterrence in the Twenty-first Century

JOHN SIMPSON

The current strategic era can be regarded as having both continuities and discontinuities with the past. This is particularly the case with regard to the nuclear and other deterrence policies of the two European nuclear-weapon states, France and the United Kingdom. As a consequence, the analysis that follows will use as its starting point the late-twentieth century perspectives of these states on their deterrent forces and concepts.

Before looking at the elements of continuity and discontinuity in the policies of both states, it is necessary to highlight the analytical and policy distinction between the existence of a nuclear *capability* and the existence of a nuclear *deterrent relationship*. On the one hand, the existence of a proven or believed capability to make nuclear weapons, most credibly by having conducted a test of a nuclear device, is a necessary element in a nuclear deterrent relationship.[1] On the other, a state could credibly claim to have a nuclear-weapon capability, but not have any overt doctrine for its use as a nuclear deterrent, whatever the perspectives of other states on this matter.

As a consequence, this analysis will address two distinct issues. One is the motivations that led both states to acquire and sustain a nuclear-weapon capability. The second is to examine the generic situations that would cause their current nuclear and other capabilities to be used in a deterrent mode, either as a general threat to influence the behaviour of a target state or as an overt or implicit military threat to destroy specific targets.

Motivations for French and UK Acquisition and Possession of Nuclear Weapons

Until 1991, consensus existed between France and the United Kingdom that their major security threat came from the nuclear weapons and other military capabilities of the former USSR and the Warsaw Pact. France and the United Kingdom differed, however, on the role to be played by the US in confronting that threat, and how much reliance each should place upon both the US extended deterrent capabilities and NATO in assuring their respective security.

Initial rationalizations of the French deterrent capabilities by President de Gaulle in the early 1960s had focused on the argument that no US President would order an attack on Moscow in response to the destruction of Paris, because of the risks this would pose to US cities. This led the President to discard US offers of extended deterrence guarantees against an attack from the Warsaw Pact as having no foundation. Only the possession by France of a capability to inflict unacceptable damage upon the former USSR was seen to deter it from attacking French targets in a nuclear war. At the same time, a refusal to subordinate French forces to a US Supreme Allied Commander Europe (SACEUR) led the President to withdraw France from participation in the evolving North Atlantic Treaty Organization (NATO), the North Atlantic Treaty's permanent military arm. This was to pre-plan the responses of its members to potential Warsaw Pact attacks, using national forces committed to NATO. This French decision also led to the withdrawal of US forces from French soil.[2]

This argument against the credibility of extended deterrence remained the main underpinning of the French strategic deterrent force through to 1991. However, responding, among other things, to memories of the ground invasions and occupations France had suffered in the past, both a pre-strategic and a strategic force were seen to be required. It was envisaged that the pre-strategic forces would be used in both a deterrent and war-fighting role. As a deterrent, they would serve as a 'warning-shot' to demonstrate French willingness to use strategic nuclear weapons if its territory should be invaded. As a defence capability, their use would be to attack any Warsaw Pact invasion force moving through German territory on its way to the French border.

Britain tested its first nuclear device in 1952, a decade earlier than France, and had been an active participant in the wartime US Manhattan project. This co-operative relationship had been terminated in 1946 as a consequence of decisions by both the US executive and legislature, leaving the United Kingdom no choice but to move ahead alone with an independent programme. At this stage at least two roles were seen for a UK nuclear-weapon capability: defence of Western Europe, including the UK homeland; and Imperial and Commonwealth defence.

The United Kingdom saw United States participation and leadership in the defence of Western Europe as essential, and had from the late 1940s regarded this as something that could only be assured through permanent institutional arrangements. It also regarded US nuclear capabilities as an essential deterrent to a Russian attack on Western European targets, and to a Warsaw Pact invasion. In pursuit of this goal, it had agreed by the end of the 1940s to allow US aircraft capable of delivering nuclear weapons to be based in England. This, however, raised the issue of the United Kingdom's ability to participate in decisions to use these weapons.

In 1958, just as the French nuclear-weapon programme started to gather momentum, the United States agreed to reinstate UK-US co-operation over nuclear weapon design and allow trade with the United Kingdom in nuclear-weapon materials. In addition, the initial deployment of UK nuclear weapons and the medium-bombers to carry them contributed to the United Kingdom being able to participate in US strategic nuclear-planning activities, including co-operation over targeting in the event of war.

At the same time, the United Kingdom was anxious to retain a national nuclear capability under its own independent control. One motivation for this was that the United States was not prepared to discuss co-ordination of nuclear targeting outside Europe. Another was to be able to influence US decisions on the use of nuclear weapons, especially those based in the United Kingdom. A third was to enhance deterrence of a USSR attack on UK soil by offering an additional independent threat of strategic retaliation against the USSR.

This posture contained an element of 'catalytic' deterrence, given that any attack by the United Kingdom on the former USSR was likely to be indistinguishable by it from an attack by US forces based in the United Kingdom, and thus result in a USSR attack on the United States. However, it was not until the 1980s that official UK defence documents argued this 'catalytic' concept openly through a 'second centre of decision' doctrine. This doctrine asserted that the ability of the United Kingdom to respond independently to an attack on Western Europe would reduce any USSR doubts about the willingness of the United States to respond with nuclear weapons to such an attack.

In parallel with these developments, the United Kingdom moved to accept US weapons for use on its own delivery systems in the event of a Warsaw Pact attack, in common with other NATO members, as well as committing these nuclear-capable forces to SACEUR's command. The United Kingdom also accepted the evolving NATO strategies of graduated deterrence and escalation dominance to deter an invasion of Western Europe. Its strategic nuclear policy was also linked to this role after 1962, when it agreed to commit to SACEUR the four nuclear missile submarines it was to construct. This was one of the conditions for the sale to the United Kingdom by the United States of their Polaris missiles. However, the United Kingdom retained a residual capability for independent national use. This 'Europeanization' of the UK nuclear force was taken a stage further in the later 1960s with the creation of the NATO Nuclear Planning Group (NPG), which pre-planned the use of alliance nuclear weapons in any conflict with the Warsaw Pact.

The Impact of the End of the Cold War on the French and UK Deterrent Forces and Doctrines

By the end of 1991, although a residual concern for the future of the large nuclear forces possessed by the successor states of the USSR remained, the threat of a land invasion from the east had largely dissipated. With this went the need for anything other than a token US nuclear presence in NATO Europe to provide an extended nuclear security guarantee. This led to major reductions in UK national and NATO nuclear capabilities; considerable concern and confusion in France as to the future role of its nuclear forces; and the initiation of a formal dialogue or commission in 1992 on nuclear policy and doctrine between the two states. The dialogue, made permanent in 1995, generated a new and more intimate relationship between them on such matters, centred around a recognition of similarities and common points of interest in doctrine and a recognition that the vital interests of one state were also likely to be those of the other.[3]

France and the United Kingdom emerged from the 1990s with both strategic and sub-strategic nuclear forces, albeit in reduced numbers. Missile submarines were to continue to provide France's strategic nuclear capabilities, while the pre-strategic role was to be played by aircraft-delivered gravity bombs. The United Kingdom, by contrast, decided to rely on only one deterrent system, the Trident missile, which by the late 1990s was to have both a pre-strategic and strategic role. One consequence was that the two systems deployed by France appeared to offer greater flexibility than those of the United Kingdom. Its pre-strategic systems could be used as political instruments by visibly moving them close to the state mounting a threat, whereas the UK force would remain hidden under the sea at all times. However, at the same time, both emphasized that they would not use their nuclear weapons in battle, and sought to substitute precision-guided conventional weapons for the nuclear ones earmarked for this role in the Cold War period.[4]

As it reduced the numbers and variety of its nuclear-weapon systems, the United Kingdom also moved away from preparations and expectations of fighting a main-force armoured battle in central Europe and towards a focus on peacekeeping operations on the NATO periphery and elsewhere. France did the same, and specifically declared that 'nuclear dissuasion no longer occupies the same position as it did during the cold war ... it is no longer possible to make the entire military system dependent on it, and place must be made for the strategy of action which is based on conventional forces'.[5] It also became less overtly hostile to co-operation with NATO, while the United Kingdom appeared more open to French ideas of a distinct European defence capability, albeit within NATO. Both states retained a strategic targeting policy that by default focused on Russian cities, though this was formally eliminated in May 2000 when all the nuclear weapon states agreed not to target each other in a joint statement made to the 2000 NPT Review and Extension Conference.[6]

These events left both France and the United Kingdom with non-specific nuclear-weapon and deterrent doctrines.[7] For different reasons, both rejected any 'no first use' posture.[8] Their nuclear weapons appeared to have become a strategic insurance against an uncertain future through their ability to act as an ultimate deterrent against military attack, invasion or defeat, but also much less central to their security policies than before. For example, the July 2002 statement by the United Kingdom on the current tasks and roles of its armed forces argued that its nuclear weapons had a 'continuing use as a means of deterring major strategic military threats' and 'in guaranteeing the ultimate security of the UK'.[9] However, the statement also recognized that this role was much more limited than in the pre-1991 period, and some of its targets were also radically different by making it 'clear, particularly to the leaders of states of concern and terrorist organizations, that all our forces play a part in deterrence, and that we have a broad range of responses available'.[10] In addition, 'Where necessary, military and other action will be taken to disrupt the political, economic, military and technical means by which aggression is pursued' including 'the possibility of action in the face of an imminent attack'.[11]

This made clear that the United Kingdom now saw deterrence in the first decade of the twenty-first century as residing in its possession of 'a wide and flexible range of military options, including conventional weapons with a capacity for precision and penetration so as to minimize incidental damage'.[12] In addition, the 'only certainty we should offer is that we shall respond appropriately if we need to, using any of the wide range of options open to us'.[13] This appears to indicate a policy of graduated and proportional deterrence aimed at actions by both state and non-state actors, including the possibility of pre-emptive actions involving a wide range of military capabilities, in the core regions where UK interests are to be found, namely 'Europe, the Gulf and the Mediterranean',[14] though by 2004 these core regions were migrating south in Africa. At the same time, the UK MoD was describing the role of the UK nuclear force in rather less positive terms: 'the continuing risk from the proliferation of nuclear weapons, and the certainty that a number of other countries will retain substantial nuclear arsenals, mean that our minimum nuclear deterrent capability ... is likely to remain a necessary element of our security.' In addition, it noted that 'Decisions on whether to replace Trident ... are likely to be required in the next (Parliament). We will therefore ... ensure that the range of options for maintaining a nuclear deterrent capability is kept open until that decision point.'[15]

France and the United Kingdom have thus moved towards a similar focus for their nuclear deterrent activities, though the former remains outside the NATO NPG arrangements and the other within them. France also differs from the UK in having a more detailed and overt deterrence policy than the UK in at least three areas. The first is that it is concerned with deterring long-range threats to its interests, especially in Asia and specifically involving China. The UK by contrast has attempted to limit its geographical scope to the European periphery.[16] Second, French spokespersons have stated that faced with a threat from a regional power, France would target 'in priority its political, economic and military centres of power'. This formulation would appear to be an attempt to threaten directly 'dictators for whom human life does not count and who would be ready to sacrifice their countries'.[17] Third, France adheres to the idea of an *ultime avertissement* or 'final warning'. This would involve a single, limited strike on a military target as a prelude to a massive strike. President Chirac described this in June 2001 as 'the capability to signal ... to a potential enemy, both that our vital interests are at stake and that we are determined to safeguard them'.[18]

Future Security Threats and the Relevance of Deterrent Capabilities

In this new strategic context, where security concerns are much broader in their nature than those pre-1991, and where nuclear deterrent forces are non-specific in their overt targeting, the future roles of the French and UK nuclear and non-nuclear deterrent forces appear increasingly problematic. To try to investigate these roles, it may be useful to examine the nature of the security threats both states may need to address in future; the relevance of specific capabilities in deterring those threats; and the type of alliance context they will operate within.

At least four scenarios offer a means of analysing potential security threats to France and the UK:

- invasion of, and attacks on, the French/UK homeland;
- invasion of, and attacks on, EU/NATO European states other than France/UK;
- destruction/neutralization of EU/NATO/UN intervention forces by WMD within or outside the two state's 'Core Areas'; and
- acquisition of WMD and their means of delivery by potentially hostile states.

Invasion of, and Attacks on, the French/UK Homeland

Following their wartime experiences and their assessments of Warsaw Pact military capabilities in the years that followed, threats of military invasion and mass-destruction underpinned both French and United Kingdom thinking about security and deterrence. In the current Western European strategic and security context, however, such threats are no longer credible in the immediate future. Indeed, thanks to the collapse of the Warsaw Pact and the disintegration of the USSR, plus the existence of NATO and the European Union, the states of Western Europe now enjoy greater inter-state security than at any time in the last century.

The French and UK security frontier is now far to the east of the inner-German border that delineated it until 1990. Their security concerns are increasingly focused on terrorist acts whose source is to be found in regional conflicts outside the EU or claims for regional autonomy within it. Moreover, although France may regard some states on the southern shores of the Mediterranean as potential invasion threats, they are not likely to be so for decades to come.[19] Given the more favourable geographical position of the United Kingdom, such concerns have been almost entirely removed from the agenda, unless both the EU and NATO were to collapse, something that under current circumstances appears almost inconceivable. It thus seems that invasion is no longer a realistic concern to either state. This appears to remove any short- and medium-term need for an ultimate weapon to deter this threat.

As a consequence, French and UK security concerns have now started to move towards threats originating in other geographical areas and of a different nature. In that context, the view of the French and UK governments appears to be that their nuclear forces are sufficient to deter attacks upon their homelands with WMD. In this they appear to differ from the United States, which is committed to deploying a homeland defence against a limited attack on its cities by missiles armed with WMD, and thus by implication has less confidence in the effectiveness of nuclear deterrence in these circumstances. Although the two states' views may change if credible and affordable technology becomes available for a national defence system, demands to acquire non-strategic missile defence capabilities to support expeditionary forces, and enhanced logistical and other capabilities to support such forces, currently take precedence over national missile defences.[20]

Events on 11 September 2001 and their own recent experiences have inevitably raised concerns about the potential terrorist threats against both states from WMD. However, the idea of deterring such attacks by threatening a nuclear response appears totally inapplicable. Instead, the requirement is, as Bowen indicates above, for good intelligence, timely measures to interdict such devices en-route to their targets and a proven ability to track them back to their source. Again, differences between the two states and the United States appear to exist over this, although both have to confront the implications that their intelligence on Iraq's WMD in the 2002–3 period was inadequate and as a consequence inaccurate. Similarly, France and the United Kingdom appear to regard the disruption of electronic communications, commerce and military command and control networks by computer viruses and other such methods as actions that would need to be dealt with by defensive measures and direct action against the perpetrators. Finally, the international criminalization of such non-state activities may be a more effective type of deterrent for France and the United Kingdom than threats

134   DETERRENCE AND THE NEW GLOBAL SECURITY ENVIRONMENT

of military responses: again, however, US and European views on this may differ significantly.

Invasion of, or Attacks on, EU/NATO European States Other than France/UK

In the Cold War context, neither France nor the UK was prepared to make 'no first use' pledges concerning their nuclear weapons. In addition, neither was prepared to give unconditional negative nuclear security assurances to any non-nuclear weapon aggressor state associated with a nuclear-weapon state.[21] This position has not changed since 1991. Thus any invasion or threat of attack against a member of the North Atlantic Treaty, and in all probability against an EU state that was not a member, would potentially result in a French and UK deterrent commitment to use all their forces, including their nuclear ones, in its defence.

The extent of such a commitment would, of course, depend on which states will become members of NATO, or any EU defence arrangement, in the future. In the latter case, any new EU constitution could play a significant role. It would also be affected by the arrangements that existed at the time of any invasion or attack for consultations over nuclear weapon use. In that context, the positions of France and the United Kingdom differ appreciably in current circumstances.

As discussed above, the United Kingdom is a member of the NATO NPG and its nuclear weapons are committed to SACEUR. Its threat of the use of nuclear weapons would be subject to multilateral consultations with the state or states under threat and with other NATO members. France, by contrast, is still not a member of the NPG, and in the past has placed low value on extended deterrence commitments, though in January 1995 Alain Juppé, the then Minister for Foreign Affairs did suggest that 'After developing a joint doctrine between France and the United Kingdom, should our generation fear the prospect, not of a shared deterrent, but at least discussing the issue of *dissuasion* with our main partners?'.[22] Moreover, unlike the United Kingdom, it does have an ability to demonstrate visibly its intent to use its nuclear weapons by, for example, moving some of its nuclear-capable aircraft to bases in the states concerned if, as currently appears unlikely, it was prepared to offer nuclear security guarantees to others.

The existence of such commitments and capabilities does beg several questions about what current and enlarged NATO, and possibly EU, membership might mean for both the French and UK deterrent forces. Setting aside the possibility of conflict arising between NATO and Russia over former Warsaw Pact members, the Baltic States and Ukraine, there is also the front-line position of Turkey in respect of Middle-Eastern conflicts. To this may be added Cyprus, an EU Middle-Eastern frontier state. Thus, the willingness of France and Britain to make extended deterrent commitments to their eastern or southern European neighbours, through both their nuclear and advanced conventional military capabilities, may become an increasingly important consideration when discussing the roles and future existence of their deterrent forces – and their own need to sustain them for national defence purposes.

More controversial and difficult to assess, however, will be their position in this respect if the EU develops further the defence and security aspects of its activities, as well as its political and economic roles. Here, one can see at least four major questions arising. The EU, unlike NATO, includes several states that remained overtly neutral during the Cold War, such as Austria, Ireland and Sweden. They were, and are, leading advocates of global nuclear disarmament. Under current circumstances, it is difficult to see how the member states could take a common position over an EU policy of extended nuclear deterrence unless these former neutrals were to change radically their positions on nuclear disarmament and weapons.

Second, the EU would need to acquire a decision-making structure comparable to, if not going beyond, NATO's NPG for such a commitment to be seen as credible. Third, a decision would have to be taken on the technical nature of the force that would back-up such a commitment (e.g. using aircraft, land-, sea- or air based ballistic or cruise missiles as delivery means), and the financing and deployment of the necessary supporting infrastructure, such as reconnaissance satellites. Finally, the force itself could be either an EU one, or just involve operational co-operation or 'concertation' between France and the UK, which would remain the owners and operators of the force.

At the time the NPT text was negotiated, it was understood that the EU could become a nuclear-weapon state if it became a state-like entity and was regarded as a successor state to France or the United Kingdom. However, as has been discussed above, the technological origins of the two national capabilities are radically different, making integration in procurement difficult. The French capability is an independently developed and manufactured one: the UK one is closely linked with the United States and committed to NATO, and thus would probably require US agreement for it to be used as part of any European force.

Much will therefore depend on United States attitudes towards France and the United Kingdom, in the latter case both while the current Trident system remains in service and at the point when a decision would need to be taken on the procurement of a new UK delivery system. The timing of this procurement decision could be at any point between 2006 and 2025, depending on a range of technical and political considerations. The key variables in this situation may be whether the United States has chosen to withdraw its forces and/or its extended deterrence guarantees from Europe, and whether France and the United Kingdom can unite with other EU states to replace them with a new European-led security system. However, if it was advanced conventional forces that were needed to deter such actions, and they were regarded as usable in a pre-emptive role, this may be a capability that could be procured and deployed on a European basis without the need for US agreement.

The type of force that this would imply would be one using either air- or sea-launched conventionally armed cruise missiles. Such a force is now being deployed by the United States in a new form, using conventionally armed, vertical-launch cruise missiles carried by four *Ohio* class former ballistic-missile submarines. In theory there would be no reason why similar vessels could not be deployed by France and the United Kingdom for deterrent purposes, either in the form of submarines equipped with conventionally armed systems only or as a mix of conventional cruise missiles and nuclear ballistic-missile ones.[23] However, the United Kingdom may be more prepared than France to use conventionally armed missiles in a pre-emptive role, especially if it was operating in concert with the United States.

It is thus concerns over events on the eastern and southern peripheries of Europe that may provide an additional and more immediate justification for the ultimate deterrence role of the French and UK nuclear forces over the next two decades. For the degree to which deterrence of invasion and attack in these areas can be effectively and credibly offered by advanced conventional capabilities, rather than nuclear ones, is at best problematic. Under such circumstances, one compromise would be to convert some or all existing delivery platforms to a conventionally armed role, and place their current nuclear ordnance in storage. This could sustain perceptions of its latent nuclear deterrence capability through the virtual or recessed deterrent threat inherent in such an arrangement, as well as offer an immediately usable conventional capability.

Destruction/Neutralization with WMD of EU/NATO/UN Intervention Forces

Both France and the UK have been major contributors to international peacekeeping and peace enforcement activities over the last decade, and also were involved in both the Gulf War in 1991 and the 'war on terror' in Afghanistan in 2001. They now regard such activities as the core active roles their military forces are likely to perform in the near future, rather than as pre-1991 engaging in tank-battles and theatre WMD warfare in Europe. However, such activities bring with them basing requirements, long logistic chains and a need for extensive maritime and air support facilities. The threat to such forces in the field from attacks with WMD is one that has to be assessed and safeguarded against, especially if such intervention involves a state with extensive military capabilities. Indeed, plans are already moving forward to field a NATO Theatre Ballistic-Missile Defence (TMD) capability to combat such possibilities. What is less clear is the degree to which deterrence through the threat of retaliation, as against defence, may be seen to be credible in such circumstances.

Some of the scenarios likely to be encountered can be predicted fairly confidently by reference to the Gulf Wars of 1991 and 2003. Attacks with conventionally armed ballistic missiles require both defences and, if possible, destruction of the missiles before they are fired. This appears to require real-time intelligence, and conventionally armed rapid response capabilities. Chemical attacks may require passive defences, and interdiction and destruction of delivery systems. Uncertainty will always exist over whether such use would justify nuclear retaliation, though it is arguable that this was an effective deterrent against the use of chemical and biological weapons by Iraq in 1991 (and contributed to the instructions in 2003 to ensure that all its stocks had been eliminated).

In the case of biological weapon attack the potency of such an attack to neutralize an expeditionary force, as well as cause major casualties among the host populations, might well be seen in some quarters to justify the issuing of overt nuclear deterrent threats, despite the constraints imposed by the existence of negative security assurances. Whether such retaliatory threats would be effective in preventing the use of biological weapons, as the UK decision in the late 1950s to close down its offensive biological weapon programmes appeared to imply, seems likely to remain a subject of continuing debate. But the very existence of such threats to French and UK expeditionary forces, as well as the more remote possibilities of radiological and nuclear attack, is likely to be seen as one justification for their continued deployment of nuclear deterrent forces. In the UK case, this is illustrated by statements made by Mr Hoon, the Minister of Defence, in March and April 2002, prior to hostilities with Iraq in 2003, on the plausibility of a British nuclear response to a CBW attack on UK deployed forces.

Acquisition of WMD and their Means of Delivery by Potentially Hostile States

In the post-Cold War context, the main security threats to Western states have been seen to arise from the proliferation of state WMD capabilities, as well as those that might be acquired by terrorist organizations. Although the global WMD non-proliferation regimes have remained a major instrument in controlling proliferation, they have not in themselves been able to prevent it, as became clear in the case of Iraq in 1991. The regimes have thus been seen as an increasingly ineffective obstacle to proliferation by a small number of 'states of concern'. As a consequence, other means of deterrence and dissuasion, including the pre-emptive use of military force, have acquired increasing significance as non-proliferation strategies.

By 2002, this threat of pre-emption had been implicitly extended beyond Iraq to Iran and the DPRK through President Bush's 'Axis of Evil' speech.

One implication is that the United States now appears to be implementing a policy of deterring WMD proliferators, or more accurately the ones regarded as hostile to the United States, by the threat of pre-emptive military action and, in cases such as Iraq, forcible change in the governing regime. While France and the United Kingdom are both opposed to further WMD proliferation, their views have differed on how to handle Iraq. France has taken an independent position on such matters while, as in the past, the United Kingdom has tended to act in concert with the United States. It has also acquired US-built, conventionally armed cruise missiles, used its air force in 1998 against suspected Iraqi WMD capabilities and in 2003 participated in an invasion of Iraq nominally triggered by the WMD stocks and capabilities that it was believed to possess.

This situation seems likely to generate two uncertainties for French and UK deterrence policies. One is that it could lead to acute differences of opinion with European partners over any pre-emptive military action taken by the United States against suspected proliferators as occurred in the UN Security Council and elsewhere over Iraq in 2003. How further action of this type would affect the positions of France and the United Kingdom within the EU is far from clear, as is the effect of such actions upon some of their NATO partners. The second is that it could generate a need for an independent UK deterrent capability to deter attacks on the UK homeland and its overseas bases in the event of joint US–UK actions against such proliferating states. Alternatively, it could seek US extended deterrent or defence guarantees.

This situation would be exacerbated further if the United States engaged in two types of possible anti-proliferation activities. One would be to take military action against states that several European states and Russia did not regard as overt proliferators, such as Iran. The second would be if it used nuclear weapons against sites where chemical and/or biological agents were stored, on the basis that such weapons alone could guarantee the total destruction of these agents.

It appears unlikely in either of these cases that France would go along with the United States and actively support its actions. The United Kingdom, however, would find itself in a much more delicate and difficult position. To support actively the United States might isolate it further from its European partners, but not to do so could mark the end of 60 years of continuous UK international deterrent policies based on standing alongside the United States in order to benefit from its military strength and, at the same time, to be in a position to influence its actions. It might also threaten the end of the US–UK nuclear and intelligence relationships. How the UK government of the time would handle such a choice, one that it would undoubtedly do its best to avoid, is difficult to predict. However, the way the UK government handled the Iran situation in 2003–6 suggests that it could act in concert with its key allies, France and Germany, while yet sustaining its close relationship with the United States.

France, the United Kingdom and Deterrence in the Twenty-first Century: Some Tentative Conclusions

This analysis has sought to indicate the continuities and changes in both French and UK deterrence policies that are becoming apparent in the first decade of the twenty-first century. It has described how their motives for possessing nuclear weapons, the procurement strategies for them and the deterrent and other arguments surrounding them have changed since 1991. In particular, it has demonstrated that two states, separated by a narrow stretch of water, had radically different views on these issues through to that point and then wrestled with a common problem: how relevant were their nuclear deterrent capabilities likely to be in the new world environment? This resulted in a move towards similar force structures, but a failure to bridge the gap between the independent position of France established by President De Gaulle four decades ago, and the US- and NATO -oriented position sustained by the United Kingdom in both procurement policy and, increasingly, in WMD anti-proliferation policies.

The implication of the remainder of the analysis is that while the nuclear capabilities of both France and the United Kingdom have been retained, the focus of their deterrence policies, insofar as it exists, has switched to new, but more generic rationales. Moreover, if one examines the military threats that it seems reasonable for France and the United Kingdom to plan against in managing the further evolution of their deterrent forces, both strategic and sub-strategic, four independent variables appear to be dominant. One is the evolution of the institutions of European political, economic and security co-operation, and particularly NATO and the EU. The second is the degree to which the states of Europe, and particularly France and the United Kingdom, will continue to play a role in intervention or peace enforcement operations outside core European territory, and in doing so generate military threats against themselves.

The third is the impact of changes in the focus of threat in the WMD area from almost exclusive concern with the use of nuclear weapons and its prevention, to other forms of WMD. This in turn seems likely to generate increasing debate on whether nuclear capabilities provide deterrence against the use of these other weapons, particularly biological agents and, perhaps more significantly, whether the theoretical ability of nuclear explosives to destroy other WMD justifies their use in this role, despite the destructive effect this will almost certainly have on the international nuclear non-proliferation regime.

Also, whether possession and pre-emptive use of advanced conventional capabilities may be a more effective deterrent against proliferators than sustaining the current type of nuclear capability designed to survive a surprise first strike of significant size.

Finally, there is the issue of the relationship between the future policies of the United States, now the world's sole military super-power, and the deterrent capabilities and policies of France and the United Kingdom. In particular, at what point may the United Kingdom have to make a choice between its enduring relationship with the United States and its evolving one with the increasingly integrated EU economic and political entity.

What emerges from a systematic analysis of future threats to the two states is that the risks of invasion or massive nuclear attack on the French and UK homelands now seem remote, and thus the arguments for a continued nuclear deterrent against these possibilities are currently weak. What is more open to debate is the need for a nuclear deterrent against a lesser attack, or against an invasion or massive WMD attack on other states of Europe, particularly those on its eastern and southern peripheries. As has been indicated earlier, however, such a capability begs many questions about which Europe, that of NATO or that of the EU, is to provide such a capability, and whether its nature would be different from that needed to provide a 'concertation' of the national deterrents of France and the United Kingdom.

What may be more central to future debates over French and UK deterrence capabilities and forces is their use to deter attacks on European forces intervening in core areas of interest to France and the United Kingdom or, particularly in the UK case, to deter retaliation against national territory if it were used by the United States to mount attacks on a third country. This latter scenario is, of course, more likely to apply to the United Kingdom than France under current circumstances, and it could be argued that the events of 11 September 2001 and early 2003 have offered the UK force an additional rationale in this context.

The future of the deterrent strategies of both France and the United Kingdom will be determined, of course, by the need to invest in the continued development and operations of the French and UK nuclear forces, in competition with the demands for new conventional weaponry which is usable in a pre-emptive manner against both state and non-state entities. A key difference between their positions, however, may arise from their differing procurement methods. The French procure their strategic nuclear submarines and missiles using a continuous building cycle, whereas the United Kingdom renews its flotilla every 25–40 years on a batch manufacturing basis. Every nuclear procurement decision is thus a major UK political event, whereas the same is not the case for a French decision to build an additional submarine.

Setting aside the Iraq 2003 case and the legitimacy and morality of embarking on pre-emptive military action, with or without UN authority, it seems probable that the allocation of scarce resources between their nuclear and non-nuclear forces is one of the major issues that French and UK military planners will have to struggle with over the next decade. One consequence may be, as was suggested above, conversion of some or all of their strategic nuclear capabilities to carry more usable conventional warheads, either in combination with their nuclear capabilities or by placing the latter in reserve. One continued difference between them is that while the UK seems content to have a military *deterrent capability*, France continues to seek a *deterrent relationship* with potentially hostile states by seeking to elucidate how its forces would be used, even if only in generic terms.

Elements of change will thus continue to run alongside the elements of continuity in the deterrent policies of both France and the United Kingdom. The core elements of continuity within these policies may now be the existence of such weapons in their arsenals, and the major political decisions and consequences that would be involved if they were to dispense with them.

The main element of change is in the role of nuclear deterrence and nuclear weapons in addressing proliferation threats. On this, US and French policies appear to differ significantly, although closer inspection suggests they may not be far apart militarily. This could include the strategic use of advanced conventional weapons along similar lines to the US 2002 Nuclear Posture Review.

Whether the United States and the United Kingdom will eventually part company over these matters is difficult to predict. If they do, the result will be both the largest discontinuity in the US–UK relationship for more than half a century and an opportunity for France and the United Kingdom to move closer together on deterrence policy, and to advance the dialogue on such issues which was started and then stalled in the first half of the 1990s. Yet if the United States and the United Kingdom remain closely linked in their policies, the effect upon the further development of the EU may be profound. Thus while French and United Kingdom nuclear deterrent policies appear to be about security, in reality they camouflage a range of much wider issues and choices that will be decisive in determining their persistence during the twenty-first century.

NOTES

1. This is the criterion found in the text of the Treaty on the Non-Proliferation of Nuclear Weapons of 1968, though it is now generally acknowledged that certain types of fission devices are technically credible without having been fully tested in this manner.

2. For a more detailed account of the evolution of French policy see Beatrice Heuser, *Nuclear Mentalities? Strategies and Beliefs in Britain, France and the FRG* (Basingstoke: Macmillan, 1998), pp.75–178.
3. Pascal Boniface, *French Nuclear Weapons Policy after the Cold War*, Occasional paper (Washington: The Atlantic Council of the United States, 1998), p.11.
4. Ibid. pp.6–7.
5. President Jacques Chirac, *Defense Nationale*, (Aug.–Sept. 1996), p.9 as quoted in Boniface, *French Nuclear Weapons Policy after the Cold War*, p.4, ref.9.
6. NPT/CONF.2000/2000/21, 1 May 2000.
7. Arguably this has always been a characteristic of French, though not UK policy. It's best known early exposition was Charles Ailleret 'Defense dirigée ou defense tous azimuts', *Defense Nationale* (Dec.1967).
8. In the UK case this was because NATO continued with the posture they had adopted when facing a perceived superior WTO conventional threat. In the French case the argument was that it was consistent with the right to national self defence recognized by Article 51 of the UN Charter: see Bruno Tertrais, 'National Policy: France Stands Alone', *Bulletin of Atomic Scientists*, July/August 2004, Vol.4, p.51. Tertrais also argues that both France and the UK subscribe to the norm of 'belligerent reprisals', which implies that any non-nuclear weapon state breaking its non-proliferation commitments automatically forfeits the protection offered by its nuclear security assurances.
9. *The Strategic Defence Review: A New Chapter*, Cm5566, Vol.1 (London: HMSO, 2002), p.12 para.21.
10. Ibid.
11. Ibid. paras 21, 22.
12. Ibid. para.23.
13. Ibid. para.22.
14. Ibid. para.26.
15. *Delivering Security in a Changing World Defence White Paper*, HMSO, London, December 2003, Cm6041-I, p.9.
16. Tertrais, op cit., p.51.
17. Ibid, p.52, quoting General Henri Bentegeat, Chief of Defence.
18. Ibid.
19. For a French assessment of the current situation see Therese Delpech, 'The Proliferation of Weapons of Mass Destruction in the Mediterranean', *RUSI Journal*, Vol.147, No.4 (August 2002), pp.46–52.
20. For a comprehensive analysis of this issue, see Ian Kenyon, Mike Rance, John Simpson and Mark Smith, *Prospects for a European Ballistic Missile Defence System*, Southampton Papers in International Policy, No.4 (Southampton: Mountbatten Centre for International Studies, 2001).
21. The most recent version of these commitments were annexed to letters sent to the Secretary-General of the United Nations by the Permanent Representatives of China (A/50/155-S/1995/265), France (A/50/154-S/1995/264), Russia (A/50/151-S/1995/261), the United Kingdom (A/50/152-S/1995/262), and the United States (A/50/153-S/1995/263) in New York on 5–6 April 1995.
22. Allain Juppé, 'Quel Horizon pour la politique étrangère de la France?', *Politique Etrangére*, (Spring 1995), p.147 as quoted in Boniface, *French Nuclear Weapons Policy after the Cold War*.
23. One reason for having easily recognisable distinctions between conventional and nuclear delivery systems, or having nuclear warheads known to be in storage, would be to prevent self-deterrence. This could arise in situations where nuclear and conventional warheads were deployed on the same delivery system, and an opponent was believed to be operating a nuclear force on the basis of 'fire on warning'. In that situation, a conventional attack could be inhibited by the fear that it would generate an automatic nuclear response.

PART IV: DETERRENCE PRACTICE – REGIONAL DYNAMICS

Positions on Deterrence in a Non-WMD Country: The Case of Germany

BERND W. KUBBIG

Germany, Its Current State of Internal Affairs and Its Security Environment

At the beginning of the twenty-first century, more than ten years after the historic fall of the wall, the unified and sovereign Federal Republic of Germany (FRG) is encircled by friendly countries, most of them stable or young democracies. The Federal Republic is embedded in a dynamically enlarging European Union, integrated in an intensely self-transforming NATO, and building comprehensive relations with the former enemy Soviet Union, now the somewhat democratizing Russia. No hostile neighbour is on the horizon. From this purely territorial perspective Germany is secure.

When security is defined in a comprehensive way, one gets a different – and more adequate-picture. Germany's economy, although basically fairly solid, is plagued by a constant combination of high unemployment and low growth rates, its territory is illegally penetrated by foreigners (at least in the view of a certain number of Germans), its ecology factually and potentially jeopardized by a variety of local, regional and global causes, its political system somewhat challenged by outspoken right-wing extremists, and its societal peace still a little bit disturbed by inequalities between the Eastern and Western parts of the unified country. After 11 September 2001, it became an unpleasant truth that undetected terrorist sleepers in various neighbourhoods were identified as a real or potential threat. Germany is country No.2 on the list of terrorist targets. Terrorism has a new and brutal foreign policy dimension, too, as the death of several German tourists in April 2002 on the Tunisian island of Djerba has shown.

All this indicates that the political landscape in which Germany is embedded has dramatically changed. To be sure, because of the unification the FRG is also in geographical terms no longer the same. It is not the enlargement as such but the changed geopolitical role that has turned the former front-line-state of the Cold War into a country that now, like many other states, is confronted with the problem of weapons of mass destruction (WMD).

Nevertheless, the FRG is characterized by the fact that it has in a legally binding way rejected all nuclear, biological and chemical WMD. This social norm of foreign-policy restraint, which was initially imposed on Germany by the winners of the Second World War, has been meanwhile internalized and accepted by the FRG as self-restraint. It has become an integral part of the political culture, which in turn constitutes the core of Germany as a model of the democratic and primarily civilian-oriented, trading state.[1] But to portray Germany as a non-WMD country is only one part of the story. For during the entire Cold War years this status was only possible because the FRG had borrowed its security from the United States, which as a traditional hegemon put Germany under its (nuclear) umbrella.

This fundamental ambivalence has led to inconsistencies and dilemmas which relate to the aspect of deterrence. They are specified in this paper in two respects. First, they regard the contradictions between the norm of self-restraint on the one hand and the presence of US nuclear tactical weapons in Europe, the first-use option and US counter-proliferation policy on the other hand. Second, they regard the decoupling issue in the current debate on ballistic missile defence (BMD).[2] It is noteworthy that deterrence[3] has not been discussed as such, but is only a by-product of the combined BMD/WMD debate. Thanks to this discourse, the central issue of decoupling comes to the surface, i.e. the FRG's long-standing dependency on US nuclear guarantees. How do the politically relevant actors in the Parliament *(Bundestag)* and the red–green government deal with the inconsistencies described above and with the decoupling issue in the light of the fact that the security peg of the Cold War no longer exists as the Soviet threat is no longer there? By attempting to give an answer to these two questions, this paper presents two specific aspects of the German situation as a non-WMD state after the end of the East–West conflict.

US Tactical Nuclear Weapons in Europe, the Nuclear First-Use Option and Counter-Proliferation: Inconsistencies with the German Norm of Self-Restraint

As part of its initial strategy of de-legitimizing nuclear weapons, the *Bündnis 90/Die Grünen*, which together with the Social Democratic Party (SPD) form the government in Berlin, succeeded in including 'the complete disarmament of all weapons of mass destruction' in the red–green coalition agreement of 1998. The Federal government has pledged to participate together with partners and allies in initiatives for implementing this objective. In spite of the fact that especially the Greens, with their long history of support of nuclear-weapon free zones in Europe, came to power in 1998, the new government did not endorse a nuclear-free Germany in reality.

While the conservative–liberal Kohl/Genscher government[4] had traditionally opposed such a political concept, the red–green coalition has established a specific policy of non-support of nuclear-weapons free zones: it dodges the issue.

All official reports on arms control and disarmament praise such zones as an important tool for supporting the non-proliferation regime.[5] At the same time, they emphasize that according to the Bush/Gorbachev initiative in 1991, NATO has reduced its sub-strategic arsenal by 85 per cent (compared to the eighties).[6] In other words, not all tactical nuclear weapons have been removed and destroyed. This is inconsistent with all official pledges for strengthening the non-proliferation regime by a consistent strategy of de-legitimizing nuclear weapons. The reasons for this inconsistency are the same as those I will now discuss with respect to the no-first-use issue.

On this closely related subject, the coalition agreement of 1998 stated that 'the new government ... will make strong efforts for the no-first-use of nuclear weapons'. Again, the clear green handwriting in the political system was a response to its committed electorate. This declared political effort of a non-nuclear country meant stirring a viper's nest. In particular, Foreign Minister Fischer tried to fundamentally change NATO's New Strategic Concept, which was under development at that time. The new government learnt that its preference for multilateralism to implement German interests worked both ways – its unilateral move basically to remove a cornerstone of NATO's strategy encountered stiff opposition from all member states (with the exception of Canada). During his visit to Washington in November 1998, where he addressed this issue, Fischer was politically and emotionally burned.

The Clinton administration let it be known that the no-first-use question was anathema, it did not want to discuss this topic, neither in bilateral talks nor in the official NATO committees. Washington was disappointed that such an attempt to undermine nuclear deterrence came from a member state of the Western alliance which had lived for decades under its nuclear umbrella. Although this idea was on the agenda of NATO's High Level Group meetings at that time, the New Strategic Concept left the first-use strategy of the Alliance virtually untouched. It states in an admittedly general way that 'nuclear weapons will continue to fulfil an essential role by ensuring uncertainty in the mind of any aggressor about the nature of the Allies' response to military aggression'.[7] Moreover, the Alliance claims the right to use military force outside its territory and, in extreme cases, to do so even without a UN mandate.[8]

But at German (and Canadian) request, the New Strategic Concept contained a paragraph in which the use of nuclear weapons was regarded only as an extremely remote possibility. Moreover, on NATO's Fiftieth

Anniversary Summit in May 1999 in Washington, the member states agreed to discuss the contentious nuclear issue in the broader framework of WMD proliferation, confidence-building measures and arms control. The result was a study published one year later, which positioned the no-first-use topic in a broad and general approach. From the perspective of the 'nuclearists', this important issue was actually buried, from the view of the red–green government a *modus vivendi* of letting sleeping dogs lie was initiated within NATO that would satisfy the Berlin coalition and the once angry members of the Alliance.

The first-use option is associated with another contentious aspect – whether nuclear weapons should be used as a deterrent against non-nuclear threats posed by biological and chemical weapons of mass destruction. The New Strategic Concept that the Alliance agreed upon at its Washington summit is not specific on this issue either. It does not explicitly limit NATO's nuclear deterrence function exclusively to nuclear threats. The general remarks in the New Strategic Concept[9] can be interpreted in a broader sense, i.e. including the countering of biological and chemical weapons as well. What is more, President Clinton signed in November 1997 National Security Decision Directive No. 13 which reportedly acknowledges the relationship between nuclear deterrence and the threat posed by biological and chemical WMD.[10]

For years, the issue of whether nuclear weapons should be considered a legitimate counter-proliferation instrument against non-nuclear threats remained dormant, at least in German public discourse. It was occasionally brought up in connection with the Second Gulf War. US President George Bush reportedly signalled to Saddam Hussein that a use of Iraqi chemical weapons could prompt a US nuclear response. This example is widely cited to show that nuclear deterrence can work, even against seemingly non-deterrable dictators.

Triggered by recent reports of Pentagon plans possibly to attack Iraq with mini-nukes, this topic suddenly came up, started a lively discussion, and prompted the Foreign Ministry to react. State Minister Ludger Vollmer addressed the implications of what such a counter-proliferation option means for non-nuclear Germany with its tradition of the importance of norms, international treaties, and the primacy of non-military means. Vollmer, who attempted to play down the entire matter by characterizing the US plans as a national issue and not as a NATO topic, pointed to the obvious 'new quality' of the nuclear-use option in US military thinking and planning.[11] US nuclear WMD would be directed against a non-nuclear weapons state which has signed the Nuclear Non-Proliferation Treaty (NPT). It has been the declared policy of all nuclear powers to provide so-called negative security assurances to all non-nuclear members of the

NPT (in the US case, unless they attack the United States and its allies with the support of another nuclear-weapons country). The official German excitement on this occasion has been very low-key, but it nevertheless demonstrates a deep-rooted and constant feature of Germany's non-nuclear policy of not being discriminated against.[12] It should not be forgotten that the norm of self-restraint in the WMD field did not fall from heaven but was a painful social process, the beginning of which was characterized by statements by leading German politicians who condemned the first drafts of the NPT as a 'second Yalta' (Chancellor Adenauer), a 'second Morgenthau Plan' (Minister of Finance Franz-Josef Strauß), or as a 'Versailles of cosmic dimensions' (Chancellor Kiesinger).[13]

Nuclear counter-proliferation plans are not compatible with the unequivocal obligations of the United States. The US negative security guarantees were a major incentive to have the non-nuclear weapon states join this treaty and forswear the nuclear option. The non-proliferation regime is in jeopardy, as State Minister Vollmer has emphasized.[14] Nuclear counter-proliferation plans raise doubts among 'nuclear have-nots' that they cannot be sure of not being attacked. What sense does it make for them to forego the nuclear option? Thus, nuclear counter-proliferation strikes are likely to strengthen the appetite for nuclear weapons and will thus be counterproductive. Moreover, from the view of BMD and nuclear critics/opponents, this option is not compatible with the Article VI obligation by the nuclear powers of complete nuclear disarmament – the reason being that additional testing may be regarded as indispensable for the further miniaturization of nuclear WMD (this in turn will reduce the chances of ratifying the Comprehensive Test Ban Treaty). These old questions, which so far have been by and large discussed on paper, are likely to be part of the debate on the adequacy of a pre-emptive strategy towards Iraq.[15]

In this respect there may be one good piece of news from the 'Revolution in Military Affairs' (RMA). Because of the increasingly indistinguishable nuclear and non-nuclear capabilities, nuclear deterrents against small states of concern may not be required any more. This will enormously reduce, if not lift, the inherent tensions discussed in this analysis, provided that countries such as the United States forego the further miniaturization of nuclear weapons ('mini-nukes').[16]

The Decoupling Issue and the Current Debate about WMD and BMD

Both the strong and pragmatic proponents of ballistic missile defence, who can be found in the Christian Social Union (CSU), the Bavarian branch of the Christian Democratic Union (CDU) and within the Christian Democratic Union, respectively, have addressed the decoupling issue in a fundamental way. Leading politicians of the Christian Social Union such as the chairman of the CSU Parliamentary Group (*Landesgruppe*), Michael Glos, have in partly highly emotional words praised the United States as the constant provider of the security guarantee *(Schutzmachtgarantie)* after 1945.[17] In their corresponding motions and position papers the strong and pragmatic supporters of all variants of BMD have included the decoupling dimension as a major element of their political strategy toward the United States. Therefore they aim at strengthening – and not reducing or even jeopardizing – NATO's political and military cohesion in the sense of preventing a decoupling effect, i.e. the emergence of two zones of security. This is also a central criterion for assessing American missile defence proposals. Needless to say, the elimination of the 'N' in National Missile Defence by the Bush administration has made the currently vague US plans more acceptable by both wings of the conservatives.

In the current ballistic missile defence debate, the decoupling dimension is 'for the supporters of BMD' only a new variant of the traditional dilemma[18] of the non-nuclear state, which has borrowed its security from a close relationship with the United States. Extended deterrence[19] is still alive among conservatives and has to be dealt with properly, i.e. by an allied defence system that includes Europe. The conservatives' view of new threats from countries such as Iraq and Iran is the major reason for their concern about decoupling. It has replaced the security peg of the Cold War.

After the terrorist attacks of 11 September, the BMD proponents inside and outside the *Bundestag* have underscored the need for additional protection beyond deterrence. From their perspective, it is not at all certain that either fanatical dictators or terrorists can be reliably deterred in the future.[20] Here their premise is that those tyrants do not behave in a rational way, i.e. not according to the expectations of BMD proponents. Building both active and passive defences[21] sends a signal to terrorists that the civilized world is not completely at their mercy, which in turn can have a deterring or de-escalating effect on their activities.[22] Like the BMD proponents in the United States, their political allies in Germany hope that a combination of nuclear weapons and efficient defences will deter dictators from starting a WMD programme, as it can easily be overwhelmed. Here their premise is that fanatical dictators behave in a rational way, i.e. according to the BMD proponents' expectations. General (ret.) Klaus Naumann, former Chairman of the NATO Military Committee, has combined both demands for a stronger defence of German territory and for its expeditionary forces deployed in an EU or NATO setting.[23] To go ahead with programs such as the Medium Extended Area Defense System (MEADS) would increase the expected German room for maneuver[24] – the alternative would be self-deterrence in a given regional WMD context.

For the sceptics of ballistic missile defence, who can largely be found within the small opposition party of the liberals *(Freie Demokratische Partei*, FDP), the decoupling fear is less obvious.[25] And for the critics and opponents within the Social Democratic Party, the *Bündnis 90/Die Grünen*, and especially in the Party of Democratic Socialism (PDS) extended deterrence, as we have known it, is regarded as no longer necessary. Many critics and certainly all BMD opponents start from the assumption that the security peg has gone with the end of the Cold War and that the emerging or future risks and threats that have yet to be assessed are not an equivalent. Accordingly, the fear of decoupling is virtually non-existent among the critics of ballistic missile defence within the Social Democrats[26] or the Greens.[27] For many critics and for all opponents, the traditional American role as the provider of military security is certainly no longer needed. This does not mean at all that they reject the US presence in Europe in general and in Germany in particular. But they ask for a qualified presence. Depending on whether one is a BMD sceptic or critic/opponent, the American presence and the transatlantic bonding via variants of ballistic missile defence is conditioned to strict criteria or is regarded as more harmful than helpful.[28]

The traditional decoupling argument is still present in the issue of US tactical nuclear weapons on European soil, Germany included, although it is not being discussed explicitly. This makes it impossible to analyse the positions of the various political parties.[29] From both sides of the Atlantic, the major argument for the presence of these entirely anachronistic bombs which have no deterrent value at all *vis-à-vis* WMD[30] still goes as follows. The Americans claim that the Germans (Europeans) still want to have them for reasons of coupling as a visible and material residual capability of traditional extended deterrence. By contrast, the Germans (Europeans) assert that the United States is interested in the deployment as a symbol of US presence on the Old Continent.[31] From the German perspective, it may indeed express a residual and deep-rooted fear of becoming decoupled from the US hegemonic security provider. Moreover, to treat this question as anathema may also reflect how cumbersome is the process of getting accustomed to a new German role in world politics.[32]

Summary and Conclusions

This paper has attempted to present the positions on two deterrence-related issues in Germany, a country that has renounced the possession of all kinds of WMD, but which at the same time has not been a country that has rejected the presence of American nuclear WMD on German soil. This ambivalent status has created inconsistencies. The American nuclear tactical weapons in Germany/Europe, the first-use option and US counter-proliferation policy on the one hand collide with the norm of self-restraint and the rhetorical claim for a nuclear weapons free zone on the other. How do the politically relevant actors in German democracy deal with the inconsistencies? This was the first deterrence-related question the paper tried to explore. The answer is somewhat embarrassing for a democratic state when it comes to the aspect of the nuclear weapons free zones: the entire issue is dodged. The reason for this is very simple, the German public is not interested in this topic. As noted in the introductory remarks, security is defined in different terms.

As to the problem of a compatible counter-proliferation policy, the question of norm adherence is aggravated for the non-WMD country of Germany by the new dimension of pre-emption, publicly endorsed for the first time by US President George W. Bush in his West Point speech on 2 June 2002. Moreover, even an invasion by conventional means was problematical as it was neither legitimized by an international body such as the United Nations nor based on the criteria of clear-cut evidence that a state such as Iraq possesses WMD *and* has helped terrorist activities against the United States – these are additional features of the German civilian-oriented trading state model.

Decoupling, the second deterrence-related issue, consists of two dimensions. The traditional one, which expresses itself in the presence of US tactical nuclear weapons on German and European territory is not discussed. The new variant of the old decoupling topic relates to the necessity of various kinds of BMD. There is no consensus on the relevance of military decoupling. For the strong and pragmatic BMD supporters, the issue still has to be addressed because of new threats, especially from Third World countries. For the BMD sceptics the military decoupling is much less important, and for the critics/opponents the issue has become moot, as they see the WMD issue not in terms of threats but more of risks and challenges. Therefore, they favour politico-diplomatic means to counter the proliferation and WMD problem.

Here, the dual debate on weapons of mass destruction, ballistic missile defences and on counter-proliferation merge. If terrorism is the major form not only of threats but of wars, what is the general role and importance of traditional deterrence and of BMD? The current discussion on pre-emption is living proof that pre-emption (doubtful as it is) is considered within the current US government to be the right answer in certain cases – with or without BMD. Thus, the Bush administration's (nuclear) pre-emption strategy has sharply devalued the importance of traditional deterrence as well as of BMD, whose budgets nevertheless have been growing dramatically.

Against this backdrop, the ballistic missile programs look like a relic of the state-centred, pre-11 September world. Certainly we still have to cope with the problem states, but the relevance of BMD has dramatically decreased. After the Saddam Hussein regime in Iraq has been successfully toppled by offensive means, only two countries – North Korea and Iran – remain as states of concern on the official National Intelligence Estimate provided by all eleven US secret services. It remains to be seen to what extent the shifts in American strategy will influence the German debate on the appropriate mix of means to tackle the BMD problem in general and the deterrence issue in particular.

Whatever the German answer in this specific policy field may be, all the major German actors want to avoid jeopardizing the transatlantic relationship. The majority agrees that the United States is needed on the Old Continent for reasons well beyond deterrence and decoupling – not as the traditional security provider but as the protector of democracy, order, and political stability. This explains why, until 2003, the Germans behaved toward their most important ally as if the security peg of the East–West conflict still exists.

NOTES

This chapter, originally drafted in 2002, describes the state of the art well before the Iraq war. The intense discussions in Germany and the United States about the war against Saddam Hussein indicate that a new chapter in German–American relations has begun, in which the issues discussed have to be framed in the context of a more assertive German policy that aims at a greater degree of independence from the United States.

1. For more detail on this see Bernd W. Kubbig, 'Coping with Weapons of Mass Destruction', paper presented to the Annual Review Meeting, Mountbatten Centre International Missile Forum, 26–29 May 2002, Southampton, available at <http://www.hsfk.de/abm/forum/pdfs/mciskubb.pdf> (rev. 12 Oct. 2004).
2. A point of terminological clarification: Ballistic Missile Defense (BMD) = (National) Missile Defense ([N]MD) + Tactical Missile Defense (TMD) in terms of regional defense/Eurodefense.
3. Of course 'deterrence' is a constructed term itself. For a helpful working definition which I implicitly use in this paper see Colin S. Gray, 'Deterrence in the 21st Century', *Comparative Strategy*, No.19 (2000). pp.255–61: 'Deterrence is what social scientists pompously and obscurely call a "relational variable". Both of those words really matter. Deterrence is the product of a relationship, it is not something one can generate unilaterally. And it is a variable; it is a shifting value. To go back a step, *deterrence is a condition wherein a deterree* – the object of deterrent menaces – *chooses not to behave, in ways in which he would otherwise have chosen to behave, because he believes that the consequences would be intolerable.* Deterrence, the theory, is quite independent of the means one has available or the strategies one favors. Deterrence is deterrence. Nuclear deterrence, conventional deterrence, deterrence for fear of asymmetric action, deterrence for fear of punishment of your society, deterrence for fear of military defeat in war (and its consequences) – it is all deterrence, the same theory and subject. Deterrence in the 21st century is no different in theory, and in the structure of practice, from deterrence in the 20th century or indeed in the fifth century BC. You may, or may not, find nuclear holocaust more deterring than the prospect of mass rape, slavery, and impalement (among other less than wholly amusing consequences of defeat), but the prospect of either basket of unpleasantness may well deter. How does deterrence work? This deceptively simple question requires the most uncompromisingly sharp-edged answer. Specifically, deterrence works because a policy maker (or a polity, collectively) decides that it is deterred'.
4. See Alexander Kelle, 'Germany', in Harald Müller (ed.), *Europe and Nuclear Disarmament. Debates and Political Attitudes in 16 European Countries* (Brussels: European Interuniversity Press, 1998), p.97.

5. See, for example, *Bericht der Bundesregierung zum Stand der Bemühungen um Rüstungskontrolle, Abrüstung und Nichtverbreitung sowie über die Entwicklung der Streitkräftepotentiale,* Jahresabrüstungsbericht 2000, (Berlin: Bundesregierung, 2001), p.52. The same holds true for the most recent annual report, 2001. See *Bericht der Bundesregierung zum Stand der Bemühungen um Rüstungskontrolle, Abrüstung und Nichtverbreitung sowie über die Entwicklung der Streitkräftepotentiale,* Jahresabrüstungsbericht 2001 (Berlin: Bundesregierung, 2002), pp. 53–4.
6. Jahresabrüstungsbericht 2000, p.44 and Jahresabrüstungsbericht 2001, p.44.
7. Quoted in 'NATO, The Alliance's Strategic Concept', statement by the heads of state and government participating in the meeting of the North Atlantic Council in Washington DC, 23–24 April 1999, available through ⟨http://www.nato.int/docu/pr/l999/p99-065e.htm⟩.
8. Harald Müller, *Nuclear Weapons and German Interests: An Attempt at Redefinition,* PRIF Reports No.55 (Frankfurt am Main: Peace Research Institute Frankfurt, August 2000), p.14.
9. It states that nuclear weapons 'will be maintained at the minimum level sufficient to preserve peace and stability'. Quoted from Karl-Heinz Kamp, 'NATO's Nuclear Future: A Rationale for NATO's Deterrence Capabilities', paper presented at the International Conference on European Security and Translanticism at the beginning of the 21st Century, Vancouver, Canada, 15–19 May 2001, p.17.
10. Ibid., p.17.
11. Interview with Ludger Vollmer in *Frankfurter Rundschau,* 14 March 2002.
12. Müller, 'Nuclear Weapons and German Interests'.
13. Quotations in Erwin Häckel, *Die Bundesrepublik und der Atomwaffensperrvetrag. Rückblick und Ausblick,* Arbeitspapiere zur Internationalen Politik No.53 (Bonn: Forschungsinstitut der deutschen Gesellschaft für Auswärtige Politik e.V, April 1989), p.20.
14. Interview with Ludger Vollmer.
15. See for example an interview with Herman Scheer, a leading SPD member of the *Bundestag* criticizing the government for being too soft on its reaction to the Pentagon plans, in *Spiegel online,* 15 March 2002, ⟨http://www.spiegel.de/politik/deutschland/0, 1518,187108,00.html⟩.
16. On this see Harald Müller and Niklas Schörnig, *'Revolution in Military Affairs': Abgesang kooperativer Sicheritspolitik der Demokratien?,* HSFK-Report 8/2001 (Frankfurt am Main: Hessische Stiftung Friedens- und Konfliktsforschung, 2001), esp. pp.20–24.
17. Quotations in statement by Michael Glos during the BMD-related discussion on transatlantic relations in the *Bundestag,* 15 March 2001, in *Deutscher Bundestag, 14. Wahlperiode, 158. Sitzung,* 15 March 2001, ⟨http://dip.bundestag.de/btp/l4/14158.pdf⟩, pp.18, 20.
18. See Müller, 'Nuclear Weapons and German Interests', esp. p.5.
19. As to the traditional notion of extended deterrence see the definition by the Committee on International Security and Arms Control, in *The Future of the US.–Soviet Nuclear Relationship* (Washington, DC: National Academy of Sciences, 1991), p.15: 'any concept of "extended" deterrence, to deter massive non-nuclear attack on one's own country or its allies, suffers from a basic tension of values. The credibility of a US threat of nuclear retaliation against a non-nuclear attack, however dire its consequences, is impaired if the US homeland would then itself be subject to a nuclear counterstrike (as symbolized by the remark that the United States would not have traded New York for Paris). Therefore an aggressor planning to initiate a massive non-nuclear attack may or may not be willing to accept the risk of nuclear escalation'.
20. See the statement by Ruprecht Polenz, in: *Deutscher Bunderstag, 14. Wahlperiode, 193. Sitzung,* 12 October 2001, (http://dip.bundestag.de/btp/l4/14193.pdf), pp.18888–90.
21. On this see Oliver Thränert, *Terror mit chemischen und biologischen Waffen. Risikoanalyse und Schutzmöglichkeiten,* SWP-Studie S14 (Berlin: Stiftung Wissenschaft und Politik, April 2002).
22. Quotations in Oliver Thränert, 'Nach dem Terror: Ein Schutzschild bleibt notwendig', *Neue Gesellschaft,* Vol.48, No.11 (Nov. 2001), p.656.
23. General (ret.) Klaus Naumann, 'What Defence does Europe Need?', AECMA Evening Lecture, Brussels, 25 September 2001, p.8: 'This [vulnerability of Western societies, B.W.K.] underlines the necessity to put more emphasis on defence than hitherto instead of

deterrence. The reason for that is very simple: Western superiority means that the opponents will use terrorism, WMD and cyberattacks. They will try to hit Western nations at their Achilles' heels, i.e. the home territories and the deployed forces. Emphasis on defence therefore means to gain strategic flexibility which will be further enhanced the less dependent a country or an alliance are on access and basing rights.'

24. On the need to protect German expeditionary forces see Torsten Sohns, 'Protection Against Weapons of Mass Destruction. A German Perspective', in Oliver Thränert (ed.), *Preventing the Proliferation of Weapons of Mass Destruction: What Role for Arms Control? A German–American Dialogue*, (Bonnl/Berlin: Friedrich-Ebert-Stiftung, 1999), pp. 141–52.
25. See the statement by Günther Friedrich Nolting, in *Deutscher Bundestag*, 14. Wahlperiode, 108. Sitzung, 8 June 2000, ⟨http://dip.bundestag.de/btp/l4/14108.pdf⟩, p.10258; see also the motion of the Parliamentary Group of the Free Democrats as of 14 March 2001 which does not mention the decoupling issue. See *Drucksache* 14/5570.
26. See the statement by Uta Zapf, in *Deutscher Bundestag*, 14. Wahlperiode, 108. Sitzung, 8 June 2000, ⟨http://dip.bundestag.de/btp/l4/141.pdf⟩, p.10257.
27. There is one minor exception: Representative Wolfgang Gehrcke, a member of the Party of Democratic Socialism, which categorically opposes the American BMD plans, has used this argument, too. But none of the PDS motions introduced against BMD mentions it.
28. For more detail on this see Bernd W. Kubbig 'Coping with Weapons of Mass Destruction'.
29. The fact that this question is hardly debated in the political system may have to do with old Cold War thinking, bureaucratic inertia, lack of interest, and the fear of waking up barking and biting dogs (peace movement).
30. As the actual numbers are classified, publicly available figures vary widely. 13 years after the fall of the Berlin wall, between 150 and 700 tactical nuclear bombs are stored in several NATO countries, including Germany (supposedly at Ramstein air base). None of the original rationales apply any longer. Neither do they enable the European partners within the Alliance to participate in nuclear consultations and planning processes within NATO nor do they contribute to NATO's credible nuclear-deterrent capability. In case of a conflict in the Middle East or a concrete WMD threat, the Alliance would probably send its message of deterrence on the basis of US (nuclear) cruise missiles or submarine-launched ballistic missiles, and not via European-based nuclear bombs. They have to he put under a *Tornado* aircraft to be flown over vast distances into the given crisis region. Moreover, the nuclear weapons in Europe do not provide an indispensable political and military link between the old and the new continent, symbols of cohesion within NATO and of Alliance solidarity need not be demonstrated by these tactical nuclear weapons. See Kamp, *NATO's Nuclear Future*, p.20.
31. As far as the US position is concerned, the Pentagon briefing on the Nuclear Posture Review (NPR) made no reference to tactical nuclear weapons, of which the United States not only deploys several hundreds as mentioned but stockpiles in operational condition more than 1,000. See Philipp C. Bleek, 'Nuclear Posture Review Released, Stresses Flexible Force Planning', *Arms Control Today*, Vol.32, No.1 (Jan./Feb. 2002), ⟨http://www.armscontrol.org/act/2002_01-02/nprjanfeb02.asp⟩.
32. Nevertheless, the last White Paper by the Ministry of Defence in 1994 is living proof that the withdrawal option had at that time already conquered the military minds in Germany at least on paper. It surprisingly treated the 'complete withdrawal of nuclear weapons ... from German territory' as a *fait accompli* – the *Weißbuch* in 1994 was way ahead of its time. *Bundesministerium der Verteidigung, Weißbuch 1994: Weißbuch zur Sicherheit der Bundesrepublik Deutschland und zur Lage der Bundeswehr* (Bonn: 1994), p.24.

Regional Dynamics and Deterrence: South Asia (1)

WAHEGURU PAL SINGH SIDHU

Since India and Pakistan went nuclear in May 1998 at least three myths related to regional dynamics and deterrence have been challenged in South Asia. First is the belief that going overtly nuclear automatically ensures the cessation of all conflict – conventional and nuclear – and leads to the creation of strategic stability between two adversaries.[1] Following the Kargil crisis of 1999 and the eyeball-to-eyeball confrontation in early 2002, which came in the wake of the attack on the Indian Parliament on 13 December 2001 by terrorist groups reportedly operating from Pakistan, this belief has been shaken. In fact, Kargil showed that an overt dyad nuclear relationship is not inherently stable but can lead to situations where it may actually provoke one side (or both sides) to take steps to undermine the stability. Second, the belief that a conflict can be maintained at the conventional level without going nuclear has also been brought into question. Although India's Defence Minister George Fernandes in a speech in January 2000 promoted the concept of 'limited war' and reaffirmed the need for adequate conventional military capability so as to 'ensure that conventional war ... is kept below the nuclear threshold',[2] this concept has not been accepted by Pakistan. At a press conference on 1 June 2002, Pakistan's Ambassador to the United Nations, Munir Akram cautioned that Pakistan could resort to the use of nuclear weapons even in a conventional conflict if Pakistan considers the losses to be unacceptable.[3] Indeed, given the linkage in South Asia between missiles and nuclear weapons, there is a distinct possibility that even the use of conventionally armed missiles in a non-nuclear confrontation might prompt a nuclear exchange. Third, overt nuclearization in South Asia has challenged the perception that in the post Cold War world borders – however tenuous or contested – can be altered by force. In fact the experience of the 1999 Kargil crisis and 2002 stand off has proved that in this post-Cold War period the Line of Control (LoC) between India and Pakistan has gained the sanctity that the Iron Curtain had in Cold War Europe. The sanctity of this line is partly guaranteed by the presence of nuclear weapons and partly by the reaction of the international community, which has not tolerated a single cross-border intrusion since the end of the Cold War.

When considering the dynamics of deterrence in South Asia the region is inevitably confined to the dyad nuclear relationship between India and Pakistan.[4] However, for New Delhi the region of strategic concern, traditionally called South Asia or Southern Asia, 'extends from the Persian Gulf in the west to across the Straits of Malacca in the east, and from the Central Asian Republics in the north to the equator in the south'.[5] This strategic environment encompasses the member countries of the South Asian Association of Regional Co-operation – SAARC – (India, Pakistan, Nepal, Bhutan, Bangladesh, Sri Lanka and the Maldives), China, Central Asia, Iran, Afghanistan, Oman, the United Arab Emirates, Indonesia, Malaysia, Thailand, and Myanmar. By contrast, Beijing has traditionally excluded itself from India's strategic space and has narrowly confined South Asia to include only the SAARC countries.[6] On the other hand, as Indian analyst Sujit Dutta has argued, China became an 'integral part of the Southern Asian geopolitical and strategic environment' when it took over Tibet.[7] Since then China was involved in the Afghan wars of the 1980s, sold nuclear capable missiles to Saudi Arabia, has a growing nuclear co-operation with Iran, in addition to its already well established strategic links with Pakistan, initiated the Shanghai Co-operation Organisation (SCO), which exclusively focuses on Central Asia, and is developing close ties with Myanmar (now also an ASEAN member).[8] This, from New Delhi's perspective, makes China an important actor in South Asia's regional dynamics and deterrence. By the same token Washington's ongoing military operations in Afghanistan and the presence of US troops in Pakistan, Uzbekistan and Tajikistan also makes the United States a key player in understanding the regional dynamics and deterrence in South Asia.

This analysis will begin with a brief evaluation of the evolution of the regional dynamics of South Asia as well as the evolution of deterrence in South Asia both during and after the Cold War. It will then examine how the regional dynamics and deterrence have changed in the post-Cold War world, particularly since May 1998 when two new nuclear weapon states emerged in South Asia, and to what extent the events of 11 September 2001 have impacted on this change. Finally, the article will explore the possible future course of regional dynamics and deterrence in South Asia.

The Evolution of Regional Dynamics in South Asia

Although independent India, based on its size and geography, economic and political strength, dominates the South Asian geo-political space and considers itself to be the successor state to the British Indian empire, this status has been constantly challenged; first by the 565 princely states that were located within the British Indian empire and then by both Pakistan and China. Pakistan has consistently refused to accept the *status quo*, particularly with regard to Kashmir, and unsuccessfully attempted to wrest this territory in 1948 and 1965. Since 1990 key elements within the Pakistani establishment have reportedly been involved in sustaining the ongoing 'cross-border terrorism' or 'proxy war' in Kashmir.[9] Similarly, China's occupation of Tibet in 1950 followed by the Sino-Indian war of 1962 not only curtailed India's geo-political space by removing a critical buffer but also severely dented India's reputation as the dominant regional power. Subsequently, China's growing strategic partnership with Pakistan was also perceived in New Delhi as an attempt to box it in on two fronts. This strategic partnership is of concern to India even today. During this period both the superpowers also combined forces to curtail India's position in the region, as was evident during the 1965 war when both imposed an arms embargo.

Since 1971, when India's war with Pakistan led to the emergence of Bangladesh and, consequently, a dramatic decline in Pakistan's power and position in the region, India emerged as the dominant power at least in the SAARC area. The Simla Agreement of 1972 between India and Pakistan also helped to consolidate India's position. Simultaneously, the rapprochement between Beijing and New Delhi, which began in the late 1970s and evolved into a slow détente in the 1980s, also provided a tacit endorsement by China of India's dominant position in the SAARC area. One indication of this was China's increasing neutrality on the Kashmir issue and its repeated assertion that Kashmir could only be resolved through bilateral negotiations. By the late 1980s, following India's neutrality on the Soviet intervention in Afghanistan, the United States, which remained suspicious of India's leadership of the non-aligned movement nonetheless appears to have tacitly acknowledged New Delhi's dominant role in the SAARC region.

Following the collapse of the Soviet Union and the end of the Cold War a number of factors prompted both India and the United States to improve their bilateral ties in the early 1990s. These included the growing trade and economic ties, driven to a large extent by Indian expertise in information technology and the desire of US firms to build links to these software experts. In addition, the US interest in India was also marked by Washington's identification of India as one of ten Big Emerging Markets. For India, by the mid-1990s, the United States had emerged as the biggest and most important trade partner. These developments in turn prompted Indian and US leaders to attempt to resolve or put aside their non-proliferation differences, which were becoming more acute in the 1990s.[10]

Ironically, it was the emergence of the United States as India's key extra-regional relationship which prompted New Delhi to seek greater autonomy in its own decision-making by going nuclear. Although the Indian political leadership has consistently supported the 'weapon option' policy since its inception in the 1950s, they were reluctant to exercise this primarily because they felt that it would not provide any particular advantage to them.[11] However, in the 1990s successive governments, irrespective of their political leanings, seriously considered exercising the nuclear option.[12] This was primarily because they felt that in the absence of a reliable protector India needed to ensure its own autonomy of decision-making and concluded that the acquisition of nuclear weapons would afford such ability.[13]

There were other factors that also prompted New Delhi to exercise its nuclear option. According to Ashley Tellis:

> This need became more pressing after ... the newly acquired nuclear capabilities of its traditional antagonist, Pakistan; and the new growing economic and military capabilities of its prospective competitor, China. In addition, the indefinite extension of the Non-Proliferation Treaty in 1995 and the successful conclusion of the Comprehensive Test Ban Treaty in 1997 increased – from New Delhi's perspective – the costs accruing to its traditional posture of ambiguity ('keeping its options open') with regard to nuclear weaponry [and this marked a] critical shift in India's strategic direction.[14]

For its part India attempted to deal with the fallout of its nuclear tests in two ways: first, to justify its *de facto* right to bear nuclear arms and also to provide some element of *de jure* recognition of this right. Second, to portray and prove itself as a responsible member of the exclusive nuclear weapon club through its declarations and actions. Thus, soon after the tests while India declared its desire to create a 'minimum credible deterrence' it also offered a qualified 'no-first use guarantee'. In a curious move, soon after the tests, India also offered to join the NPT, but only as a nuclear weapon state. India also readily agreed to provide negative security guarantees for proposed nuclear-weapon-free zones in its vicinity.[15] This move was not entirely altruistic: it was aimed at acquiring *de facto* recognition of India as a nuclear weapon state. Similarly, India followed by Pakistan also declared a unilateral moratorium on further nuclear tests. Subsequently India created an elaborate nuclear posture that was designed to achieve both objectives. The revelations of the extensive proliferation network established by rogue Pakistani scientist Dr Abdul Qadir Khan in early 2004 not only validated India's position as a responsible nuclear state but also vindicated its concerns regarding the developments across its borders.

In yet another ironic twist, despite the tests (or perhaps because of them) India and the United States embarked on an unprecedented and prolonged dialogue on security issues from 1998 to 2000. Although the mandate for this dialogue came ostensibly from the UN Security Council Resolution 1172 and was primarily to preserve 'the viability of the global non-proliferation regime', it led to the first serious and substantial engagement between the world's two largest democracies in the post-Cold War era.[16] This engagement culminated in the visit of President Bill Clinton to India in March 2000 and the signing of the joint Vision Statement.[17] The advent of the Bush administration saw a dramatic change in Indo-US relations. This was evident even during the election campaign when Bush declared '[w]e should work with the Indian government, ensuring it is a force for stability and security in Asia'.[18] Significantly, the same speech made only a perfunctory reference to Pakistan, thus indicating that under a Bush White House it might be possible for New Delhi to establish relations with Washington without always being linked (often in the same sentence) to Islamabad. Until 11 September 2001, this trend had been reinforced by high-level visits between the two capitals. According to Chintamani Mahapatra, 'Indo-US official engagements have never been as frequent and intense during the initial months of a new administration as has been the case during the current [Bush] administration'.[19]

In the wake of the events of 11 September 2001 and within hours of President Bush's declaration of war against terrorism, India offered to provide all assistance in this war.[20] While there was some surprise at the *carte blanche* nature of India's support, New Delhi could not have done otherwise, given its own decade-long war against cross-border terrorism and the possible link between the militancy in Kashmir and Al Qaeda; the fear that a large number of the victims in the twin towers in New York were of Indian origin; and the existence of a Joint Indo-US working group on terrorism. As Praful Bidwai noted, 'since the militancy erupted [in Kashmir] 12 years ago, India has been pleading with the United States to recognise "terrorism" as a major global menace and as a common platform for a special alliance of "democracies" to the exclusion of Pakistan'.[21]

However, for a number of reasons, primarily logistical, operational and tactical, Washington preferred Islamabad's less than forthcoming offer of assistance, much to the shock of many Indian strategists who argued that Pakistan was not only an unreliable but a dangerous ally in the war against terrorism.[22] In addition, Washington also cautioned New Delhi not to take advantage of the situation and attempt to put pressure on Islamabad, thus reverting India and Pakistan back to a hyphenated relationship. However, the dramatic suicide attack on the Jammu and Kashmir Assembly in Srinagar on 1 October 2001 and the attack on the Indian Parliament on 13 December 2001, by Pakistan-backed militant groups indicated that such a message, even if delivered to Islamabad, went unheeded or unimplemented.[23] Although it would appear that India's regional dominance was dramatically challenged following the events of 'Terrible Tuesday', these developments might well have strengthened India's role in the South Asian region. These attacks and the subsequent US pressure on Islamabad publicly to rein-in the terrorist groups operating in Pakistan and to sever ties between the Pakistani establishment (represented by the Inter Services Intelligence agency) and these groups is likely to stem the cross-border terrorism in Kashmir. Significantly, New Delhi is also not averse to the US presence in Central Asia, despite the fact that such a presence would irk India's erstwhile ally, Russia as well as China. In fact Foreign Minister Jaswant Singh also endorsed the presence of US forces in Pakistan as a guarantor for its stability.[24]

The Evolution of Deterrence in South Asia

Until 1971 deterrence in South Asia was purely of a conventional nature. Although Pakistan's membership of SEATO and CENTO (in 1954 and 1955 respectively), China's nuclear and missile development (after 1964) and India's 'Treaty of Peace and Friendship' with the Soviet Union (in 1971) did, in theory, introduce the nuclear dimension to the region, it was not considered to be particularly significant for deterrence purposes. Since 1974, however, when India conducted its first nuclear test, Pakistan embarked on its nuclear weapon programme and China refined its nuclear and missile capabilities, the nuclear dimension became increasingly significant for deterrence in South Asia. Between December 1971, when India and Pakistan fought their last full-fledged war, and the Kargil crisis of June 1999 South Asia has been in a state of 'violent peace' – a state where though there have not been any wars – declared or undeclared – military confrontations, albeit of a limited nature, have erupted regularly. These crises, particularly in the 1980s, all of which stopped short of full-scale war, were, clearly, played out against the emerging nuclear scenario in the sub-continent. These 'wars that never were' occurred in 1983–84, 1986–87 and 1990.[25]

In 1983–84 there were persistent reports that India would attack Pakistan's nuclear weapon production facilities and Pakistan threatened to retaliate with a similar attack on Indian facilities. The crisis in 1986–87 occurred when India conducted exercise *Brasstacks*, its biggest military exercise ever, close to the border. Pakistan, fearing that the exercise might be converted into an attack, launched its own defensive disposition – *Operation Sledgehammer*. The Indians then responded with a mobilization to counter Pakistan's deployment – *Operation Trident*. Although the crisis was resolved, Pakistan indicated that it had acquired nuclear weapons capability. The 1990 crisis developed soon after Pakistan conducted its biggest military exercise, *Zarb-i-Momin*, in late 1989. In the wake of this exercise, there was a sudden spurt in the insurgency movement in Kashmir, allegedly operating out of camps in Pakistan. India, while accusing Pakistan of training and supporting the militants, rushed reinforcements to the Valley and threatened to carry out 'hot-pursuits' across the border into Pakistan to strike the alleged training camps. Pakistan considered this a hostile act and at the height of this tension, Islamabad is reported to have threatened to weaponize its nuclear capability to counter any Indian attack. Although none of these crises was conducted with the possession of nuclear weapons, they were all certainly about nuclear weapons – the threat to build them; the threat to prevent their construction; and the threat of future use of them. Again, while the nuclear dimension may not have been explicitly conveyed to the other side, it was always present in the background and would have had a bearing on the decisions taken by policy-makers on both sides of the border. Scholars have variously called this condition 'recessed deterrence', 'non-weaponized deterrence' or 'existential deterrence'.[26] And to that extent, these were nuclear-related crises even though there was no overt deployment of weapons.

The Kargil confrontation of 1999, however, was markedly different in many respects.[27] This was the first major crisis after both India and Pakistan had tested several nuclear devices and declared themselves to be nuclear weapon states in May 1998. Unlike the past (where there may have been some doubt about the nuclear weapons capability of the other) in this instance both sides were well aware of the presence of nuclear weapons in each other's arsenal. In fact, according to one account, India is reported to have prepared at least half a dozen nuclear weapons for delivery during the course of the conflict.[28] Similarly, Pakistan too is reported to have moved its missiles into launch positions.[29] Second, in the South Asian context, this was the first time since 1984 (when India launched a pre-emptive assault to occupy the Siachen Glacier area) that one side had occupied a disputed territory. Thus the Pakistani action of crossing the LoC in the Kargil area of Jammu and Kashmir signalled a major breakout and challenged the relative stability that had been established under the non-weaponized deterrence relationship between the two antagonists since the early 1980s. Finally, Kargil was different because it was the longest, and perhaps bloodiest, military confrontation between the two countries, which (unlike the others) did not end with a bilaterally negotiated peace treaty. To a large extent the crisis was resolved at the behest of a third party – the United States. Thus the Kargil conflict was, perhaps, the first confrontation between two nuclear weapon states that was not resolved bilaterally but by another nuclear weapon state.

In the 2002 confrontation, while India mobilized its conventional strike forces and argued for a 'limited war', India's Prime Minister Atal Behari Vajpayee issued what can only be described at a nuclear threat. Speaking in Lucknow on 3 January he declared 'no weapon would be spared in self-defence. Whatever weapon was available it would be used no matter how it wounded the enemy'.[30] Within days of this statement India also test-fired the 700-kilometer range *Agni-I* on 25 January 2002. Although Islamabad was notified of the test, this launch was, clearly, regarded as an attempt to intimidate Pakistan. Subsequently, Pakistan's President Pervez Musharraf too issued a nuclear threat in April 2002 and test fired three surface-to-surface ballistic missile systems of the *Hatf* series: the *Ghauri*, *Ghaznavi* and *Abdali* in late May 2002.[31] Both sides were also reported to have put their nuclear weapons on high alert. The nuclear brinkmanship was further compounded by both sides closing down their official channels of communication and not allowing any back channel of communication (as was the case during the Kargil crisis). In this scenario it was left to some countries, notably the United States and Great Britain, to convey their alarm by asking their nationals to withdraw from both India and Pakistan. Eventually, high-level shuttle diplomacy on the part of Washington ensured that deterrence worked, but only just. Clearly, both India and Pakistan are still trying to grapple with making deterrence based on overt capabilities work and are learning through trial and error, which might not be best way when nuclear weapons are involved.

Following Kargil a senior Pakistani official justified the crossing of the LoC and occupying Indian territory on the grounds that similar action by the Soviet Union in Hungary (in 1956) and Czechoslovakia (in 1968) had been accepted by the United States. The official also argued that this action was aimed to counter the Indian occupation of the Siachen glacier.[32] Similarly, Indian officials too have often cited the Ussuri river clash between China and the Soviet Union in 1969 to justify their own concept of limited war.[33] These arguments reflect not only the misperception that a Cold War justification is likely to be accepted in post-Cold War scenario but also the lack of acknowledgement that such action was based on a long process of building strategic stability between the two original nuclear foes and later China and the Soviet Union.

In the wake of the Kargil conflict while Pakistan, which has a tacit first-use-doctrine, elaborated its nuclear command and control structure India, which has a declared no-first-use doctrine and is working towards a second strike capability, articulated a draft nuclear doctrine.[34] While both of these reflect the differing priorities for both Islamabad and New Delhi, they also indicate a basic desire to communicate these priorities to the other side. However, given the crisis-prone nature of the relationship there is very little opportunity for either side to absorb the messages being offered, let alone discuss them. For instance, while India has frequently declared its concept of a 'limited war' it is not clear whether it has even acknowledged the Pakistani message that even a conventional 'limited war' could lead to a nuclear response by Islamabad.[35] As both sides are still in the process of formulating their concepts of nuclear deterrence, the messages are at best not delivered or at worst are often contradictory. For instance, while Pakistan's President Pervez Musharraf 'dismissed the threat of nuclear war on June 1 [2002], his envoy at the United Nations reiterated, a few hours earlier, that Pakistan could resort to the use of nuclear weapons even in a conventional conflict'.[36] Similar contradictions are evident on the Indian side. For instance, APJ Abdul Kalam, a key figure in the Indian nuclear and missile programme and the President of India, confidently declared that 'nuclear deterrence on both sides helped [them] not to engage in a big war [and] avoid a nuclear exchange'.[37] Indian military officials, however, are not so sanguine. General Ved P. Malik, the former army chief cautioned that if 'Pakistan persists with its proxy war or trans-border terrorism policy, an Indo-Pak war cannot be ruled out'.[38]

The situation is likely to be even more complex if the China factor is also taken into consideration. For instance, while there is little possibility of a conventional war, let alone a nuclear war breaking out between India and China, such a possibility cannot be entirely ruled out if there is a nuclear exchange between India and Pakistan. For instance, if India were to absorb a first strike from Islamabad and launch a second strike against Pakistan, could New Delhi be certain that it would not be struck by Pakistan's closest ally, China, especially when India would have used most if not all of its second strike force? Also, would China be relieved of its no-first-use pledge once India had struck?

In addition to the triangular nuclear relationship between China, India and Pakistan, the events of 11 September 2001 and their aftermath have also highlighted the role of a new player: non-state actors armed with weapons of mass destruction. First, it brought to the fore the critical but tenuous links between Al Qaeda, the Taliban and Pakistan-based terrorist groups such as Jaish-e-Mohammad (JeM) and the Lashkar-e-Toiba (LeT), operating in Kashmir, as well as a tentative connection between acts of terror committed against India and the United States.[39] One indication of this relationship was the listing of India, along with the US, Russia and Israel, as 'enemies of Islam' by the Al Qaeda spokesman Suleman Abu Ghaith.[40] This link in turn also highlighted the pivotal role played by Pakistan's Inter Services Intelligence (ISI) agency in coordinating, if not sustaining, the relationship between these three groups of terrorist entities.[41] Revelations of this triumvirate, coupled with the proliferation antics of Dr Khan and the alleged quest for chemical, biological, nuclear or radiological weapons by Al Qaeda, raised concerns that the armed groups in Kashmir might also acquire such weapons.[42]

While terrorists armed with radiological weapons remain only a potential threat, the prospect of cross-border terrorism triggering a conventional conflict that could quickly lead to a nuclear escalation remains a clear and present danger. It is pertinent to remember that the two occasions that India and Pakistan have been locked in an eyeball-to-eyeball confrontation since going nuclear in 1998 were precipitated by the actions of terrorist outfits operating across the LoC.

Similarly, the presence of US troops, particularly in Pakistan is likely to be a consideration for Indian and Pakistani planners as they contemplate their deterrent relationship. Would Washington be willing to stand by and allow Islamabad to launch a nuclear strike against India knowing that India would then be compelled to respond and also inadvertently attack US troops based in Pakistan? Or would the US presence guarantee that Pakistan does not use its nuclear capability, thus providing India with the assurance that, even if it launched a conventional attack, Pakistan would not be able to retaliate with its nuclear capability. Is, therefore, the continued US presence in Pakistan to the advantage of India as Jaswant Singh indicated? Alternatively, would the US presence in Pakistan embolden the military leadership in Islamabad to use its nuclear capability with the assurance that India would not dare launch a retaliatory attack for fear of attacking US troops and thereby entering into a nuclear conflict with the world's sole superpower?

Clearly, these possibilities pose formidable challenges for determining the nature of post-Cold War deterrence in South Asia. One way forward might be for the four key nuclear players – China, India, Pakistan and the United States – to deliberate the prospects of deterrence in the region with a view to establishing a modicum of strategic stability. Given the regional dynamics and the unique position of the United States both globally and in this region such a dialogue will inevitably have to be initiated by Washington. The US initiative could certainly ensure the start of such a dialogue although even the world's only superpower cannot assure its successful conclusion.

NOTES

1. See Dilip Lahiri, 'Formalizing Restraint: The Case of South Asia', in James Brown (ed.), *Entering the New Millennium: Dilemmas in Arms Control* (Albuquerque: Sandia National Laboratories, 1999), p.105. Lahiri, an Indian Foreign Service Officer, reflected the Indian position following the May 1998 nuclear tests. See also the remarks made by Director General (South Asia) Zamir Akram, a senior Pakistani diplomat at a conference on Trust- and Confidence-Building Measures in South Asia, organized by the United Nations Institute for Disarmament Research at Palais des Nations, Geneva, 23–24 Nov. 1998.
2. Inaugural address by Raksha Mantri (Defence Minister) George Fernandes, 5 January, at National Seminar on The Challenges of Limited War: Parameters and Options, organized by the Institute for Defence Studies and Analyses (IDSA), New Delhi, 5–6 Jan. 2000. This has also been emphasized in the draft Indian nuclear doctrine, which insists 'effective conventional military capabilities shall be maintained to raise the threshold of outbreak both of conventional military conflict as well as that of threat or use of nuclear weapons'. See 'Draft Report of the National Security Advisory Board on Indian Nuclear Doctrine', para.3.2, at ⟨http://www.meadev.gov.in/govt/indnucld.htm⟩.

3. T. Jayaraman, 'Nuclear Crisis in South Asia', *Frontline*, 21 June 2002. The Pakistani perspective has also been affirmed in a separate report put out by the Italian Union of Scientists for Disarmament. See *Nuclear Safety, Nuclear Stability and Nuclear Strategy in Pakistan*, a concise report of a visit by Landau Network – Centro Volta.
4. The problem of defining 'South Asia' was initially raised in Waheguru Pal Singh Sidhu, 'South Asia', *International Perspectives on Missile Proliferation and Defenses*, Special Joint Series on Missile Issues, Occasional Paper 5, Center for Non-proliferation Studies and the Mountbatten Centre for International Studies (March 2001), p.61, n.1.
5. Ministry of Defence (MOD), *Annual Report 2000–2001* (New Delhi: Government of India, 2001), p.7.
6. For instance, a recent Chinese book on Sino-South Asian studies defines the region as mostly containing the SAARC countries. See Lin Liangguang, Ye Zhengjia, and Han Hua, *Contemporary China's Relations with South Asian Countries* (Beijing: Social Sciences Documentation Publishing House, 2001).
7. Sujit Dutta, 'China's Emerging Power and Military Role: Implications for South Asia', in Jonathan D. Pollack and Richard H. Yang (eds), *In China's Shadow: Regional Perspectives on Chinese Foreign Policy and Military Development* (Santa Monica: RAND, 1998), p.99.
8. Defense Intelligence Agency, *China and Afghanistan: PRC Concerns and Ability to Influence Events (U)*, DDE-2200-179-83 (Washington, DC: DIA, March 1983); Yitzhak Shichor, *East Wind over Arabia: Origins and Implications of the Sino-Saudi Missile Deal*, China Research Monograph No.35 (Berkeley: Institute of East Asian Studies, University of California, 1989); Swaran Singh, 'Sino-Pak Defence Co-operation Joint Ventures & Weapons Procurement', *Peace Initiatives*, Vol.5, No.3–6 (May–Dec. 1999), pp.1–15; Karan R. Sawhny, 'The Sino-Pakistani Nuclear Alliance: Prospect & Retrospect', *Peace Initiatives*, Vol.5, No.3–6 (May–Dec. 1999), p.27; Bates Gill, 'China's Arms Exports to Iran', *Middle East Review of International Affairs*, Vol.2, No.2 (May 1998), pp.55–70; Bertil Lintner, 'Chinese Arms Bolster Burmese Forces', *Jane's Defence Weekly*, 27 Nov. 1993, p.11, and *idem.*, 'Allies in Isolation: Burma and China Move Closer', *Jane's Defence Weekly*, 15 Sept. 1990, p.475.
9. See Rahul Bedi, 'Infiltration worries', *Frontline*, 5 July 2002.
10. See Waheguru Pal Singh Sidhu, 'Enhancing Indo-US Strategic Cooperation', *Adelphi Paper 313* (Oxford: Oxford University Press for IISS, 1997).
11. There is near unanimity among students of India's nuclear programme that the option to make weapons was built into the programme from its inception in the early 1950s. This built-in ability to weaponize came to be known as the 'weapon option', a phrase most probably coined by India's first Prime Minister, Jawaharlal Nehru. See George Perkovich, *India's Ambiguous Bomb* (Berkeley: University of California, 1999); Itty Abraham, *The Making of the Indian Atomic Bomb: Science, Secrecy and the Postcolonial State* (London: Zed Books, 1999); Peter R. Lavoy, 'Learning to Live with the Bomb: India and Nuclear Weapons 1947–1974', unpublished PhD dissertation (University of California, Berkeley, 1997); Waheguru Pal Singh Sidhu, 'The Development of an Indian Nuclear Doctrine Since 1980', PhD dissertation (Cambridge: University of Cambridge, 1997); and Zafar Iqbal Cheema, 'Indian Nuclear Strategy 1947–1991', unpublished PhD dissertation (London: University of London, 1991).
12. For the political pressure to exercise the nuclear option see Waheguru Pal Singh Sidhu, 'India's Nuclear Use Doctrine', in Peter R. Lavoy, Scott Sagan and James J. Wirtz (eds), *Planning the Unthinkable: New Proliferators and the use of Weapons of Mass Destruction* (Ithaca: Cornell University Press, 2000), pp.145–8.
13. Jaswant Singh, 'Against Nuclear Apartheid', *Foreign Affairs*, Vol.77, No.5 (Sept./Oct. 1998), pp.41–52.
14. Ashley Tellis, *India's Emerging Nuclear Posture*, RAND Research Brief, No.63, available at ⟨http://www.rand.org/publications/RB/RB63⟩. See also Jaswant Singh, 'Against Nuclear Apartheid'.
15. During the late July 1999 Singapore meeting of foreign ministers of ASEAN, China announced that it had decided to sign the protocol to the SEANWFZ Treaty (Treaty of Bangkok). India too announced that it would 'endorse' the treaty and was ready to sign the

protocol but it was noted that according to Article 3 of that instrument this is open to signature only by the five recognized nuclear-weapon states. See 'Non-Proliferation Developments', *PPNN Newsbrief*, No.47 (3rd quarter 1999), p.1.
16. Strobe Talbott, 'Dealing with the Bomb in South Asia', *Foreign Affairs*, Vol.78, No.2 (March/April 1999), pp.120–21 and *Engaging India: Diplomacy, Democracy, and the Bomb* (Washington, DC: Brookings Institution Press, 2004).
17. See Rajeswari Pillai Rajagopalan, 'Indo-US Relations in the Bush White House', *Strategic Analysis*, Vol.25, No.4 (July 2001) pp.545–56.
18. George W. Bush, 'A Distinctly American Internationalism', foreign policy speech at the Ronald Reagan Library, 19 Nov. 1999.
19. Chintamani Mahapatra, 'The New Bush Administration and India', IPCS Article No.536, 10 Aug. 2001, available at ⟨http://www.ipcs.org/issues/articles/536-usr-chintamani.html⟩.
20. Aarti R. Jerath, 'Hoping for Leg-up, India gives US a Hand', *Indian Express*, 13 Sept. 2001.
21. Praful Bidwai, 'Terrorism: India's New Strategic Chance?', *InterPress Service*, 13 Sept. 2001 available at ⟨http://www.tni.org/archives/bidwai/chance.htm⟩.
22. See, for instance, T.V.R. Shenoy, 'Tomorrow it Could Be Us', *Indian Express*, 13 Sept. 2001 and Dr Subhash Kapila, *India's Foreign Policy Challenges Post-Sept. 11, 2001: An Analysis*, South Asia Analysis Group, Paper No.361, 13 Nov. 2001.
23. Atul Aneja, 'Its Time to Restrain Pak., PM tells Bush', *The Hindu*, 3 Oct. 2001.
24. Jim Hoagland, 'India Looks With New Favor on a "Natural Ally"', *International Herald Tribune*, 22 Jan. 2002.
25. Only recently have scholars studied these crises in some detail. For the 1984 crisis see Ravi Rikhye, *The Fourth Round* (New Delhi: ABC Publishing House, 1984) and Waheguru Pal Singh Sidhu, 'The Development of an Indian Nuclear Doctrine Since 1980', pp.119–43. For discussion of the *Brasstacks* crisis, see Kanti Bajpai *et al.*, *Brasstacks and Beyond: Perception and Management of Crisis in South Asia* (New Delhi: Manohar, 1995); Inderjit Badhwar and Dilip Bobb, 'Game of Brinkmanship', *India Today*, 15 Feb. 1987; and 'The War that was not – Happily', *Sainik Samachar*, 19 April 1987. On the 1990 crisis, see B.G. Deshmukh, 'Spring 1990 Crisis', *World Affairs* Vol.3, No.2 (Dec. 1994), pp.36–7; General V.N. Sharma's interview, 'It's All Bluff and Bluster', *Economic Times*, 18 May 1990; Dilip Bobb and Raj Chengappa, 'War Games', *India Today*, 28 Feb. 1990; C. Uday Bhaskar, 'The May 1990 Nuclear Crisis: An Indian Perspective', *Studies in Conflict and Terrorism*, Vol.20 (1997), pp.317–32; Devin Hagerty, 'Nuclear Deterrence in South Asia: The 1990 Indo–Pakistani Crisis', *International Security*, Vol.20, No.3 (Winter 1995/96), pp.79–114; William E. Burrows and Robert Windrem, *Critical Mass* (New York: Simon and Schuster, 1994), pp.349–77; Seymour Hersh, 'On the Nuclear Edge', *The New Yorker*, 29 March 1993, pp.56–73 and Michael Krepon and Mishi Faruqee (eds), *Conflict Prevention and Confidence Building Measures in South Asia: The 1990 Crisis*, Occasional Paper No. 17 (Washington, DC: The Henry L. Stimson Center, April 1994).
26. See Devin Hagerty, 'Nuclear Deterrence in South Asia: The 1990 Indo-Pakistani Crisis', *International Security* Vol.20. No.3 (Winter 1995/96), p.87; George Perkovich, 'A Nuclear Third Way in South Asia', *Foreign Policy*, No.91 (Summer 1993), p.86; and Air Commodore Jasjit Singh, 'Prospects for Nuclear Proliferation', in Serge Sur (ed.), *Nuclear Deterrence: Problems and Perspectives in the 1990s* (New York: United Nations Institute for Disarmament Research, 1993), p.66.
27. For details of the Kargil conflict see Waheguru Pal Singh Sidhu, 'In the Shadow of Kargil: Keeping Peace in Nuclear South Asia', *International Peacekeeping*, Vol.7, No.4 (Winter 2000), pp.189–206.
28. Raj Chengappa, *Weapons of Peace* (New Delhi: Harper Collins, 2000), p.437. This, however, has been denied by Indian officials.
29. Bruce Riedel, *American Diplomacy and the 1999 Kargil Summit at Blair House*, Policy Paper Series (Philadelphia: Center for the Advanced Study of India, 2002).
30. T. Jayaraman, 'Nuclear Crisis in South Asia'.
31. Ibid.; and idem, 'N-Deterrent gave India Second Thoughts: Musharraf', *Times of India*, 18 June 2002.

32. This argument was presented at a seminar on Strategic Stability in South Asia organized by the International Institute for Strategic Studies at Mauritius, 21–24 June 2000.
33. See inaugural address by Raksha Mantri [George Fernandes] at National Seminar on The Challenges of Limited War: Parameters and Options, 5 Jan. 2000.
34. See Rodney W. Jones, *Minimum Nuclear Deterrence Postures in South Asia: An Overview*, Report prepared for the Defense Threat Reduction Agency, 1 Oct. 2001, p.38.
35. According to *Nuclear Safety, Nuclear Stability and Nuclear Strategy in Pakistan*, a concise report of a visit by Landau Network – Centro Volta, there are at least four scenarios under which Pakistan could exercise its nuclear option: space threshold; military threshold; economic strangling; and domestic destabilization. The last two in particular are more difficult to pinpoint precisely and therefore could dramatically lower the threshold for retaliation, based on the perception of either an economic stranglehold or domestic destabilization.
36. See T. Jayaraman, 'Nuclear Crisis in South Asia'.
37. Sanjoy Majumdar, 'Indian president-to-be bares his soul', *BBC News*, 19 June 2002.
38. 'VP Malik politely tells Kalam: You're Wrong on N-deterrence', *Indian Express*, 20 June 2002.
39. See, for example, K. Santhanam, Sreedhar, Sudhir Saxena and Manish, *Jihadis in Jammu and Kashmir: A Portrait Gallery* (New Delhi: Sage Publications, 2003), pp.25–37; Satish Kumar, 'Reassessing Pakistan as a Long Term Security Threat', *Centre for Policy Research Lecture Series: Public Lecture No.7*, 3 March 2003, p.8; J.K. Baral and J.N. Mahanty, 'The US War Against Terrorism: Implications for South Asia', *Strategic Analysis*, Vol.26, No.4. (October–December 2002), pp.508–18; and Jessica Stern, 'Pakistan's Jihad Culture', *Foreign Affairs*, Vol.79, No.6 (November/December 2000).
40. Santhanam *et al., Jihadis in Jammu and Kashmir*, p.32.
41. Sreedhar, 'Challenges After 11 September 2001', *Aakrosh*, Vol.5, No.14 (January 2002), pp.61–75. According to one estimate the ISI spends about Rs 2 billion per year to 'fuel J&K militancy'. See Santhanam *et al., Jihadis in Jammu and Kashmir*, p.35. Yet another estimate puts the total cost of financing terrorism in J&K at Rs 4–5 billion per year. See N.S. Jamwal, 'Terrorist Financing and Support Structures in Jammu and Kashmir', *Strategic Analyses*, Vol.26, No. 1 (January–March 2002), pp.140–52.
42. Rashed Uz Zaman, 'WMD Terrorism in South Asia: Trends and Implications', *Journal of International Affairs*, Vol.7, No.3 (September–November 2002), and Matin Zuberi, 'Nuclear Terrorism: High Risks, Low Probability?' *Aakrosh*, Vol.6, No.18 (January 2003), pp.15–36.

Regional Dynamics and Deterrence: South Asia (2)

NAEEM AHMAD SALIK

Nuclearization of South Asia has not only shaken the foundations of the existing non-proliferation regime, it has raised the spectre of a catastrophic nuclear war between India and Pakistan, resulting from miscalculations, misperceptions, misinterpretation of intelligence information, false warnings or accidents. Given a long history of mistrust and hostility, accentuated by the festering dispute over Kashmir, the prophets of doom can find all the ingredients for an impending disaster. Small wonder then that South Asia has often been characterized as a nuclear flashpoint and the most likely venue for a nuclear exchange. The situation, therefore, demands a dispassionate and objective analysis of the peculiar dynamics of the emerging nuclear deterrent equation in South Asia, which distinguish it from the traditional Cold War models. However, before attempting to address the issue it would be appropriate to study its background and historical context in order to place it in the right perspective.

The Baggage of History and the Burden of Geography

South Asia is a conglomeration of states ranging from India with a population of over a billion people and an area in excess of 3 million square kilometres, to the tiny island state of Maldives with a population of around 0.3 million and a land area of merely 300 square kilometres.[1] Geographically, India occupies the pivotal position and shares common land borders with Pakistan, Bangladesh, Nepal and Bhutan, while a narrow strait separates it from Sri Lanka. As a geographical unit South Asia is bounded in the north and north-west by the mighty Himalayan and Hindu Kush Mountains, in the south by the Arabian Sea, in the east it shares its borders with the ASEAN region and in the west it links up with West and Central Asia. The region as a whole is home to one fifth of humanity. However, from the point of view of power potential and politico-diplomatic significance India and Pakistan are the two paramount states in the region and their mutual hostility and unresolved disputes have always cast a dark shadow on the overall regional environment with regard to peace, security and mutual cooperation. Mainly for this reason the South Asian Association for Regional Cooperation (SAARC) has failed to realise its full potential and emulate the example of other regional groupings such as ASEAN and the European Union. The overt nuclearization of India and Pakistan in May 1998 has brought this region to the forefront of international attention as is evident from former US President Clinton's characterization of the region as a 'nuclear flash point'. For the purpose of this paper, therefore, the focus will remain on India and Pakistan and the evolving deterrent equation between the two South Asian rivals.

Indo-Pakistani antagonism has its roots deeply embedded in history long before their post-independence period. Muslims of India fearing domination by the Hindu majority after the departure of the British from their most valuable colonial possession, and after having failed to obtain constitutional guarantees to safeguard their legitimate rights, demanded a separate homeland based on the Muslim majority areas mainly in the north-west and south-east of the Indian sub-continent. This demand was based on the 'two nations theory' – the argument that Hindus and Muslims despite co-existence for a thousand years had maintained their distinctive identities and despite mixing with each other had never fused into a single nation.[2] The demand for a separate homeland, which meant bifurcation of 'mother India', was unacceptable to leaders like Gandhi and Nehru. However, while some of the Muslim political parties representing mainly religious groups were opposed to the creation of Pakistan, some very prominent Hindu leaders came out in support of the idea.[3] Interestingly, though, the last chance to maintain the unity of post-independence India, which presented itself in the form of the Cabinet Mission Proposals of 1946, was lost due to the arrogance of Jawaharlal Nehru while the Muslim League under the leadership of Muhammad Ali Jinnah had accepted the proposed plan.[4]

The partition of India came about through a mutually agreed and legal process. However, the mass migration and large-scale communal violence following the decision has left such deep scars on the psyche of the two nations that they have not been able to grow out of the traumatic experience even after the passage of more than half a century. The Congress leadership had accepted the creation of Pakistan grudgingly with the hope that it would be a short-lived phenomenon.[5] As such Pakistan's existence as an independent state was never accepted at heart and it took 52 years for an Indian Prime Minister to acknowledge this reality by visiting the monument erected at the site where the Muslim aspirations for a separate homeland were codified in an historic resolution which has come to be known as the 'Pakistan Resolution'.

Geostrategic/Security Environment

Once the British left, India viewed itself as the rightful successor to the British Empire. However, it couldn't fulfil its ambitions of replaying the 'Great Game' in the north-west and found its access to West and Central Asia impeded by what was then known as West Pakistan. In the north, the options were in any case restricted by the gigantic Himalayas, while the Arabian Sea in the south, in the absence of a sea-going tradition and an adequate naval force, didn't allow much freedom of action either. Unable, therefore, to project it's power beyond its geographical confines and forced to deploy its forces inwards on the newly created borders, India felt frustrated and irritated by Pakistan. A similar situation has been witnessed in the recent past when, despite all its enthusiasm, India couldn't play a direct role in the ongoing war against terrorism in Afghanistan due to limitations imposed by the geographical realities. Pakistan was again viewed as the stumbling block, leading to an acute sense of frustration and anger which has manifested itself besides other causes, in the 2001–2 military stand-off.

Pakistan, on the other hand, despite its location at the crossroads of West, Central and South East Asia and overlooking the entrance to the strategic Persian Gulf Region, suffers from some serious misfortunes of geography. Firstly, it is shadowed on three sides by three of the world's most populous and largest states, namely Russia, China and India, which tend to dwarf it. A country with over 140 million people and a land area of over 0.8 million square kilometres would otherwize have been a major player in any other region of the world. Secondly, the rectangular shape of the country with its longest borders in the east being shared with a hostile and antagonistic India and in the West with a turbulent Afghanistan mean that the country has minimal strategic depth and an enormous burden of defence. The emergence of the Kashmir problem, soon after independence, which still remains unresolved despite half a century of confrontation with a much larger neighbour, has meant that preservation of national security and integrity has been its predominant concern throughout its history. Until the creation of Bangladesh in 1971, out of the former East Pakistan, the two wings of the country were separated by 1,000 miles of Indian Territory, which greatly compounded its security problems. However, due to this peculiar geography Pakistan was at the same time part of south-west as well as south-east Asia, which facilitated its entry into military alliance systems spanning both the regions.[6]

Pakistan, therefore, attempted to counterbalance the Indian preponderance in conventional security means by entering into alliances with powerful outside powers and by developing close security ties with the Muslim states in the Middle East and West Asia. This approach manifested itself in the form of Pakistan's participation in multilateral treaties such as SEATO and

CENTO in 1954 and 1955 respectively, and a bilateral security arrangement with the US in 1959.[7] However, during the 1965 and 1971 wars with India these alliances proved to be of little consequence in terms of their impact on the course and the ultimate outcome of the wars. This frustrating experience led to Pakistan's ultimate withdrawal from these treaties by the mid-1970s. By the late 1970s differences over Pakistan's nascent nuclear enterprise led to the imposition of military and economic sanctions by the US. In the 1980s the Soviet invasion of Afghanistan turned Pakistan into a frontline state with its attendant benefits as well as dangers.[8] On the positive side, it restored the American military and economic assistance, which enabled Pakistan to embark on a limited programme of military modernization and replacement of some of its obsolescent military hardware.

The succour provided to Pakistan by the Afghanistan interlude was, however, to be short lived and the umbilical chord was abruptly snapped in 1990 due to US concerns over the direction of Pakistan's nuclear programme. This episode, coupled with the traumatic memories of dismemberment of the eastern wing of the country through military intervention, confirmed Pakistan's belief that at the end of the day Pakistan itself has to take whatever steps are entailed to ensure its safety and no outside power could be expected or relied upon to underwrite its security.

India, on the other hand, while espousing non-alignment was able to develop a close strategic/security relationship with the erstwhile Soviet Union and with its successor, the Russian Federation.[9] The 'Treaty of Peace and Friendship' signed between the two countries in August 1971 for 15 years and constantly renewed since then was nothing but a mutual security arrangement. Its immediate dividend for India was to curtail any possibility of a Chinese intervention on Pakistan's side in the 1971 War.[10] While Russia remains the main supplier of arms and equipment to India, it didn't prevent India from receiving whatever military equipment it could purchase from the West. More recently, it has developed a significant military procurement relationship with Israel resulting in purchases of state of the art equipment worth billions of dollars. At the same time it is expanding its military ties with the US and entering into agreements for the purchase of hi-tech items of military hardware.

Evolution of Indian Nuclear Programme

It is not possible to trace the detailed history of development of the Indian and Pakistani nuclear programmes within the scope of a short paper. However, an attempt will be made to briefly trace the major landmarks in the evolution of the respective nuclear capabilities of the two countries. The origins of India's nuclear ambitions predate India's independence in 1947 by almost three years and the first ever tests of atomic bombs in 1945 by around a year.[11]

The architect of India's nuclear programme, Homi Bhabha, recognising the potential of this new technology, set about establishing an 'Institute for Fundamental Research' in Science and Technology under the auspices of the Sir Dorabji Tata Trust. As a result India already had a cadre of trained scientists and technicians at the time of independence. It therefore quickly moved to establish a Department of Atomic Energy in 1948, barely a year after independence. India's nuclear programme was initiated ostensibly to exploit the peaceful potential of nuclear energy in contrast to the other nuclear powers whose programmes started with the specific purpose of achieving nuclear weapons capability. However, successive Indian leaders pursued the development of military potential of the programme within the purview of an overall nuclear development programme.

In a 1948 address to the Parliament, Mr Nehru stated that, 'Of course if we are compelled as a nation to use it for other purposes, possibly no pious sentiments will stop the nation from using it that way'.[12] As far back as 1960 Major General (Retired) Kenneth D. Nichols, while on a visit to India as a consultant to Westinghouse to discuss plans for building India's first nuclear power reactor, briefed Prime Minister Nehru in the presence of Homi Bhabha. Nichols recounts that Nehru turned to Bhabha and asked:

> 'Can you develop an atomic bomb?' Bhabha assured him that he could and in reply to Nehru's next question about time, he estimated he would need a year to do it. I was really astounded to be hearing these questions from the one I thought to be one of the world's most peace loving leaders. He then asked me if I agreed with Bhabha, and I replied that I knew of no reason why Bhabha couldn't do it.... He concluded by saying to Bhabha, 'Well don't do it until I tell you to'.[13]

In a memorandum for the National Security Council meeting in 1966, acting Secretary of State, George Ball asserted that, 'India is almost certain to develop nuclear weapons', and argued that, 'efforts to influence India's decision ... are not likely to achieve more than a short-term delay'. Rajiv Gandhi who had presented an action plan at the UN to eliminate nuclear weapons, had in 1988–89 quietly given the green signal to the head of the Defence Research and Development Organization (DRDO) and the Chairman of the Atomic Energy Commission to begin creating an Indian Nuclear Deterrent.[14] Even the suave and docile Inder Kumar Gujral is known to have seriously considered the possibility of conducting a nuclear test,[15] obviously to raise his political stock. The development of the Indian nuclear programme can be divided into various phases as under:

- *The Pre-1974 Phase.* This was the formative phase in which the various elements of the nuclear fuel cycle were put into place with a view to achieving autarky. Besides establishment of the CIRUS research reactor as a source of fissile material, the other development of great significance was the establishment of a French supplied reprocessing plant, which was inaugurated by Prime Minister Shastri in 1965. India thus became the first Asian country to achieve this distinction. On the policy front Shastri authorized preparations for subterranean nuclear explosions (SNEs), which laid the groundwork for India's first nuclear explosion in 1974.[16]

- *The Consolidation Phase – (1974–1998).* This phase began with India's first nuclear test, code named 'Smiling Budhha', on 18 May 1974, which at the time it chose to call a 'Peaceful Nuclear Explosion' (PNE). Recently, however, Raja Ramanna, a former DAE Chairman who was in charge of the 1974 project, has publicly acknowledged that it was, in fact, a weapons test.[17] India, however, didn't claim the status of a Nuclear Weapons State following this test, mainly due to a lack of requisite delivery means. The focus then shifted towards the development of delivery systems by way of initiating the Integrated Guided Missile Development Programme. During this phase attempts were made to conduct more nuclear tests first in 1982–83 and then in December 1995. However, Indira Gandhi buckled under international pressure and in 1995, when imminent preparations for the test were picked up by US satellites, the Narasimha Rao government backed down under US pressure.[18] Another abortive attempt was made in the spring of 1996, when Vajpayee was sworn in as the Prime Minister and was given 15 days by President Sharma to muster the required majority in the Parliament, which he failed to achieve and had to quit on the expiry of the deadline. However, one of the first things Vajpayee did in his rather brief stint in power was to give a signal to Abdul Kalam and Chidambaram, who were in charge of India's nuclear weapons programme, to proceed with nuclear weapon tests. The scientists immediately initiated the required steps in that direction and had reportedly emplaced at least one nuclear explosive in a test shaft. However, the execution of the intended tests was subject to the outcome of the 'confidence vote' and fell through when it failed to materialize.[19]

- *The Overt Nuclearization – May 1998.* Budhha smiled again in the desolate wilderness of the Pokhran Desert on 11 May and then again on 13 May 1998. This time around however, the 'grin' was much broader with a total of 5 tests claimed in all including a thermonuclear test. In contrast to 1974 however, nuances such as 'PNE' were not used and Prime Minister Vajpayee pronounced India to be a nuclear weapon power, at the same time declaring a unilateral moratorium on further testing. India, after having announced an ambitious nuclear doctrine, is now moving on towards operationalization of the capability.[20]

Pakistan's Nuclear Programme

Pakistan didn't evince the kind of interest in nuclear technology shown by India and was slow to venture into the nuclear field. It was not until 1954 when the American exhibition on 'Atoms for Peace' toured Pakistan and aroused interest in the potential of this new technology for national development.[21] Chronologically, Pakistan's nuclear programme can be described in the following phases:

- *The Early Phase: 1954–74*. During this phase the necessary administrative infrastructure was established to promote peaceful – uses of Atomic Energy. The thrust of the programme remained unambiguously peaceful uses in the fields of medicine, agriculture and nuclear power. The progress was, however, sluggish due to bureaucratic impediments and poor funding. The decision to acquire the first nuclear research reactor was taken in 1958 and it was expected to be operational by 1960. However, it became critical only in 1965. One of the major impediments was the absence of a core of specially trained nuclear scientists and technicians. The absence of indigenous training facilities meant that arrangements had to be made to send a number of scientists abroad for training in countries like Britain, France, Canada and the US.[22] The assumption of the office of Prime Minister in December 1971 by Mr Z. A. Bhutto who earlier, as Minister of Fuel and Power in President Ayub Khan's Cabinet, had enthusiastically advocated the development of the nuclear programme, gave a much needed fillip to the programme. However, the May 1974 Nuclear Test by India became the defining moment for the future direction of Pakistan's Nuclear Programme and significantly increased the momentum towards the achievement of indigenous capabilities which would in due course provide Pakistan with the wherewithal for a military nuclear option which could be exercised in response to Indian actions in this regard.[23]
- *Expansion/Consolidation of the Capability: 1974–98*. Pakistan's immediate response to the Indian nuclear test was to despatch its Foreign Minister to Washington, London, Paris and Beijing to seek a nuclear umbrella[24] failing which it had to take action to safeguard its long-term security interests. Pakistan also made a proposal in the United Nations General Assembly for a Nuclear Weapons Free Zone for South Asia. This proposal was passed by the UNGA with an overwhelming majority and continued to be endorsed every year until 1998, but it couldn't be implemented because of Indian opposition. This particular phase was marked by technological developments such as the achievement of Uranium Enrichment Capability and mastering of techniques to develop various components which when put together would constitute a nuclear device. Pakistan,

however, exercised great restraint and, despite the availability of technological capabilities to do so by the mid-1980s, refrained from conducting a nuclear explosive test. The 1980s also saw the revival of a security relationship with the US, which enhanced Pakistan's confidence in its conventional deterrence capability, thereby reducing the incentive for going nuclear. At the same time, in response to the initiation of testing of ballistic missiles by India, Pakistan also embarked on development of its own delivery systems.

- *Overt Nuclearization: May 1998.* On 28 May Pakistan announced the testing of five nuclear devices in response to the Indian tests of 11 and 13 May. These were followed by another test on 30 May.[25] Following the tests Pakistan also announced a unilateral moratorium on further testing but, unlike India, it didn't claim a nuclear status for itself. Since then Pakistan has demanded from the international community a similar status to the one which will ultimately be conceded to India. Pakistani leaders have reiterated on a number of occasions conventional disparity with India. To accentuate the situation was the possibility of nuclear blackmail by India, and Pakistan's worst nightmares were confirmed by India's 1974 nuclear test. Pakistan thus redoubled its efforts to ensure its security and to hedge against the possibility of nuclear arm-twisting by India if the latter was allowed to monopolize the nuclear capability in South Asia. In the aftermath of the tests Pakistan has therefore neither demanded any special status for itself nor has it staked claims for a permanent seat in the UN Security Council.[26]

Characteristics of the South Asian Nuclear Environment

Before embarking upon a survey of the evolution of Indian and Pakistani nuclear programmes and policies it is important to have an overview of the prevailing nuclear environment in South Asia, which provides the backdrop which has influenced the direction of these doctrines/policies. Some of its key features are:

- Indian and Pakistani nuclear forces are still in their infancy and these relatively vulnerable assets are likely to provide tempting targets for a pre-emptive strike at least in the short term, irrespective of the probability of success of such a strike.
- India has a fairly advanced space programme and Pakistan is likely to move down the same road in due course. However, at the moment both countries lack real-time surveillance, early warning and target acquisition means, which will not only limit employment options, but will also enhance crisis instabilities.

- Doubts about the reliability/survivability of command, control communications and intelligence infrastructure will reinforce the perception of threat of a decapitating strike, thus encouraging pre-emptive tendencies thereby leaving little time for crisis bargaining/de-escalation.
- The incentive for development of an assured 'second strike' capability is likely to be fairly strong on both sides; however, deterrence instability will prevail in the short term.
- India's induction of Russian supplied 'Klub' class cruise missiles, and likely acquisition of the Israeli Arrow, the US Patriot PAC-3 or Russian AWACs and S300 ABM systems are likely to upset the evolving strategic balance and will lead to a catastrophic nuclear/missile arms race.
- Contiguity of the two countries and short flight times of ballistic missiles is likely to result in hair-trigger postures and may lead to adoption of launch-on-warning strategies which, due to technical deficiencies in the surveillance and early warning systems, increases the chances of weapons being launched in response to inaccurate or misinterpreted information.
- Peculiar value systems, emotive tendencies and proclivity for risk taking coupled with politically weak governments will create uncertainties of responses in crisis situations.
- Absence of institutionalized crisis management mechanisms will result in impulsive decision-making.
- There is a general lack of awareness of the devastating effects of a nuclear conflict amongst the masses on both sides. This ignorance of the gravity of the situation will generate undesirable public pressure on decision makers during crises.

Indian Nuclear Doctrine/Policy

On 17 August 1999, India's National Security Advisor, Mr Brijesh Mishra, announced what he termed 'India's Draft Nuclear Doctrine'. This ambitious doctrine was announced in a peculiar set of circumstances, coming close on the heels of the Kargil conflict in Kashmir and in the midst of an election campaign forced by the fall of the Vajpayee government. Interestingly, though, even after the passage of more than six years its status still remains ambiguous. It is either embraced or disowned by the Indian leaders depending on the expediency of the situation. Some of the salient features are:

- India shall pursue a doctrine of credible minimum nuclear deterrence. The actual size of the force has, however, not been quantified.
- India will have a 'no first use' policy, but will respond with punitive retaliation should deterrence fail.

- India will maintain sufficient, survivable and operationally prepared nuclear forces, capable of shifting from peacetime deployment to fully employable force in the shortest possible time.
- A robust command and control system with effective intelligence and early warning capabilities will be established, for which space based and other assets shall be created. Authority for release of nuclear weapons will vest in the person of the Prime Minister of India, or his designated successor(s).
- Comprehensive planning and training for operations will be carried out in line with the strategy.
- India will demonstrate the political will to employ nuclear forces.
- Highly effective conventional military capabilities will be maintained to raise the threshold of outbreak of both conventional as well as nuclear war.
- India will have effective, diverse, flexible and responsive nuclear forces based on a triad of land based missiles, aircraft and sea based assets.
- Survivability will be ensured through redundancy, mobility, dispersion and deception.
- India shall not accept any restraints on its R&D capability and will continue to conduct sub-critical nuclear tests even if it decides to sign the CTBT at a future date.
- India will not use nuclear weapons against non-nuclear weapon states (NNWS), *other than those which are aligned to any nuclear power.*

On 4 January 2003, more than four and a half years after the Pokhran-II tests, India finally announced the broad contours of its Nuclear Command and Control Structure and reiterated some key elements from its draft doctrine while modifying others.[28] Whether these can now be taken as the official policy parameters of India's nuclear doctrine is not clear and so is the case with the status of the 'Draft Nuclear Doctrine'. It has not been clarified as to whether the Draft Doctrine is still valid or has been superseded by the new document. Some of the salient aspects of the Document issued by the Cabinet Committee on Security on 4 January 2003 are:

- Building and maintaining a credible minimum deterrent.
- A posture of 'no first use'.
- Retaliatory attacks can only be authorized by the civilian political leadership through the NCA.
- Non-use of nuclear weapons against non-nuclear weapon states.
- In the event of a major attack against India or Indian forces anywhere, by biological or chemical weapons, India will retain the option of retaliating with nuclear weapons.

- A continuance of controls on export of nuclear and missile-related materials and technologies, participation in the Fissile Material Cut-Off Treaty negotiations and observance of the moratorium on nuclear tests.[29]

Analysis

In the new document, while reiterating the essence of Draft Nuclear Doctrine, some new elements have been introduced:

- Declaration of the option to use nuclear weapons against any use of 'Nuclear', 'Chemical' or 'Biological' weapons against Indian territory, or Indian Armed Forces anywhere in the world, thereby not only extending the threshold of nuclear use but also expanding its geographical scope. It has virtually neutralized the 'no first use' commitment.
- Strict control over the export of sensitive technologies and materials. This appears to be designed to allay prevailing international concerns over the alleged transfer of sensitive materials and technological know-how from the secondary proliferation sources and thus project India in a positive light.
- A clear commitment to participate in FMCT negotiations.
- Continued observance of 'moratorium' on nuclear tests.
- A reaffirmation that India 'will not use nuclear weapons against non nuclear weapon states', however, the caveat in the original doctrine *'other than those aligned with nuclear weapon states'* has been removed.

Organization of Indian NCA[30]

The newly announced Nuclear Command Authority (NCA) comprises a Political Council (PC), chaired by the Prime Minister, as the sole body empowered to *authorize* the use of nuclear weapons; an Executive Council (EC), chaired by the National Security Advisor, with a dual role of 'providing inputs for decision making by the NCA' and 'execution of directives issued by the PC'. The third tier is a Strategic Forces Command (SFC), which is a tri-service command headed by a commander-in-chief, who is entrusted with the responsibility to manage and administer all the strategic forces (see Figure 1).

India's nuclear doctrine carries far-reaching implications for various facets of India's nuclear programme and policy and for the dynamics of threat to Pakistan. Some of the more important ones are:

- By declaring its intention to raise a triad-based nuclear force, India has effectively scuttled all proposals relating to establishment of a Strategic Restraint Regime in South Asia.
- India's declaration of a 'no first use policy' is aimed at gaining the high moral ground and degrading Pakistan's nuclear deterrence. This

FIGURE 1
ORGANIZATION OF INDIA'S NCA

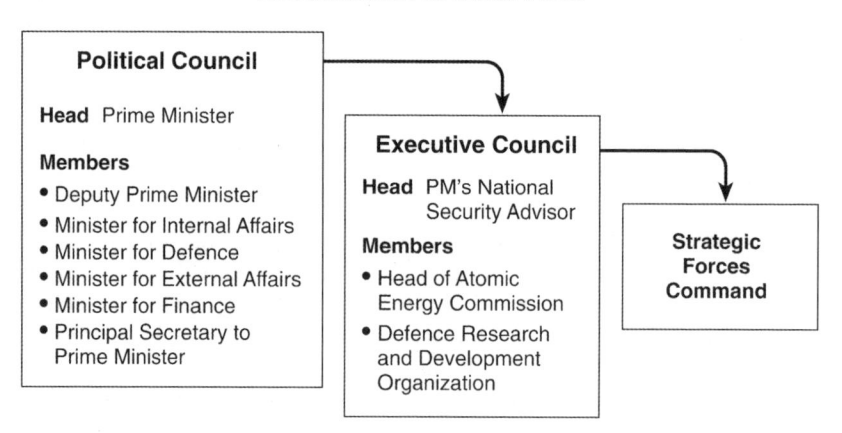

Political Council

Head Prime Minister

Members
- Deputy Prime Minister
- Minister for Internal Affairs
- Minister for Defence
- Minister for External Affairs
- Minister for Finance
- Principal Secretary to Prime Minister

Executive Council

Head PM's National Security Advisor

Members
- Head of Atomic Energy Commission
- Defence Research and Development Organization

Strategic Forces Command

commitment has been watered down in the January 2003 document. Probably taking a cue from the US Nuclear Posture Review, the Indians also pronounced that they would retaliate with nuclear weapons against a chemical or biological attack against India or its forces anywhere.
- India has declared its intentions to upgrade its conventional forces to 'raise the threshold' of both nuclear as well as conventional conflict. However, by accentuating the existing conventional imbalance, it will have the effect of lowering Pakistan's nuclear threshold, thereby reducing the credibility of its nuclear deterrence.
- By not specifying the source of nuclear threat to its security, India has kept the size of its 'minimum' deterrent open ended.
- The timing of announcement of the draft doctrine in August 1999 suggested that the BJP government wanted to convince the domestic public that it has the requisite resolve to take the process initiated in May 1998 to its logical conclusion.
- There is an implicit attempt by India to drag Pakistan into a nuclear as well as conventional arms race to exploit its economic weaknesses and engineer an economic collapse (US vs USSR syndrome!).

Perceived Goals and Objectives

There are differing perspectives and views with regard to the ultimate goals and objectives of India's nuclear policy and it may be instructive to review some of these to provide an insight into the parameters of the Indian nuclear discourse. In a RAND publication entitled 'India's Emerging Nuclear Posture', Ashley Tellis has attempted to rationalize India's nuclear policy and has even attempted to fill in the gaps and clarify the ambiguities in the 'Indian Nuclear Doctrine'. Tellis, in his seminal study, has explored five possible options ranging from 'Renunciation of Nuclear Option' to a 'Ready Arsenal', with 'Regional Nuclear Free Zone', 'Maintenance of Nuclear Option' and 'Recessed Deterrent' lying in the middle. He has concluded that India is most likely to choose a 'Force-in-being' option falling in between the recessed deterrence and ready arsenal. The implication of this posture would be that Indian nuclear capabilities will be 'strategically active', but remain 'operationally dormant'. Translated into practical terms this would afford India the ability to undertake a retaliatory strike within hours to weeks. This kind of posture will be demonstrative of Indian restraint while providing it deterrence capability *vis-à-vis* both China and Pakistan. The other advantages would be avoidance of the costs of maintaining a ready arsenal, while ensuring the retention of civilian politico-bureaucratic control over the nuclear assets, which, in the case of a ready arsenal, would automatically be passed over to the military.[31] How realistic this appraisal is, is difficult to say but in view of the noises coming out of Indian strategic circles, this may well turn out to be a rather benign view of India's nuclear ambitions.

On the domestic front, a survey of the public opinion polls conducted in the aftermath of the 1998 tests saw 'self esteem' and 'pride' emerge as pre-dominant themes. In a poll conducted by the Indian Market Research Bureau (IMRB), 91 per cent of the respondents felt a sense of pride at India's pronouncement of its nuclear status. The same argument was echoed by Prime Minister Vajpayee when he declared at the floor of the Indian Parliament that, 'It is India's due, the right of one sixth of humanity'. In a 1994 poll 49 per cent of those favouring weaponization of the nuclear option advocated development of nuclear weapons by India to 'improve its bargaining position in international affairs', while another 38 per cent favoured the acquisition of nuclear weapons to enhance India's 'international status'. In two other opinion polls conducted in June 1974 and May 1998, the results were identical: around 90 per cent people felt proud of this achievement and thought that it had raised India's stature in the comity of nations.[32]

Statements by various Indian leaders also betray this self-consciousness of India's greatness. For instance Foreign Minister Jaswant Singh, in an interview with the National Public Radio in the United States, said that, 'All that we have done is give ourselves a degree of strategic autonomy by acquiring those symbols of power ... which have universal currency.'[33]

The issue of viewing nuclear weapons as means of power and prestige is a recurring theme elsewhere as well. To quote former Prime Minister I. K. Gujral,

> An old Indian saying holds that Indians have a third eye. I told President Clinton that, when my third eye looks at the door into the Security Council Chamber it sees a little sign that says, 'only those with economic wealth or nuclear weapons allowed'. I said to him, 'it is very difficult to achieve economic wealth'. The implication was clear; nuclear weapons were relatively easy to build and detonate and could offer an apparent short cut to great power status.[34]

Bharat Karnad, one of the well known Indian analysts representing hawkish views and a former member of the Nuclear Security Advisory Board (NSAB), responsible for formulating the 'Draft Nuclear Doctrine', arguing that India needs to rationalize its nuclear testing and weaponization programmes, rather than pursuing the abstract goal of disarmament, stated that:

> Collateral security objectives of dampening Pakistani ardour for mindless confrontation but, more importantly, for containing a wily and wilful China and of deterring an over-reaching and a punitive minded United States leading the Western combine of nations, will be realized provided the deterrence solution is right.[35]

Mr Karnad is critical of any decision by India to sign either the CTBT or FMCT because in his view these will limit India's weapons yield to below a megaton and cap the number of nuclear weapons respectively, thereby endangering national security. He goes on to add that, 'for a self-proclaimed nuclear weapon state disarmament is a manifestly counter productive policy'. Karnad pleads that India should bargain hard to obtain as many concessions as possible in return for its signatures to the CTBT and FMCT. To him the minimum acceptable results should be provision for India to conduct additional thermonuclear tests and to accumulate enough fissile material stocks for 1,000 plus nuclear warheads. He implicitly threatens that failing to get an attractive enough bargain, India could export its nuclear technology and materials. Characterizing the 'no first use doctrine' as merely a hoax, he comments that, 'it is one of those restrictions which countries are willing to abide by except in war'. He supplements his argument by quoting from Herman Kahn, who had stated that, 'No first use stops just where war begins,' and Michael Quinlan, who calls it, 'political posturing that cannot alter strategic reality'. In the same breath he also dismisses the notion of a 'minimum nuclear deterrence' relying once again on Kahn's statement that, 'it is a new kind of Maginot mentality'.[36]

However, he contradicts his earlier argument later in the same chapter by saying that:

> The Indian offer of no first use was timely, will go a long way in making the Pakistanis rethink their demonology and should be unilaterally subscribed to. More convincing proof that India is not gearing up for a nuclear war could be provided by Indian force design. Not nuclearizing the short range Prithvi and, in fact, withdrawing it from present near-border deployment, should constitute the core concept.[37]

Contradictions inherent in India's nuclear stance are exposed by one of the more objective Indian analysts, Kanti Bajpai when he says that, 'New Delhi's pronouncements suggest that China is the more important threat. But the rhetoric from South Block and India's day-to-day diplomatic and strategic moves indicate that Pakistan is a co-equal if not greater threat.' According to Bajpai, the Indian strategic community also keeps giving vent to its concerns *vis-à-vis* the US mainly in the context of the potential threat to India posed by America's counter-proliferation policy and its hostility against rising powers like India on account of geo-political factors. At the moment, however, this criticism is muted but more open references to the American threat should be expected when the ICBM and SLBM capabilities come on line and it will become technically feasible to strike against the continental United States.[38]

Bajpai holds India responsible for Pakistani nuclear weaponization and believes that Islamabad would not have gone all the way if New Delhi had unambiguously closed off the nuclear option in the 1960s. He goes on to argue that:

> A second opportunity to avoid a nuclear arms race was lost in the 1970s and 1980s when Pakistan stated publicly, on several occasions, that it would sign any de-nuclearizing agreement India was prepared to accept. Islamabad's various offers were seen as tactical manoeuvres, designed to embarrass India diplomatically. But if India had called Islamabad's bluff it is difficult to see how, given the weight of world opinion, as well as influential sectors of its domestic opinion, Islamabad could have reneged on its own commitments.[39]

Rebutting the argument with regard to the inevitability of Pakistani nuclearization, he expresses his belief that, 'talks on Kashmir plus a conventional force agreement would have stood a very good chance of reassuring Pakistan and stopping the advance of its nuclear weapons programme'.[40]

Pakistan's Nuclear Doctrine/Policy

Unlike India, Pakistan's nuclear policy is driven entirely by security considerations. The discourse on the direction, aims and objectives of the nuclear policy is mainly confined to officialdom and public debate on such issues is not very broad based and the published literature on the subject is very limited compared to the volume of published material emanating from India's academic circles and think tanks. It would, therefore, be in the fitness of things to quote from two of the key spokesmen for the Government of Pakistan. Speaking at the National Defence College in May 2000, Foreign Minister Abdul Sattar stated that:

> For the past decade or so, nuclear capability has been the bedrock of our defence and security policy ... its sole purpose is to deter and prevent war. Unlike some other countries, Pakistan neither aspires to great power status or permanent membership of the Security Council nor nourishes any design for regional dominance ... We support a global, non-discriminatory international regime of nuclear and missile restraints, voted for the CTBT, will participate in negotiations for FMCT, and are prepared to strengthen our existing stringent controls against export of strategic weapons technology. Our policy of Minimum Credible Deterrence will obviate any strategic arms race ... *the idea of no-first-use of nuclear weapons needs to be expanded into a no-first-use of force*, lest the former should be interpreted to sanction first use of conventional weapons.[41]

In his keynote address at the Carnegie International Non-Proliferation Conference on 18 June 2001 at Washington D.C., Mr Abdul Sattar declared that, 'Pakistan was not the first to conduct nuclear tests, similarly we will not be the first to resume tests. In effect Pakistan is observing the CTBT in anticipation of its coming into force.' Outlining Pakistan's Command and Control mechanisms, he stated that:

> We have over the last two years upgraded command and control mechanisms. A National Command Authority, chaired by the Head of the Government and including three Federal Ministers and Chiefs of Armed Services, provides policy direction, oversees development and employment of assets, and approves measures to ensure custodial safety and complete institutional control over fissile materials and sensitive technology. Procedures have been implemented to minimize the chances of accidental or unauthorized launch. We are studying the US Personnel Reliability and Nuclear Emergency Support Teams concepts for adaptation.[42]

On the issue of nuclear safety and security and export controls he elaborated:

> We have also taken measures to further tighten administrative and legal mechanisms to prohibit and prevent export of fissile materials and leakage of sensitive technology... the Government has also established Pakistan Nuclear Regulatory Authority, another monitoring body for safety and checks.[43]

It has been repeatedly stated that the Scarlet Thread of Pakistan's nuclear policy is 'restraint and responsibility'. Pakistan has, therefore, adopted a 'Minimum Credible Deterrence' policy and has deliberately eschewed a nuclear/missile arms race with India. Foreign Secretary Inam-ul-Haq further magnified this contrast, in the goals and ambitions of the two countries, when he declared that 'instead of a triad of nuclear forces Pakistan seeks a triad of peace, security and progress'.[44] He went on to suggest a Strategic Restraint Regime, involving measures for nuclear and missile restraints as well as conventional balance. He expressed Pakistan's readiness to enter into reciprocal arrangements with India to agree on:

- Non-deployment of ballistic missiles.
- No operational weaponization of nuclear capable missiles.
- Formalization of the existing understanding on pre-notification of missile flight tests.
- Declaration of a moratorium on the development, acquisition or deployment of ABM systems.

In Inam-ul-Haq's view, the three pillars of South Asian Peace, Security and Progress are 'a high level dialogue to resolve Jammu and Kashmir, mechanism to promote trade and economic cooperation, and a strategic restraint regime would complement, sustain, support and reinforce each other'.[45]

Pakistan's Nuclear Command and Control[46]

Recognizing the need for establishment of an effective and reliable command-and-control system to assure the nation as well as the international community that Pakistan's nuclear capability is being managed in a professional and responsible manner, Pakistan announced the establishment of a National Command Authority (NCA) on 7 February 2000. The urgency with which this task was undertaken has been acknowledged by many experts as is evident from the following quotation from *India's Nuclear Bomb*, written by George Perkovitch in 2000:

> High levels of the Pakistani military and civilian leadership have displayed their seriousness as nuclear stewards by creating a new,

overarching institution to manage their strategic assets, formalization of a chain of command over nuclear weapons and setting up of several functional departments. Pakistan's leadership takes nuclear weapons very seriously and has moved rather quickly to effect orderly processes for managing their capabilities.

Pakistan's strategic command organization comprises three tiers (see Figure 2):

- *Constituent 1*: National Command Authority (NCA). This is the highest decision-making body comprising two main committees, under the chairmanship of the President with the Prime Minister as the vice chairman. An Employment Control Committee, which is a politico-military

FIGURE 2
ORGANIZATION OF PAKISTAN'S NCA

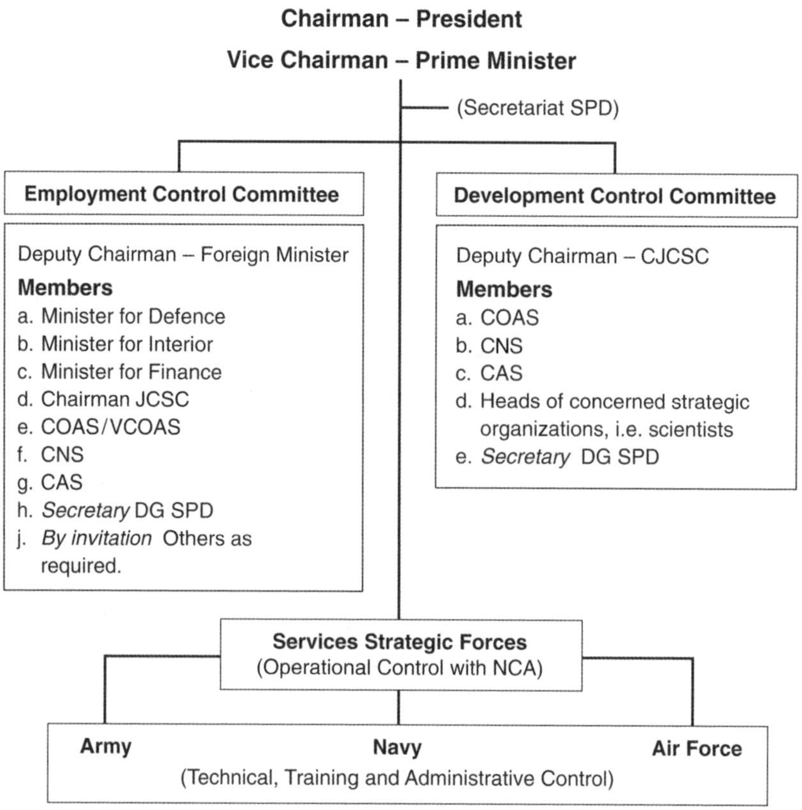

Chairman – President
Vice Chairman – Prime Minister

(Secretariat SPD)

Employment Control Committee

Deputy Chairman – Foreign Minister
Members
a. Minister for Defence
b. Minister for Interior
c. Minister for Finance
d. Chairman JCSC
e. COAS/VCOAS
f. CNS
g. CAS
h. *Secretary* DG SPD
j. *By invitation* Others as required.

Development Control Committee

Deputy Chairman – CJCSC
Members
a. COAS
b. CNS
c. CAS
d. Heads of concerned strategic organizations, i.e. scientists
e. *Secretary* DG SPD

Services Strategic Forces
(Operational Control with NCA)

| Army | Navy | Air Force |

(Technical, Training and Administrative Control)

committee with ministers of Foreign Affairs, Defence, Interior and Finance as its members besides the Chairman Joint Chiefs of Staff and the three services chiefs. The second committee is the Development Control Committee, which is basically a military–scientific committee with Chairman Joint Chiefs of Staff and the services chiefs as its members alongside the heads of various strategic organizations.

- *Constituent 2*: Strategic Plans Division. This acts as the secretariat of the NCA and is responsible not only for formulating policy options for decision making by NCA but also to oversee the implementation of these decisions.
- *Constituent 3*: Strategic Forces Commands. Unlike India, which has a single tri-service command, Pakistan has three separate services strategic force commands, which are responsible for technical, training and administrative control over the delivery systems. The operational control, however, remains with the NCA.

How Viable is South Asian Nuclear Deterrence?

South Asian Nuclear Deterrence is tenuous at best and a cause of concern for not only the two South Asian nuclear rivals but for the world at large. There are certain characteristics of South Asian nuclear competition, as alluded to earlier, which are distinctly different from the Cold War nuclear stand-off between the two super powers. According to Ambassador Thomas Simons, characteristics peculiar to South Asia are Geography (contiguity of the two countries), Asymmetry (in terms of size and potential of the two South Asian rivals) and Third Party Role (the China factor).[47] Interestingly, for almost two decades prior to the overt nuclearization, a situation variously described as 'non-weaponized', 'opaque' or 'existential' deterrence existed between India and Pakistan. The resolution of some of the crises such as the 1986/87 Brass Tacks crisis and the 1990 stand-off over Kashmir was attributed to existential deterrence. More generally, it is contended that while India and Pakistan fought three wars and a major border skirmish in the Rann of Katch in the initial 25 years of their existence as sovereign states, there was no war, nor even a serious border clash, in the next 25 years, which can be attributed to the emerging nuclear capabilities of the two South Asian antagonists. The advantage afforded by the existential deterrence was the crisis stability and the absence of dangers associated with accidental or unauthorized launch of nuclear weapons because of the inbuilt time buffers.

In the post-1998 scenario, however, the crisis-ridden and hostile relationship between India and Pakistan against the backdrop of the festering Kashmir dispute, carries the germs of a potentially hazardous and explosive security situation at least in the short term while the doctrines, command and control and safety and security mechanisms are evolving.

India's Limited War Doctrine

India's decision to test and overtly weaponize its nuclear capability came under a lot of criticism from some of the Indian analysts who argued that, by nuclear testing, India provided a perfect opportunity to Pakistan to demonstrate its own nuclear capability, thereby neutralizing not only India's nuclear capability but its conventional advantage as well. The onset of the Kargil Conflict served to confirm these views. Reacting to this criticism, India's security managers started propounding a doctrine of limited war. Former Indian Defence Minister George Fernandez stated that: 'we kept all the wars "limited" in the past.... we had understood the dynamics of limited war. ... Nuclear weapons did not make war obsolete; they simply imposed another dimension on the way warfare could be conducted'.[48]

On the issue of the deterrence value of nuclear weapons he remarked that, 'Obviously we have not absorbed the real meaning of nuclearization: that it can deter only the use of nuclear weapons, but not all and any war'. He went on cite the 1969 border conflict between two nuclear powers, the Soviet Union and China, arguing that, 'conventional war remained feasible, though with definite limitations, if escalation across the nuclear threshold was to be avoided'.[49] Speaking at the same forum, General V. P. Malik the ex-Indian Army Chief in his advocacy of the Limited War declared that, in the spectrum between low intensity conflict and a nuclear war there is room for a limited conventional war. Another former Indian Army Chief, General Padmanabhan, was reported as saying that, 'The military situation with Pakistan was serious and could spark a limited conventional war'.[50]

This advocacy of limited war in a nuclear environment entails serious security ramifications since a war may be intended to remain limited but once the hostilities commence the events tend to acquire a momentum of their own which is difficult to contain; the intensity of the enemy's reaction cannot be predicted with any certainty beforehand. Against this backdrop the danger of things getting out of hand and escalating into a nuclear exchange cannot be ruled out.

How Robust is South Asian Nuclear Deterrence?

The first serious crisis in the post-nuclearization era in South Asia was the 1999 conflict in the Kargil region of the disputed state of Kashmir. Analysts are divided in their analysis of this conflict, with one group terming it a failure of deterrence while the other cites this as another manifestation of the evolving nuclear equilibrium in South Asia. In his opening remarks before unveiling the Indian Nuclear Doctrine in August 1999, India's National Security Advisor, Brijesh Mishra, pointed to the fact that the Kargil conflict remained confined to a limited sector and didn't spill over to other parts of the Line of Control or the international border; he attributed this to the existence of nuclear deterrence.[51]

The second aspect, which is generally misperceived, is the prevailing conventional balance in South Asia. Although the balance is clearly tilted in India's favour, what is generally overlooked is the fact that India's conventional advantage is by no means overwhelming, and Pakistan has so far been able to maintain a manageable ratio of forces and is capable of holding its own for a considerable time. The doomsday scenario projecting a contemplation of the use of nuclear weapons by Pakistan at a very early stage of the conflict is, therefore, grossly misplaced. However, if India continues to acquire large amounts of state of the art military hardware from Russia, Israel and even the United States, it will not be long before the disparity will become unmanageable with the undesirable effect of lowering Pakistan's nuclear threshold. India has increased its defence outlay by a whopping 79 per cent in the last five years. Pakistan, in accordance with its declared policy of avoiding the temptation of getting embroiled into a debilitating arms race with India, has kept its own defence budget frozen over the same period.

The 2001–2 military stand off with over a million troops deployed astride the borders has tested the limits of deterrence. Fortunately, deterrence has held due to the fact that the existing conventional balance doesn't allow India the freedom of action to feel confident of making any meaningful gains. In the backdrop of a mutual nuclear deterrence situation, any military adventure entails very high risks and costs. One thing, however, has clearly emerged; that in 2002 things did not spiral out of control, but the probability of an intended or unintended disaster cannot be ruled out in the future. The propensities for sabre rattling and brinkmanship need to be curbed, and coercive use of military force cannot be employed once too often. During the 2002 military stand-off India acted to the contrary. First it tested a modified version of the MRBM Agni with a range of 700 kilometres. It was openly acknowledged that this was a Pakistan-specific missile. Second, the Indian Army Chief made a statement in which he did not display any subtlety or finesse in hurling nuclear threats. General Padmanabhan, while warning Pakistan that launching any nuclear attack would unleash a backlash from India, is reported to have remarked: 'The perpetrator of that particular outrage shall be punished – shall be punished so severely that the continuation of any form of fray will be doubtful'.[52] Such actions and pronouncements did not inspire much confidence either within the region or outside. One can only hope that with the passage of time nuclear maturity will come and due care will be taken with regard to the serious repercussions of loosely brandishing nuclear swords.

Conclusion

The best way to avoid a nuclear war is to avoid any war at all. That is why Pakistan has been advocating a 'No use of force' as opposed to 'no first use of nuclear weapons'. The best way to stabilize and strengthen nuclear deterrence, therefore, is to agree on a comprehensive 'Strategic Restraint Regime' covering nuclear, missile and conventional restraints. Pakistan offered a comprehensive proposal in this regard as far back as October 1998, but an Indian response has remained elusive. Additionally, the need for a serious and sustained dialogue for the resolution of all outstanding disputes between the two nuclear-armed rivals cannot be over emphasized. It is therefore imperative not only for the two countries to show the desired degree of patience and sagacity but for the international community as well to maintain the moral and political pressure and to continue to encourage and cajole the two sides to stay the course.

NOTES

1. *CIA World Fact Book*, ⟨http://www.odci.gov/cia/publications/factbook/index.html⟩.
2. Chaudhri Muhammad Ali, *The Emergence of Pakistan* (New York and London: Columbia University Press, 1967), p.1.
3. Hafeez Malik, *Dilemmas of National Security and Cooperation* (London: Macmillan, 1993), pp.10–15.
4. Ibid., p.11.
5. Ibid., p.5.
6. Bharat Karnad, 'India's Weak Geopolitics and What to do about It', in Bharat Karnad (ed.), *Future Imperilled* (New Delhi: Viking, 1994), p.24.
7. Kail C. Ellis, 'Pakistan's Foreign Policy: Alternating Approaches', in Hafeez Malik (ed.), *Dilemmas of National Security and Cooperation in India and Pakistan*, pp.131–3.
8. Ibid., p.141–2.
9. Hafeez Malik, *Dilemmas of National Security*, p.8.
10. Kail C. Ellis, 'Pakistan's Foreign Policy: Alternating Approaches', p.136.
11. *SIPRI Yearbook 1975* (Massachussetts and London: The MIT Press), p.17. Also see K. Subrahmanyam, 'India's Nuclear Policy', in Onkar Marwah and Ann Schultz (eds), *Nuclear Proliferation and Near Nuclear Countries* (Cambridge, MA: Ballinger Publishing Company, 1975), p.141, and Onkar Marwah, 'India's Nuclear and Space Programme: Intent and Policy', *International Security*, Vol.2, No.2 (Fall 1977), p.98.
12. Zia Mian, 'Homi Bhabha killed a Crow', in Zia Mian and Ashish Nandy, *The Nuclear Debate: Ironies and Immoralities* (Colombo: Regional Centre for Strategic Studies, July 1998), p.12.
13. George Perkovich, *India's Nuclear Bomb* (Berkeley, CA: University of California Press, 1999), p.36.
14. K. Subrahmanyam, 'Indian Nuclear Policy – 1964–98', in Jasjit Singh (ed.), *Nuclear India* (New Delhi: Knowledge World, 1998), p.44.
15. Amitabh Mattoo, 'India's Nuclear Policy in an Anarchic World', in Amitabh Mattoo (ed.), *India's Nuclear Deterrent – Pokhran-II and Beyond* (New Delhi: Har Anand Publications, 1999), p.18.

16. Ibid., p.17.
17. Ibid.
18. Ibid., p.18.
19. Perkovich, *India's Nuclear Bomb*, pp.374–5.
20. *The Hindu*, 12 May 1998; *The News*, Islamabad, 12 May 1998.
21. Shirin Tahir Kheli, 'Pakistan's Nuclear Options and US Policy', *Orbis*, Vol.22, No.2 (Summer 1974), p.358.
22. P.B. Sinha and R.R. Subramaniam, *Nuclear Pakistan: Atomic Threat to South Asia* (New Delhi: Vision Books, 1980), pp.31–2.
23. Ibid., p.37; and Charles K. Ebinger, *Pakistan: Energy Planning in a Vortex* (Bloomington, IN: Indiana University Press, 1981), p.84.
24. *Keesing's Contemporary Archives*, June 1974.
25. *The News*, Islamabad, 29 May and 1 June 1998.
26. Abdul-Sattar, 'Foreign Policy After The Cold War', address at National Defence College, Islamabad, 24 May 2000.
27. *The Hindu*; *The Hindustan Times*; *The Indian Express*; 18 Aug. 1999.
28. 'India Establishes Strategic Forces Command', *Hindustan Times*, 5 January 2003, and C. Raja Mohan, 'Nuclear Command Authority Comes into Being', *The Hindu*, 5 January 2003.
29. Ibid.
30. Ibid.
31. Ashley J. Tellis, *India's Emerging Nuclear Posture: Between Recessed Deterrence and Ready Arsenal* (Santa Monica: RAND, 2001). For a review and summary of the book, see RAND Research Brief, RB-63 (2001).
32. Mattoo, *India's Nuclear Deterrent – Pokhran-II and Beyond*, pp.11–15.
33. Perkovich, *India's Nuclear Bomb*, p.441.
34. Ibid., p.400.
35. Bharat Karnad, 'A Thermonuclear Deterrent', in Amitabh Mattoo (ed.) *India's Nuclear Deterrent*, p.111.
36. Ibid., pp.113–26.
37. Ibid., p.136.
38. Kanti P. Bajpai, 'The Fallacy of an Indian Deterrent', in Amitabh Mattoo (ed.) *India's Nuclear Deterrent*, pp.151–2.
39. Ibid., pp.153–4.
40. Ibid., p.154.
41. Abdul Sattar, 'Foreign Policy after the Cold War'.
42. Abdul Sattar, 'New Leaders, New Directions', keynote address at the Carnegie International Non-Proliferation Conference, Washington, DC, 18 June 2001.
43. Ibid.
44. Inamul Haq, foreign secretary of Pakistan, statement to the Conference on Disarmament, Geneva, 25 Jan. 2001.
45. Ibid.
46. For details of Pakistan's nuclear command and control see Major General (Retd) Mahmud Ali Durrani, 'Pakistan's Strategic Thinking and the Role of Nuclear Weapons', CMC Occasional Paper/37, Cooperative Monitoring Center, Sandia National Laboratories, Albuquerque, New Mexico, USA, July 2004.
47. Ambassador Thomas Simons (former US ambassador to Islamabad), in a seminar at Islamabad in March 2001.
48. George Fernandez, inaugural address at National Seminar organised by IDSA on The Challenges of Limited War: Parameters and Options, New Delhi, 5 Jan. 2000.
49. Ibid.
50. 'General Padmanabhan says limited war is possible', *The Hindustan Times*, 11 Jan. 2002.
51. *The Hindu*, 16 August 1999.
52. See note 50.

Regional Dynamics and Deterrence: The Middle East

ALAA ISSA

The Middle East over the past half-century has been the most heavily militarized and war-prone region in the world. It has witnessed seven major interstate wars and many other militarized conflicts short of interstate wars. The value of armaments imported into the region since the end of the Second Gulf war runs to the high end of hundreds of billions of dollars, and military expenditures continue to account for a significant proportion of the national budgets of many states. Furthermore, the pursuit, acquisition and possession of WMD and their means of delivery has been part of the military and political landscape of the region for over four decades. In tandem with these phenomena, deterrence theory and its strategic application, which had developed in the context of the relationship and rivalry between two superpowers that were geographically distant from one another, was adopted by regional actors in the geographically constricted environment of the Middle East and adapted to serve the geopolitical and military realities in the region, primarily in the context of the Arab–Israeli conflict, but also during the First and Second Gulf Wars.

Deterrence theory as we know it today developed out of the new technology of nuclear weapons and the need to deal with their military applications and their absolute destructiveness. Initially, US strategy developed along the lines of war prevention during the period when the United States enjoyed a monopoly over nuclear weapons. However, as the technology spread to the USSR in the mid-1950s and US predominance eroded, ideas related to massive retaliation and mutual deterrence evolved and eventually culminated in the concept of Mutually Assured Destruction (MAD). One concept associated with the doctrine of MAD was that of Extended Deterrence, whereby the United States extended significant commitments to defend Western Europe against a possible Soviet attack.

The concept of Extended Deterrence faced inherent difficulties, in particular because it called into question the credibility of the US policy of retaliation, which in turn was the essence of MAD. Would the US risk an all out nuclear war if Paris or any other Western European city were attacked by the USSR? If the answer was yes, then the premise of deterrence policy would remain unshaken. If, however, the answer was no, then it would ultimately undermine the foundations of the US policy of deterrence and retaliation. In responding to this problem strategic thinking developed along the path of proportionality, of developing different levels of response suited to different scenarios, as opposed to total retaliation. Doctrines relating to limited nuclear warfare were developed as well as nuclear weapon technology for tactical use.

Deterrence theorists also distinguished between general and immediate deterrence. General deterrence relates to the conditions under which a crisis may arise, be they diplomatic or military or otherwise. It presumes the presence of an adversarial relationship between two or more states, the willingness of one state to resort to force and the preparedness of the other state to respond in kind. Immediate deterrence on the other hand relates to an actual crisis and how a state can deter the adversary from undertaking a potential specific action during the crisis or conflict.

The modern experience of the Middle East is replete with examples of deterrence theory put to the test. While the region witnessed far more wars and conflicts during the past fifty years than any other region, it is important to bear in mind that the interaction was never limited to the local players. The super-powers were always ready to intervene at any time to safeguard their own interests or protect those of their allies or clients. The result was that the experience of deterrence in the Middle East did not replicate the model of engagement in the East–West struggle in a mechanistic manner.

This analysis will consider several historical incidents during the period 1967–73 and during the early 1990s where the dynamics of deterrence were visible in the Middle East, consider their success or failure, and then, briefly, the nature of some of the challenges that lie ahead.

Historical Experience in the Middle East

One state more than any other in the region, Israel, publicly adopts a strategy of deterrence *vis-à-vis* its neighbours, particularly those involved directly in the Arab/Israeli conflict. Israeli political and strategic scientists have gone to greater lengths than their regional counterparts to articulate elements of their country's policy, and they believe that it has generally been successful. A common portrayal of Israeli deterrence policy tends to identify an initial phase during the early years of the state in which deterrence took the form of punitive action against Palestinian villages in order to stem the tide of Palestinian resistance and, at a broader level, to deter a full scale war by any Arab State or group of States against Israel. In the late 1950s, particularly after the 1956 Suez Affair, and throughout the 1960s, there was a gradual articulation of a more coherent conventional deterrence posture whose objective was to force the Arab States into accepting the territorial *status quo* that existed in the region, and ultimately to enforce the acceptance of Israel.

During that period, one should consider the Israeli policy of deterrence in two respects.

The first is whether this Israeli policy of deterrence did in fact succeed in preventing the Arab States from initiating a military conflict against Israel in the years leading to 1967. This may be the case, but is difficult to ascertain because during the period 1956–67 the major Arab States confronting Israel, such as Egypt and Syria, were also preoccupied with other issues that took precedence over a military engagement with Israel. Egypt's direct involvement in the civil war in Yemen is but one example.

The second concerns the outbreak of the June 1967 War, and provides an interesting case of the dynamics of immediate deterrence and how deterrence can become a danger unto itself when the pace of crisis outstrips the pace of diplomacy. During the first half of 1967, tension and escalation along the Israel–Syria front reached a high state of intensity that augured an Israeli attack on Syria. Events unfolded in May 1967 in a manner whereby Egypt eventually began mobilizing an increased number of troops in the Sinai Peninsula with the objective of preventing an attack against Syria. Despite Israel's policy of deterrence, Egypt had been compelled to move an increasing number of forces into Sinai knowing that this action constituted a red line for Israel. The Egyptian action was in itself an act of immediate deterrence aiming to deter the adversary – Israel – from undertaking probable military action against Syria, and was not intended to initiate an attack. Israel attacked on 5 June. It is not altogether unreasonable to argue that Israel's policy of deterrence not only failed to prevent this particular action by Egypt but did in fact precipitate a full-scale war.

The years following 1967 were to prove a failure for deterrence policy in the Middle East. The 1969–70 war of attrition and the 1973 war provide vivid examples of this failure. After 1967, the conventional military balance was overwhelmingly favourable to Israel. Israel controlled the Sinai Peninsula, the Golan Heights and the West Bank. US commitment to the security of Israel was translated into arms supplies that would assure Israel of military supremacy in a future regional conflict. Moreover, the critical element of credibility that is necessary to the success of a deterrence policy existed: the perception of Israel's military invincibility was ever present in Arab minds.

Despite these factors, during 1969–70 the decision was taken by Egypt to conduct a war of attrition against Israeli forces along the Suez Canal zone at great expense to Egypt in both material and human terms. The 1973 war was no less costly for Egypt and Syria. In both instances the military balance was highly favourable to Israel and the credibility of her general deterrence posture was at an all-time high so as to deter any possible military action against her. The Israeli occupation of the Sinai Peninsula and the Golan Heights had created a national grievance in Egypt and Syria that was much deeper than Israel anticipated, and this grievance had in turn stimulated in both countries a national commitment to challenge the *status quo* that existed after 1967. Moreover, the domestic political system in Egypt and in Syria would have imposed a severe cost on the leadership in both countries had they permitted the perpetuation of that status quo. The result was that the Israeli policy of general deterrence failed to prevent the war of attrition and the 1973 war.

Furthermore, one must consider that there may have existed in 1973 an unconventional element in Israeli deterrence strategy and its possible impact. There is no evidence to suggest that the planning and execution of the Egyptian–Syrian attack in October 1973 was in any way influenced by factors that went beyond the military and strategic situation favourable to Israel after 1967, as mentioned above. Indeed, even at the apex of Egyptian–Syrian success in the early phase of the war there was no indication from any of the parties that an unconventional capacity would be introduced into the conflict. Of course one may argue, with the benefit of hindsight, that at no time during the 1973 war did Israel or the other parties face an existential threat that might have stimulated resort to unconventional capabilities, and that the intention of the Egyptian leadership all along was to conduct a limited war that would serve to break the diplomatic deadlock and perhaps pave the way for some form of negotiated solution. In any case, the situation in 1973 was such that Egyptian and Syrian planning and action were unrestrained by any Israeli policy of deterrence whatever form it might have taken.

The concept of extended deterrence also applies to the Middle East. Some countries in the Middle East region have been beneficiaries of extended deterrence from the United States or the USSR in the past and some still are to the present day. While the most prominent case is the US commitment to the security of Israel, comparable commitments exist between the United States and its key Arab allies. There were also previous commitments of a similar nature, albeit of a lesser scope, extended by the USSR to close allies or friendly states in the region. This extended deterrence took two forms.

The first was of the immediate nature that related to specific actions during ongoing conflicts or crises and involved the provider of extended deterrence such as the US, and the adversary of the recipient, such as Egypt. In one incident in the spring of 1970 the United States sought to deter Egypt from moving an anti-aircraft system from the interior of the country to the theatre of battle along the Suez Canal and conveyed a sternly worded message from Secretary of State Rogers to this effect through the USSR. This attempt at deterrence failed. Another incident occurred in September 1970 when fighting erupted between Jordanian forces and Palestinian militias based in Jordan. The US intervened on behalf of Jordan and successfully deterred Syria from committing its armoured forces in support of the Palestinian militias.

The second form of extended deterrence was of a general nature and applied in cases where the recipient in the Middle East might encounter an existential threat or danger of a severe magnitude. The salient example is probably the case of Iraq's invasion of Kuwait, where the United States led an extensive military and diplomatic initiative to roll back the invasion and enforce punitive action against Iraq. Once the seriousness of US resolve to liberate Kuwait became apparent, it served to deter Iraq from invading Saudi Arabia or any of the other Gulf states.

Iraq's invasion of Kuwait presented a fertile field for consideration of the effectiveness of deterrence or at least some aspects of its application. In the *International Herald Tribune* on 27 September 1990, Pierre Lellouche raised the question of whether, if Iraq had been in possession of nuclear weapons and the means of their effective delivery, the United States and her allies would have been so ready to deploy troops against Iraq. Lellouche argued that the same dilemma that had arisen with regard to the concept of extended deterrence several decades earlier, and led General DeGaulle to doubt whether the US would risk the destruction of New York in order to save Paris, applied in the case of Kuwait City. Although the issue raised was a hypothetical one, it did prompt a further question related to whether deterrence designed against the Soviet threat had any value for contingencies of a different nature such as the world would be facing in the post-Cold War era, including in the Middle East.

Besides the issue of nuclear weapons discussed above, Iraq's possession of, but non-use of, chemical weapons was another area for speculation about the success or failure of deterrence. Iraq's refraining from launching chemical warheads at Israel, Saudi Arabia or the US and coalition troops engaged in operation Desert Storm was attributed by some to Iraq's fear of an overwhelming and unrestrained response from Israel, and thus is presented as an example of Israel's deterrence policy at its most effective moment. Others claim that even if Iraq had deployed WMD against US troops, the United States would not have responded in kind but rather would have continued beyond the liberation of Kuwait to pursue the indictment of the Iraqi leadership for committing war crimes, and that here lay the most effective deterrent. Still another view questions the capability of Iraq to weaponize its missiles with chemical warheads once the fighting had begun, and also doubts the effectiveness of dispersing chemical weapons from Iraq's missiles, both of these elements being at the source of Iraq's restraint.

Success and Failure

In many respects, the policy and practice of deterrence in the Middle East has met with mixed results. On the one hand, the historical experience supports the conclusion that deterrence policy in the Middle East – regardless of its success or failure – was primarily of a conventional nature, as opposed to its evolution and application in the context of the US–USSR relationship where it was based on nuclear weapons.

Despite the predominance of the conventional mode of deterrence, the military balance does not seem to have been a conclusive factor as one might have expected it to be. The impact of a superior military capability was negligible in the face of a strong national commitment as occurred in the 1973 war. It may also be worthwhile today to evaluate the efficacy of Israel's military machine in deterring the stone throwing Palestinian youth in the *intifada* or suicide bombers or against a more severe conflict such as the Palestinian occupied territories have been witnessing recently. The conclusion is not likely to be a favourable one.

With regard to unconventional deterrence, it would seem that with the exception of an existential threat against a state in the region, it has had a very limited and negligible effect. It did not play any role in the deterrence equation in 1973 nor did it deter Iraq from launching missiles at Israel and Saudi Arabia during the Gulf War.

A further factor that merits consideration is the extent to which deterrence has provided security to those in the region that adopt such a policy. Whereas deterrence can be said to have provided an acceptable degree of stability, assuredness, and a framework for managing the superpower confrontation in the context of the Cold War, the experience in the Middle East bears different results. In the Middle East, deterrence has, to a certain extent, managed conflicts and suspended or frozen confrontation within specific parameters, but one cannot say conclusively that it has assured security.

Conclusion

In conclusion, there are several factors that are likely to affect deterrence policy or postures in the Middle East and its further development. The first factor is the continued presence and growth of WMD capabilities in the region and the refinement of their means of delivery despite global efforts to regulate and ban such weapons. The continued proliferation of WMD in the Middle East cannot be attributed to the rather nebulous motive of prestige on the part of possessors of WMD nor can the insistence of many key regional states to address the issues of prohibition or curtailment of WMD and missiles in a comprehensive manner. It relates rather to an increasingly deeply held belief among adversaries in the region of the need to maintain an ultimate form of retaliation against their existing or future adversary. The proliferation of missiles and missile technology in the region is in many ways, though not exclusively, related to their use for delivering WMD. Missile proliferation also relates to the perceived inherent value of missiles to bolster conventional military capacity. The fundamental point here would be whether the Middle East may be moving towards an era of strategic deterrence based on the acquisition of WMD.

A second factor relates to the introduction and development of missile defence in the region. This occurred in Israel after the end the Gulf War in 1991 and there is now a well established Israeli programme whose central component is a ballistic missile defence capacity developed with US cooperation. To the extent that a state can defend itself against incoming missile-related and WMD threats, it succeeds in nullifying the capabilities of its adversaries and their deterrence value, establishes a hegemony of its own capabilities and strengthens the belief in the utility of deterrence policy. From this point of departure one can presume that the introduction of missile defence in the Middle East might act as a drive for increased proliferation and refinement of WMD and missile capabilities in the region.

The third factor flows from its predecessors and relates directly to nuclear capabilities. Currently Iran is accused by some states of seeking to acquire a nuclear weapon capability. These claims are currently being examined by the IAEA in the light of Iran's obligations under the safeguards agreement with that agency. If the nuclear non-proliferation regime were to gradually weaken and nuclear weapon capabilities were to become more widespread in the region, then the entire spectrum of developments and dilemmas that existed in the case of the superpower relationship would unfold, but with a regional dimension.

Finally, the question of deterrence and security in the region needs to be reconsidered in the light of recent experience and the nature of future conflict in the region. Israel's deterrence policy relates to its relations with other regional states and probable conflicts in this context. Recent experience raises the probability that in the foreseeable future conflict in the region will be of low intensity rather than full-fledged inter-state wars. The question whether Israeli deterrence policy will identify a need to adapt to this trend and to the nature of conflict that will be prevalent in the occupied territories will eventually need to be considered within the broader considerations of: the definition of security applied; the contribution of deterrence policy to security; the nature of expected threats; as well as perceptions of past success or failure of deterrence.

PART V: CONCLUSIONS

Conclusions

JOHN SIMPSON AND IAN R. KENYON

Although our original intention in initiating work on *Deterrence and the New Global Security Environment* had been to focus exclusively on nuclear deterrence, it soon became clear that we had to spread our net much wider. To understand the complexities of the security challenges facing states in the post-Cold War era, it is not sufficient to consider situations where each side can threaten the other with assured total destruction. A range of asymmetrical situations are now emerging involving various combinations of large and small nuclear capabilities (with differing levels of certainty of delivery); chemical and biological weapons; highly effective conventional weapons; and, since 11 September 2001, mass casualty terrorism by non-state actors. One consequence was that when the articles were assembled together, it became apparent that their contents could most usefully be viewed as falling into three distinct categories: those dealing with generic questions concerning deterrence; those which explored the deterrent policies of the five nuclear-weapon states; and those which addressed deterrent issues in different regions – Western Europe, South Asia and the Middle East.

Deterrence Theory

As Howlett demonstrates, discussions on the conceptual and practical requirements for deterrence during the Cold War revolved around a number of recurrent generic themes. What remained constant, however, was the recognition that a nuclear bomb was an 'absolute weapon'. The risks inherent in its existence led to a difficult and dangerous process of 'nuclear learning' occurring between the US and USSR from the 1960s onwards. This was centred upon the need to manage mutual deterrence through diplomatic tools such as confidence building measures and bi-lateral arms control agreements. Indeed, these tools acquired such a significance that it took ten years after the end of the Cold War before they started to be viewed as no longer a necessary means of limiting the risks inherent in established nuclear deterrence policies, and US attempts to abandon them resulted in a climate of intense misgiving and disagreements over this move in much of the international arms control constituency.

Part of the reason for these misgivings arose from the use of similar, legally based rules and norms to address the other part of the nuclear security problem, the proliferation of nuclear weapons to additional states. Proliferation had been contained during the Cold War by the legal constraints of the NPT and alliance arrangements to provide nuclear security guarantees. However, the dramatic diminution of the threat posed by the former Soviet nuclear arsenal resulted in this being displaced by nuclear proliferation as the major preoccupation of western defence-policy makers. At the same time, events in the 1990s led to assertions that 'the non-proliferation regimes have failed' as they were incapable of stopping a handful of new players covertly equipping themselves with nuclear, chemical and/or biological weapons and the ballistic missiles to deliver them.

As a consequence of these contextual changes, most of our authors found it necessary to take a wider view and to offer some thoughts on the nature of deterrence itself. This process has highlighted five basic conceptual questions, which appear to have no simple answers. The first is the distinction between the existence of a deterrent *capability* (itself open to a wide range of interpretations) and of a deterrent *relationship*. Clearly the first is a necessary condition for the second, but it can also exist independently of the second, and increasingly may do so among the established nuclear-weapon states. The second is whether, as Quinlan asserts, deterrence is confined to situations involving *terror* and *unacceptable consequences* or, as others use the term, it also encompasses *defence* and *denial* of the ability to undertake unacceptable actions. Third is the continuing debate between *universal rationality* and *particular strategic cultures* in relation to the mechanisms and effectiveness of deterrence, and the implications for this of threats of mass destructive actions by non-state actors and perceived 'rogue states'. Fourth, there is the question of what, if anything, is understood by the term *strategic stability* in a world of only one nuclear superpower, and an increasing number of small nuclear forces. Finally, there is the role played by *deterrence* and *defence* in combating proliferation of weapons of mass destruction in comparison to that played by *legal constraints*.

It seems clear from the contributions to this volume that the principle of classical deterrence – the prevention of armed conflict between states by the threat of unacceptable consequences for the aggressor – is still as valid as ever, but that its centrality in international politics has been greatly reduced by the radical restructuring of strategic relationships that has taken place over the last decade. This change is emphasized by several of the authors, including Karp, who also suggests that as a consequence it is useful to classify deterrent relationships into three types.

The first type is that between the five long-standing nuclear-weapon states, where their nuclear weapons have served until now to prevent use against each other. However, it is also the case that their political relationships have been strengthened, and that they have collectively agreed not to target each other. This form of deterrent relationship is thus a more latent one than existed during the Cold War, and in some cases (e.g. France and the UK, and the UK with China) could be argued to be in practice politically irrelevant.

The second type is that involving the emerging nuclear-weapon states. In the eyes of those familiar with the US–USSR 'nuclear learning' process of the 1960s described by Howlett, these deterrent relationships appear to be less reliable than the first. However, Ghosh, in his discussion of the problems confronting such forces, argues that while they may not be as advanced technically or as sophisticated in their command and control systems as those of Russia and the US, their limited capabilities make for simplicity in control and protection, and thus negate these concerns about their unreliability.

Finally, there are those situations involving terrorist actors. Here the effectiveness of deterrence is more questionable. However, though both Bowen and Quinlan make the case that they can be deterred, with Bowen emphasizing the importance in this context of being known to have the capability to trace an act back to its source, the tools of deterrence for this purpose are likely to be different in nature to those involving state-to-state military force.

Karp goes on to suggest that one feature of the new and differentiated global environment within which deterrence has to operate is that the world is becoming divided into zones of war and zones of peace, with non-state terrorism emerging as the prime threat to the latter. In the zones of war and conflict deterrence is seen to retain a much greater salience, and the use of nuclear weapons and other WMD within them a continuing cause for concern. It is here that new bi- and multi-lateral arms control arrangements have been targeted since 1991. For their previous roles in stabilizing and institutionalizing Cold War nuclear deterrence appear less relevant as strengthened political and economic ties displace the conflictual military relationships that until recently dominated the old Eurocentric core of global security concerns.

At the same time, however, the states in zones of peace have become more sensitive to the threats to them from other areas, and opened debates over whether existing tools and restraints, such as deterrence and arms control agreements, help or hinder them in confronting such threats. Indeed, the removal of the threat of apocalyptic nuclear war between the established nuclear weapon-states may have paved the way for the use of 'smart' nuclear weapons to combat WMD threats arising in 'zones of war', as well as lifting the barriers to the development and deployment of those missile defences which were regarded as destabilizing during the Cold War. In short, the requirements for deterrence against threats, both state and non-state, to the zones of peace from the zones of war may now differ so radically from those deemed necessary in the Cold War period that the two may in some cases be incompatible: dealing with those 'against us' may demand a totally different code of conduct from dealing with those 'for us'.

One implication of this contextual analysis is that deterrence will remain applicable in the twenty-first century if only because, as Bowen points out, it is about maintaining the *status quo*, and not changing it. Indeed one of the problems in trying to assess its role since the end of the Cold War has been the scope and speed of political and technological change in contrast to the inertia inherent in the existence of major force structures and the reluctance in many quarters, noted above, to accept that hard won and familiar legal instruments may have become redundant. This links into Howlett's observations that during the Cold War deterrence was intimately connected to issues of nuclear order. Much of the nuclear debate from the 1960s onwards was focused on the mixture of power, co-operative rules, norms, legal agreements, non-proliferation policies and reciprocal bargains that would establish and sustain that order, and offer a basis for its continued legitimacy. The question for the twenty first century is whether this nuclear deterrent order, and the international legal agreements that sustained it, was unique to the particular political environment in which it emerged? For if this is so, three key questions arise: is the old order appropriate to the new environment; if not, can a new order be constructed or emerge, what will it be based upon and how long will it take to construct; and what types of deterrence mechanisms will be appropriate to sustain this new *status quo*?

Deterrence Practice: The Five Established Nuclear Weapon States

For the period from the early 1950s to the late 1980s the main preoccupation of world statesmen in the security field was the prevention of a Third World War through the maintenance of a stable nuclear-deterrent balance between the United States and the Soviet Union. Whilst various strategies were proclaimed at different times, such as 'flexible response', the bottom line for both the United States and USSR remained 'mutual assured destruction'. MAD was underpinned by several important bilateral agreements, starting with the 1963 'hotline' agreement and progressing to additional means to reduce the risk of outbreak of nuclear war. 1969 saw the start of negotiations between the two superpowers aimed at controlling their strategic arms race and managing their deterrent relationship so as to ensure crisis stability. These negotiations led to the 1972 SALT I Agreement, the 1972 treaty on the limitation of anti-ballistic missile systems (ABM Treaty) and the 1979

SALT II Agreement (which was never ratified but was nonetheless observed by both sides).

The next bilateral agreement was the 1987 INF Treaty dealing with the total elimination of their nuclear-armed intermediate range missiles, followed four years later by the 1991 START I Treaty, signed in Moscow less than five months before the Soviet Union itself disappeared. Throughout this process of institutionalization of the US–USSR and NATO–Warsaw Pact nuclear deterrent relationships, the other three established nuclear weapon states, China, France and the UK, played at best marginal roles. After 1991, Russia assumed the mantle of principal successor state and the START process continued, despite the fact that the United States and the Russian Federation had rapidly decreasing reasons to deter each other. It was another ten years, however, before the second Bush administration declared the process over.

There is little doubt that in this and other areas the US has been in the forefront of seeking to grapple with the problems of the transition from the deterrent world of the second half of the twentieth century to the uncharted waters of the first half of the twenty-first. Russell and Wirtz correctly characterize the strategic thinking now emerging under the Bush administration as revolutionary. The key concepts are described alliteratively in the US 2001 Quadrennial Defense Review as those of 'dissuasion, deterrence, defence and denial'. It appears that the United States now regards deterrence as principally focused upon Karp's Type II and III situations. It will operate through a capability for 'unilateral assured destruction' that, as he points out, works happily in harness with defences, unlike MAD. Russell and Wirtz point out the paradox of a renewed emphasis on US nuclear systems as weapons to be used in battle whilst, at the same time, it is suggested that precision-guided conventional weapons can accomplish many existing nuclear missions. This graded spectrum of strategic capabilities, shading from powerful conventional systems to small specialized nuclear weapons and on up to the megaton 'city-busters', backed by a stated intention to use whatever is appropriate, is intended to convey a very clear deterrent message.

Both Quinlan and Bowen in their more theoretical papers, stress that if deterrence is to work, the deterree must believe that the deterrer has the appropriate tools to carry out the threatened response (without being self-deterred through having only disproportionate means available) and has the will to do so. Russell and Wirtz themselves point to the 'new triad' unveiled in the Nuclear Posture Review (NPR) – deterrence, defence and counterforce – being focussed upon strengthening deterrence by increasing the range of options available to a US President. It is intended to guarantee that US policy makers will have appropriate tools to respond to a wide range of different forms of aggression, not just those involving nuclear capabilities.

One of these options, which is given a new emphasis, is the concept of pre-emption.

A pre-emptive strike with precision guided weapons against an opponent's WMD infrastructure and delivery systems can be supported by the deterrent threat that any attempt to use nuclear, chemical or biological weapons in a significant way would receive an overwhelming nuclear response. The opponent is left with little choice but to 'lose it rather than use it'. Yet such a response to the asymmetric threats that the United States expects to face in the new century may well generate a new form of equally asymmetric arms race. For the present the WMD of the states of concern are not highly developed and nor are their delivery systems. But equally, the ground-penetrating weapons and antiballistic missile systems needed for the new US strategy are in an early stage of development. As Ghosh points out, the less developed states can employ quite sophisticated, if 'low-tech', means of concealment of their activities and the key tools in the US arsenal may well prove to be those providing the necessary intelligence of just who has what and where – something which the Iraq experience of 2002–3 demonstrated to be highly problematic.

Pikayev, despite having so few official sources upon which to draw, paints a very convincing picture in his 'speculations' of the problems facing Russian defence planners and the likely result for the nation's deterrence policy. Faced with the revolution in thought and security policy emanating from the US and the problems of unrest within its southern borders, its policy has been reactive rather than proactive. One suspects that reliance on the existing institutional structures of nuclear deterrence has only reluctantly been forgone, as change is seen to generate greater problems than retaining well-established arrangements.

It seems certain that economic pressures will indeed both reduce the scale of Russian nuclear forces and, paradoxically, increase reliance upon them for security against a range of potential threats, mostly from the South. Just as the NATO allies refused to be bound by a policy of 'no first use' of nuclear weapons when faced with the overwhelming conventional superiority of the Soviet Union, so Russia had to renounce this policy as it faced the more than five-fold diminution in its armed forces manpower and found its material resources drained by the demands of the Chechen wars. In addition, Pikayev's suggestion that Russian planners could be prepared to countenance nuclear use 'in time of crisis' before the outbreak of hostilities reflects a similar philosophy to that behind the proposal that the United States contemplate pre-emptive nuclear strikes against 'rogue state' WMD facilities. Thus the possibility is emerging that Russia and the United States, now that they are both released from the escalatory constraints of their Cold War relationship, may feel free to threaten the use of nuclear weapons in conflict, especially if this takes place in a manner which would not cause mass casualties. What the consequences of this change will be for both global and regional deterrence, nuclear disarmament and WMD non-proliferation policies in the twenty-first century, especially if the threat was to be implemented, is almost impossible to calculate.

Perhaps the most innovative of the elements in the twentieth century process of institutionalizing nuclear deterrence relationships, briefly summarized above, was the ABM Treaty. The idea that defensive systems were destabilizing, and that both sides should be given greater confidence that their offensive systems would be effective, thereby enhancing deterrence and reducing the likelihood of their use, was a difficult and uncomfortable one for many to accept. As Karp indicates, the US decision to develop, and as soon as possible deploy, a limited missile defence for the continental United States (and its allies) at first appeared to be driving a coach and horses through the carefully constructed fabric of global strategic stability, but more careful examination shows that this has not been so.

In the Cold War period, effective and legally institutionalized mutual deterrence between those of the established nuclear weapon states that were operating under mutually antagonistic political systems was undoubtedly safer for all concerned than an unstable continuing search for advantage. It was also clear that missile defences would be a destabilizing factor in this situation. Under these circumstances the various players were agreeing to be deterred and to accept the consequent constraints on foreign policy. Such enforced acceptance of constraints is much less tolerable in the post-Cold War period where the players are less evenly matched. Possession of a few first-generation warheads on relatively primitive delivery systems poses a serious threat to a major power such as the United States or its friends, and the logical response has been the policy described by Russell and Wirtz with its important role for defences. The trick is to deploy a defensive system sufficient to negate the deterrent of the emerging opponents whilst not destabilizing the relationship with the established nuclear states.

One of the side effects of the ABMT, which was legally only binding on Russia and the United States, was that it enhanced the credibility, though not necessarily the deterrent roles, of the smaller nuclear forces of the United Kingdom, France and China. Thus the Treaty's demise had implications for these three states as well as Russia. Many commentators and political leaders expressed concern at the prospective scrapping of further hard won arms control agreements, reinforced in the case of Russia by its loss of status as the principal strategic interlocutor of the United States. This general desire to retain the existing 'rules of the road' was reinforced in the case of China by the prospect of the demise of the ABMT forcing it to reconsider its basic nuclear strategy and consider an expensive force build-up.

The Chinese view on this is set out in the article by Zhong and Pan. This places strategic stability at the core of nuclear relationships, defining it as a situation where a basic framework for strategic relationships is established on a consensual basis, giving each state an adequate sense of security and thus no incentive to seek to overthrow this *status quo*. Stability is therefore seen as essentially a political concept, with changes only occurring through mutual consent. The world is seen as one where the bipolar MAD structure continues to dominate, unlike the view from the United States described by Russell and Wirtz. After lamenting the over hasty denunciation of the ABMT by the United States, they point to the disturbances in the political harmony between the global community created by the unilateral, confrontational approach of the United States, which is seeking to build its own security on the insecurity of others.

Zhong and Pan therefore argue for a different approach to strategic stability, based on cooperation rather than confrontation, and sustaining current arrangements in the short and medium term, including MAD, while nuclear disarmament is negotiated. They point to the fact that common interests among the nuclear-weapon states outweigh differences, citing the positive impact of the terrorist threat upon international relations as proof of this. Their concept of strategic stability embraces political, economic and cultural issues as well as military ones, and greater interactions within the international community. Given this context, Zhong and Pan suggest that the world would be a safer place if nuclear relationships were in future constructed around agreed concepts of strategic stability based not on deterrence, but on pledges of 'no first use' of nuclear weapons and significant progress towards nuclear disarmament.

The end of the Cold War, and the consequent removal of the nuclear threat from the USSR, had probably its greatest effects upon the two other well-established small nuclear forces, those of France and the United Kingdom. Simpson describes the differing responses of the two states to the loss of these long-standing deterrence rationales, particularly the degree to which it has been conditioned by their Cold-War attitudes to, and military relationships with, the United States and their post-1990 experiences as members of the European Union. France positioned itself outside the unified military structure of NATO in the 1960s, and removed US forces from its soil, while the United Kingdom acquired its strategic nuclear delivery systems from the United States and placed them under the command of NATO's SACEUR, as well as providing bases for a range of US nuclear delivery systems. As a consequence, France attempted to develop independent deterrence doctrines, whereas the United Kingdom's national doctrine, as against that of NATO, was somewhat obscure from the 1960s to the 1980s, when a 'second centre of decision' role was promulgated. This argued that the UK force strengthened the Soviet belief that there would be a US response to an attack on Western Europe. In short, for both states the key objective was to have a credible nuclear force that could be used as a political tool, in the UK case in an alliance context, as well as serving as a deterrent against attack.

Simpson suggests that French and United Kingdom attitudes towards nuclear weapons still remain strongly conditioned by the Cold War arrangements within which their forces operated, despite a dialogue between them in the mid-1990s over nuclear matters. However, their nuclear deterrent postures are now directed at providing an insurance against long-term or low probability but high consequence threats, and, at least in the UK case, that if their nuclear forces did not already exist it is highly unlikely that they would now seek to acquire them. France retains an independent stance on nuclear matters, still operates outside NATO nuclear arrangements, and procures its nuclear capabilities indigenously. The United Kingdom remains closely aligned to the United States. Both France and the United Kingdom, however, confront pressures to harmonize their nuclear policies with other EU states, some of which have traditionally been opposed to nuclear weapons and deterrence.

Finally, Simpson demonstrates that the military threats that both states will confront in future are more likely to arise from intervention operations outside the NATO area, either alone or in concert with the United States, than any invasion of, or strategic strike on, NATO/EU states, including themselves. One consequence of this is the probability of a European consensus on the need to deploy theatre missile defences against attacks on expeditionary forces. The second is that the United Kingdom is currently facing major choices of whether to invest in the ability to be able to continue to operate alongside the United States in nuclear matters, or fund new conventional equipment that is more usable in joint operations.

What emerges from this group of papers is the extreme reluctance of any of the states discussed above, except the United States, to move away from the Cold War structures, security arrangements and deterrence concepts. The other side of this coin, however, is their reluctance to address the fact that the international security environment has radically changed, and their core security problems are no longer inter-state war between them, but a range of different, mostly asymmetrical threats emerging elsewhere, including from non-state actors. This reluctance is understandable as no clear vision appears to exist, except perhaps in China, of what these alternative, consensual security structures might be and the role of WMD, deterrence, and strategic stability within them. However, the discontinuities between the old world and the new are now becoming increasingly overt, and thus change in the arrangements inherited from the last century appears inevitable.

Deterrence Practice: Regional Dynamics

Europe now enjoys a security situation unprecedented for most of the last century. This has produced tensions within its non-nuclear state members over whether the way forward is to sustain existing security institutions and the potential for recreating deterrent relationships rapidly, or to push for nuclear disarmament. The situation of Germany, discussed by Kubbig, is particularly interesting in this respect. It has renounced possession of WMD, but not the presence of US nuclear weapons on its own soil and it participates in an alliance that pursues nuclear deterrence policies. During the Cold War it was geographically on the front line, forbidden by the terms imposed after the Second World War from possessing weapons of mass destruction, and reliant for its security on the umbrella of US extended deterrence and the NATO nuclear-sharing arrangements. By contrast, it is now surrounded by friendly states, has no perceived threat from Russia or any other state, and its eastern part is legally nuclear-weapon free. Moreover, unlike France and the United Kingdom, it has no recent tradition of involvement in intervention forces operating outside of the NATO area. Yet it has now realized it is likely to face terrorist problems, either in the form of attacks on its citizens or the use of its territory to plan attacks.

Like the United Kingdom, Germany has continued to regard NATO as the core of its security activities, and thus to subscribe to its collective policies. This has, however, generated tensions between the nuclear aspects of these policies, which hold nuclear weapons to be the ultimate guarantee of security, and the political demands of coalition partners in its governments for the complete global disarmament of WMD. Implicit in this have been concerns imported from the past of the 'decoupling' of European defence and security from that of the United States, most recently as a consequence of US policies over its pursuit of national ballistic missile defences.

The tensions within Europe, apart from those arising from the 2003 Iraq war, have focussed in particular upon NATO's refusal to contemplate a 'no first use' doctrine, which has generated significant political friction with the United States. Kubbig points out that this problem will be exacerbated if the United States moves towards a nuclear counter-proliferation policy, but could be ameliorated if that were to be forgone in favour of advanced conventional weapons. Above all, however, as with the United Kingdom, none of the major political actors in Germany wish to jeopardize the NATO relationship with the United States. Indeed their extreme reluctance to see the Cold War structures, including the ABM Treaty, set aside, going hand in hand with a desire to see the United States adopt a 'no first use' policy, shows how difficult it will be for it to assimilate further dramatic adjustments in the US strategic posture.

In contrast to Europe, both South Asia and the Middle East are regions where insecurity has continued in the post-Cold War period. The risks of a regional nuclear war in South Asia attracted major concerns following the respective nuclear tests by India and Pakistan in May 1998. Sidhu and Salik are well versed in both the developments in South Asia and in the theories developed during the US/USSR confrontation. However, it is evident from their articles that any 'nuclear learning' that may have occurred between Washington and Moscow over the last fifty years may have to be done anew between Delhi and Islamabad.

Sidhu, in his contribution to this volume, offers a disturbing analysis of the way several elements of Cold War 'nuclear learning' appear to have been rejected by the South Asian nuclear protagonists. He suggests declaring themselves to be nuclear weapon states has neither created strategic stability between them nor ensured the cessation of conventional conflicts. They do not appear to have been constrained from engaging in conventional conflict; overt possession of the 'ultimate weapon' has not deterred attempts to acquire additional territory; and the cardinal importance of effective and permanently open lines of communication between nuclear-armed opponents is still not fully understood. What is even more concerning is his suggestion that since the mid-1970s confrontations between the two states have been influenced increasingly by the existence of suspected nuclear weapon capabilities, and thus there has been almost three decades for relevant nuclear learning to occur.

Sidhu also highlights important differences in the dynamics of the South Asian situation to those of the Cold War. One is that the two states and China define the region differently, with the latter regarding itself as being outside it, in contrast to perceptions in India. A second is that given the linkages in South Asia between missiles and nuclear weapons, reinforced by the way missile tests have been used since 1998 to send political messages between the two states, there is a risk that the use of conventionally armed missiles in a non-nuclear confrontation could lead to a nuclear response.

Finally, there is the way the nuclear dynamics between India and Pakistan have been affected by the need for India to consider the role of China in any confrontation and, since September 2001, by the presence of US troops in Pakistan and its more active diplomatic role in the region following its declaration of the 'war on terror'. Sidhu suggests that India may have to factor into its deterrence calculations uncertainties over the role of China in any nuclear conflict it might have with Pakistan. More recently, both states have had to consider the impact of the presence of US troops in Pakistan upon any conflict between them. This raises the question of whether this external force will enhance strategic stability between the two states by constraining terrorist activities in Kashmir, or on the contrary embolden Pakistan.

This suggests that an unanticipated consequence of the 'war on terror' may have been to propel the United States into becoming a key factor in creating stable deterrence in the region, as it was for many years during the Cold War in Western Europe. This is echoed in a different vein by references in Salik's paper to work by the Indian analyst Bajpai, who suggests that some in the Indian strategic community are concerned by US counter-proliferation policy, and that one motivation for India deploying ICBMs and SLBMs may be to have a nuclear strike capability against the continental United States. This throws an interesting light upon arguments contained in both the Russell and Wirtz and the Karp papers.

One factor that is clearly different in South Asia to the situation which existed in the East/West confrontation, other than the legacy of recent armed conflicts and the continuation of low-level hostilities in the Kashmir area, is reflected in Salik's statement that the masses on both sides lack awareness of the devastating effects of nuclear conflict. At the same time he notes other causes for concern in relation to the received wisdom concerning the creation of stable nuclear deterrence relationships. These include the deterrence instability between the two sides in the short-term created by the vulnerabilities of the two states delivery systems to pre-emptive attack; concerns that a decapitating strike against the nuclear decision-making structures will encourage pre-emptive tendencies; a lack of space assets, which may enhance crisis instabilities; geographic factors and the short flight time of missiles leading to launch-on-warning policies, which enhance the risks of accidental war; unconstrained defensive deployments reinforcing existing strategic instabilities; and institutional and political factors, which may result in unpredictable crisis decision-making.

Salik also argues that at the moment Pakistan's conventional forces are capable of defending against an Indian conventional attack for a significant period of time, and thus the nuclear threshold is relatively high, but any upgrading of India's conventional forces without equivalent enhancements by Pakistan will lower its nuclear threshold, and thus enhance existing strategic instabilities. Furthermore, such a move would also be seen as a means to engineer an economic collapse in Pakistan, similar to the situation that led to the end of the USSR. Thus the linkage between conventional dissuasion and nuclear deterrence appears to be integral to any understanding of the future evolution of strategic stability in this region. Moreover, the mediating role of the United States may be crucial in engineering such stability, though its involvement could be very difficult to manage.

Another region that has witnessed both a succession of active conflicts since the end of the Second World War, and the application of dissuasion and deterrence policies in this context, is the Middle East. Issa, in his analysis of the application of deterrent policies and capabilities in this region, demonstrates that there are strong grounds for believing that neither conventional dissuasion or 'recessed' nuclear deterrence on the part of Israel, nor extended deterrence by the United States (or for that matter the USSR) were particularly effective in preventing armed attacks and warfare: they met with mixed results. He highlights the fact that neither the probable possession of nuclear weapons nor the existence of overwhelming conventional strength on the Israeli side deterred Egypt and Syria from 'crossing the red line' in 1973 when domestic political pressure became too strong to resist. He also points to the debate that has arisen since 1991 over whether the United States could have effectively deterred an overtly nuclear Iraq from attacking Saudi Arabia and the build-up of the coalition forces which ejected Iraq from Kuwait. His assessment is that while conventional deterrence or dissuasion may have helped to manage conflict in the Middle East, it has not assured security, in particular for Israel, the state that has practised deterrence most overtly.

The future of conflict in the Middle East, however, seems destined to be focussed on activities at the two ends of the military spectrum: WMD and low intensity warfare. Issa points out that the motivations for the acquisition of WMD capabilities and missiles by states in the region lies not in aspirations to prestige but in a deeply held belief among adversaries in the region of the need to maintain an ultimate form of retaliation against their existing or future adversaries. This suggests that the region may be moving inexorably towards an era of strategic deterrence but, unlike South Asia, one based upon all types of WMD, not solely nuclear weapons. He also emphasizes the trend towards introducing missile defences into the region, which may result in both those with defences believing that they enhance deterrence and their own security, though at the same time they may stimulate increased proliferation and refinement of WMD capabilities to combat this situation. Finally, commitments to the global non-proliferation regimes are currently holding in check many of these trends, especially those in the nuclear area. However, the degradation and collapse of these regimes, and the subsequent overt spread of WMD capabilities, could lead to much more complex and dangerous multi-polar deterrence relationships in the region than were ever experienced during the Cold War, either in Europe or between the United States and the USSR. Moreover, a situation where Israel seeks to nullify the deterrent capability of those of its neighbours who have sought WMD capabilities, through a combination of an undeclared nuclear arsenal and an effective anti-ballistic missile defence, offers interesting parallels with the developing US posture.

Yet it also seems clear that Israel's main security threats may now originate within its borders in the form of low intensity warfare, rather than in inter-state WMD conflicts with its neighbours. This suggests that it too is facing the same type of polarized threats that both Russia and the

United States are having to address and manage, and similar dilemmas about the reach of deterrent capabilities and the allocation of scarce military resources between them. Indeed as Karp points out, Israel's increasing need may be for defences against very short-range missiles, rather than against long-range ones.

While the deterrent situation in Europe has been transformed by the end of the Cold War, the analyses in this volume suggest that the WMD situation in both South Asia and the Middle East has become more complex and dangerous. In both regions, deterrent relations threaten to be multi-polar rather than bipolar, with the added complication in the Middle East of a mix of categories of WMD. In addition, in both cases, the United States appears likely to play a significant role in these relationships. All of which suggest that deterrence, while more difficult to engineer, might have an expanding role to play in the international politics of South Asia and the Middle East, though not in Europe.

Index

A

absolute weapons 13–15
Adams, H. 3
Afghanistan 7, 46
Akram, M. 157
Al Qaeda 46–9, 55, 56, 59, 68, 84, 160, 164; deterrence 72–4
alternative technologies: nuclear 36
American Missile Defence Act (1999) 67
anti-ballistic missile (ABM): systems 19, 213; treaty 63, 68, 69, 70, 90, 96, 101, 115, 120, 121, 123, 125, 204, 207, 210
arms control: nuclear 17–20
Asahara, S. 56
asymmetry: meaning 47–50; South Asia 187; war on terror 51

B

Ball, G. 173
ballistic missile defense (BMD) 120, 123, 146, 150, 152, 198, 210
Bhabha, H. 173
bin Ladan, O. 49, 56, 57
Biological Weapons Convention 70, 95
Blair, Prime Minister T. 58
Bush, President G. W. 34, 53, 92, 94, 96, 120, 137, 148, 150, 152, 205

C

Central Intelligence Agency (CIA) 84
Chechnya 113
Chemical Weapons Convention (CWC) 95, 117
China 6; deterrence 125; Mutual Assured Destruction (MAD) 125; nuclear 125; strategic stability 124–6
China Nuclear Energy Industry Corporation (CNEIC) 37
Christian Social Union (CSU) 149
Clinton, President B. 33, 57, 67, 68, 70, 90, 147–8, 160, 170, 182
Cold War 6; ideologies 123; multilateral contrast 123; nuclear deterrence 115; strategic stability 114–18
Collective Security Treaty 112
Collins, W. 3
Comprehensive Test Ban Treaty (CTBT) 117, 149
computer: technology 36
Cooperative Threat Reduction (CTR) (USA) 105
crisis: Brass Tacks 187; Kargil 157
Crouch, J. D. 85
Cuban Missile Crisis 29, 32

D

de Gaulle, President C. 5, 128, 139
Decoupling Issue: Germany 149–51
Defence Research and Development Organization (DRDO) 173
DeNardo, J. 19
deterrence: aims 52; Al Qaeda 72–4; catalytic 129; China 125; coercion 59; France (post-Cold War) 129–32; mass casualty terrorism 52; mechanisms 50; practice 204; punishment 54–9; regional practice 210–14; strategy 64, 213; theory 192, 201–4; Type I 64, 69, 72, 74; Type II 64, 72, 73, 74; Type III 64, 73, 74; United Kingdom (UK) (post-Cold War) 129–32; variables 50–2
deterrence policy: Israel 194; United States of America (USA) 193
deterrence strategy (USA) 87–91
disarmament 93
Draft Military Doctrine 100, 102, 178, 179
Draft Nuclear Doctrine 182

E

Europe: security system 136
European Union (EU) 133, 134, 135, 145, 170

F

Fernandez, G. 157, 188
Fissile Material Cutoff Treaty (FMCT) 40
Force de Frappe 31
France 6; deterrence capabilities 140; deterrence policy 209; nuclear motives 127–9; nuclear strategy 132; strategic capability 130, 132–9; United Kingdom (UK) relations 139
Franco-Prussian War 3
Freedman, L. 17

G

Gaddis, J. L. 20
Germany: counter-proliferation 146–9; Decoupling Issue 149–51; security environment 145–6
Ghaith, S. A. 164
global command and control systems (GCCS) 84
globalization 118
Glos, M. 150
government: Taliban 7
Guantanamo Bay 48
Gujral, Prime Minister I. K. 173, 182
Gulf War 83, 137, 197, 192; Iraq 6

H

Hekmatyar, G. 77
Herz, J. 15
history: Middle East 193–6; nuclear 12–13; South Asia 169–70
Hizbi-Islami 77
Hizbullah, H. 54
Hussein, S. 6, 58, 93, 148

I

India: nuclear goals 180–3; nuclear phases 173–4; nuclear policy 177–9; nuclear programme 172–4; Pakistan relations 161–5, 170; war policy 188
Indian Nuclear Doctrine 181, 189

International Criminal Court 8, 70
International Institute of Strategic Studies (IISS) 39
international pressure: nuclear 40–1
international threat: terrorism 74
intifada 197
Iraq: Gulf War 6; Kuwait invasion 196; Weapons of Mass Destruction (WMD) 133
Ischinger, W. 68
Israel: deterrence policy 194, 198; United States of America (USA) relations 194

J

Jaish-e-Mohammad (JeM) 164
Jenkins, B. 55
Jericho: missiles 35
Jervis, R. 63
Jinnah, M. A. 170

K

Kalam, A. 164
Kargil Conflict 29, 162, 163, 188
Karnad, B. 182
Khan, Doctor A. Q. 159
Khan, President A. 175
Kissinger, H. 5
Kosovo: war 69, 100
Kyoto Convention 70

L

Lashkar-e-Toiba (LeT) 164
Lawrence Livermore Laboratories 37
learning: nuclear 12, 21
Lellouche, P. 196
Line of Control (LoC) 157, 162, 165
Lockerbie 59

M

Manhattan: project 128
mass casualty: terrorism 52–9
mechanisms: deterrence 50

INDEX

Middle East: history 193–6
Military Doctrine (2000) 110, 111, 112
military spending (USA) 72
Milosevic, S. 8
Milstein, M. 17
Mishra, B. 177
missile: Jericho 35; Taepo-Dong 84; Trident 130, 131, 135
missile defence: disappearance 66–8; history 64–6; planning 73; superpowers 68; threat 76–8; United States of America (USA) 75
multipolarity 118
Musharraf, P. 163, 164
Mutual Assured Destruction (MAD) 29, 83, 96, 97, 115, 119, 121, 125, 192, 204, 208; China 125; United States of America (USA) 85–96
Mutual Balanced Force Reductions (MBFR) 116

N

National Command Authority (NCA) 185, 186
National Intelligence Estimate 84
national security: Russia 109
National Security Concept 101, 104; of the Russian Federation 100
National Security Council 173
natural resources: nuclear 38–9
Naumann, General (ret.) K. 150
negative assurances (USA) 93–6
Nehru, J. 170, 173
neutralization: Weapons of Mass Destruction (WMD) 136
Newhouse, J. 18
Nixon, President R. 33
Non-Nuclear Weapon State (NNWS) 20, 115, 116
non-proliferation policy 204, 207
Non-Proliferation Treaty (NPT) 93, 94, 95, 96, 109, 116, 148, 159, 202
North Atlantic Treaty Organization (NATO) 68, 70, 96, 102, 110, 111, 116, 127, 128, 132, 133, 134, 135, 145, 206, 208; arsenal 147; New Strategic Concept 147–8

North Korea 33, 65, 66
Northern Ireland 8
nuclear accidental war 39–40
nuclear alternative technologies 36
nuclear arms control 17–20
nuclear arsenal: Pakistan 39
nuclear coercion 32–3
nuclear crisis 18
nuclear deterrence 29, 31–4; Cold War 115; Russia 107, 108
nuclear economic limitations 37–8
nuclear fissile 40
nuclear goal: India 180–3
nuclear history 12–13
nuclear international pressure 40–1
nuclear learning 12, 18, 21
nuclear low-tech 35–6
nuclear methodology 29
nuclear motive: France 127–9; United Kingdom (UK) 127–9
nuclear order 13
Nuclear Planning Group (NPG) 129
Nuclear Posture Review (NPR) 82, 84, 205; United States of America (USA) 180
nuclear pre-emptive strikes 33–4
nuclear retaliation 16
nuclear security 21
Nuclear Security Advisory Board (NSAB) 182
nuclear small forces 30–1
nuclear stability 121
nuclear strategic culture 15–17
nuclear strategic stability 17–20
nuclear strategy: France 132; Russia 101–4
nuclear technology 34–7
Nuclear Weapon Capable States 29
Nuclear Weapon State (NWS) 20, 29, 30, 115
nuclear weapons: natural resources 38–9; surprise attack 15; United States of America (USA) 14
Nye, J. 14

O

operation: Desert Fox 67; Desert Storm 85, 196

P

Pakistan: Indian relations 161–5, 170; nuclear arsenal 39; nuclear command 185; nuclear phases 175–6; nuclear policy 184–5; nuclear programme 175–6; revolution 170
Partial Test Ban Treaty (PTBT) 116
Party of Democratic Socialism (PDS) 151
Permissive Action Links (PALs) 40
Permissive Enable Systems (PESs) 40
Presidential Decisions Directive 93
Project BioShield 53
Proliferation Security Initiative (PSI) 53
Putin, President V. 69–70, 86, 87, 100, 111

Q

Quadrennial Defense Review 82

R

Rajgopalan, R. 30
Regional Dynamics: South Asia 157–61
Revolution in Military Affairs (RMA) 83, 149
Rumsfield Commission Report 67, 84
Russia 6; military budget 105; military priorities 104–6; military strategy (post 2000) 111–13; national security 109; nuclear deterrence 107, 108; nuclear role 106–11; nuclear strategy 101–4; United States of America (USA) relations 86, 97, 115
Russian Security Council 103

S

Sattar, A. 184
Schelling, T. 16
security: nuclear 21
Security Council (UN) 7, 8
security environment: post-cold war 118–19

security system: Europe 136
Seng, J. 35, 39
September 11th 69–70, 72, 73, 84, 100, 118–19, 133, 140, 145, 150, 152, 160, 164, 201, 211
Sergeyev, I. 102
Shanghai Co-operation Organization (SCO) 112, 157
Shinrikyo, A. 56
Simons, T. 187
Singh, J. 161, 165
Singles Operations Plan (SIOP) 88, 96
small nuclear forces (SNF) 30, 32
Social Democratic Party (SPD) 146
South Asia: asymmetry 187; deterrence 161–5, 187–90; history 169–70; nuclear environment 176–7; Regional Dynamics 157–61; security environment 171–2; Strategic Restraint Regime 179
South Asian Association of Regional Co-operation (SAARC) 157, 158, 170
Soviet Union 65
START I Treaty 100, 105
START II Treaty 101
START treaties 69
Steinberg, G. 51, 54
strategic culture: nuclear 15–17
Strategic Restraint Regime 185; South Asia 179, 190
strategic stability: approaches 119–22; China 124–6; contrast 121; issues 122; nuclear 17–20
strategy: asymmetric 48
Suez Affair (1956) 193
superpowers: missile defence 68

T

Taliban 47, 57, 164; government 7
technology: computer 36; nuclear 34–7
Tenet, G. 48, 49
terrorism: deterrence 50–9; international threat 74; mass casualty 52–9
Theatre Ballistic-Missile Defence (TMD) 136
threat 16; missile defence 76–8

Treaty: of Moscow 88, 89; on the Non-Proliferation of Nuclear Weapons (NPT) 20; of Peace and Friendship 172
Triad: Nuclear Posture Review (NPR) 87, 87–91
Trident II 31

U

United Kingdom (UK): Arsenal 30; deterrence capabilities 140; deterrence policy 209; French relations 139; nuclear capability 130, 132–9; nuclear motives 127–9; nuclear role 128
United Nations (UN) 14, 66, 116, 141; Charter 58; Security Council 7, 8, 138; Small Arms process 70
United States of America (USA): Cooperative Threat Reduction (CTR) 105; counter force 91–3; counter-proliferation 151; deterrence policy 193; deterrence strategy 87–91; Israel relations 194; military spending 72, 89; missile defence 75; Mutual Assured Destruction (MAD) 85–96; negative assurances 93–6; new threats 83–5; Nuclear Posture Review (NPR) 180; nuclear weapons 14; pre-emptive strikes 92; Russian relations 86, 97, 115; treaty withdrawal 71

V

Vajpayee, Prime Minister 181
Vollmer, L. 148
von Clausewitz, K. 14

W

Waltz, K. 32, 33
war: Chechen 103; Falklands Island 4; Gulf 4; Korea 4; Kosovo 69, 100; Sino-Indian 158
war on terror 82, 124, 212; asymmetry 51
Warsaw Pact 102, 116, 127, 128, 129, 132, 134, 205
Weapons of Mass Destruction (WMD): acquisition 137; Iraq 133; neutralization 136
World Trade Center 49, 54, 84
World Trade Organization (WTO) 104

Y

Yeltsin, President B. 102, 103